T0330607

Integrating Sustainable Development in International Investment Law

The current international investment law system is insufficiently compatible with sustainable development. To better address sustainable development concerns associated with transnational investment activities, international investment agreements should be made more compatible with sustainable development.

Integrating Sustainable Development in International Investment Law presents an important systematic study of the issue of sustainable development in the international investment law system, using conceptual, normative and governance perspectives to explore the challenges and possible solutions for making international investment law more compatible with sustainable development. Chi suggests that to effectively address the sustainable development concerns associated with transnational investment activities, the international investment agreements system should be reformed. Such reform should feature redesigning the provisions of the agreements, improving the structure of international investment agreements, strengthening the function of soft law, engaging non-state actors and enhancing the dispute settlement mechanism.

The book is primarily aimed at national and international treaty and policy-makers, lawyers and scholars. It is also suitable for graduate students studying international law and policymaking.

Manjiao Chi is a Professor of International Law at Xiamen University, the People's Republic of China, Deputy Secretary-General, the Administrative Council of Xiamen Academy of International Law, and was a Senior Fellow at the Centre for Global Cooperation Research, Germany.

Routledge Global Cooperation Series

This series develops innovative approaches to understanding, explaining and answering one of the most pressing questions of our time – how can cooperation in a culturally diverse world of nine billion people succeed?

We are rapidly approaching our planet's limits, with trends such as advancing climate change and the destruction of biological diversity jeopardizing our natural life support systems. Accelerated globalization processes lead to an ever-growing interconnectedness of markets, states, societies, and individuals. Many of today's problems cannot be solved by nation states alone. Intensified cooperation at the local, national, international, and global level is needed to tackle current and looming global crises.

Series Editors:
Tobias Debiel, Claus Leggewie and Dirk Messner are Co-directors of the Käte Hamburger Kolleg/Centre for Global Cooperation Research, University of Duisburg-Essen, Germany. Their research areas are, among others, global governance, climate change, peacebuilding and cultural diversity of global citizenship. The three co-directors are, at the same time, based in their home institutions, which participate in the Centre, namely the German Development Institute/Deutsches Institut für Entwicklungspolitik (DIE, Messner) in Bonn, the Institute for Development and Peace (INEF, Debiel) in Duisburg and the Institute for Advanced Study in the Humanities (KWI, Leggewie) in Essen.

www.routledge.com/Routledge-Global-Cooperation-Series/book-series/RGC

American Hegemony and the Rise of Emerging Powers
Cooperation or Conflict
Edited by Salvador Santino F. Regilme Jr and James Parisot

Integrating Sustainable Development in International Investment Law
Normative Incompatibility, System Integration and Governance Implications
Manjiao Chi

Integrating Sustainable Development in International Investment Law

Normative Incompatibility, System Integration and Governance Implications

Manjiao Chi

Centre for
**Global
Cooperation
Research**

SPONSORED BY THE

Federal Ministry
of Education
and Research

Routledge
Taylor & Francis Group
LONDON AND NEW YORK

First published 2018 by Routledge

2 Park Square, Milton Park, Abingdon, Oxfordshire OX14 4RN

52 Vanderbilt Avenue, New York, NY 10017

Routledge is an imprint of the Taylor & Francis Group, an informa business

First issued in paperback 2019

British Library Cataloguing-in-Publication Data
A catalogue record for this book is available from the British Library

Library of Congress Cataloging-in-Publication Data
Names: Chi, Manjiao, 1976-, author.
Title: Integrating sustainable development in international investment law : normative incompatibility, system integration and governance implications / Manjiao Chi.
Description: New York, NY : Routledge, 2017. | Series: Routledge global cooperation series | Includes index.
Identifiers: LCCN 2017023066 | ISBN 978-1-138-18788-7 (hb) | ISBN 978-1-315-64284-0 (ebk)
Subjects: LCSH: Investments, Foreign (International law) | Sustainable development.
Classification: LCC K3830 .C55 2017 | DDC 346/.092—dc23
LC record available at https://lccn.loc.gov/2017023066

ISBN: 978-1-138-18788-7 (hbk)
ISBN: 978-0-367-26307-2 (pbk)
DOI: 10.4324/9781315642840

This work and its open access publication has been supported by the Federal Ministry of Education and Research (BMBF) in the context of its funding of the Käte Hamburger Kolleg/Centre for Global Cooperation Research at the University of Duisburg-Essen (grant number 01UK1810).

To Eva Yimei Chen and Luvia Xuchen Chi

Contents

x *Contents*

Abbreviations

AB	Appellate Body of the Dispute Settlement Body of the World Trade Organization
APEC	Asian-Pacific Economic Cooperation
ASEAN	Association of South East Asian Nations
BIT	Bilateral Investment Treaty
BYBIL	British Yearbook of International Law
CETA	Canada–European Union Comprehensive Economic and Trade Agreement
CFIUS	Committee on Foreign Investment in the United States
COMESA	Common Market for Eastern and Southern Africa
CSR	Corporate Social Responsibility
DSB	Dispute Settlement Body of the World Trade Organization
EC	European Commission
ECHR	European Court of Human Rights
EP	European Parliament
EU	European Union
EUCFT	European Union Charter of Fundamental Rights
EYBIEL	European Yearbook of International Economic Law
FCN	Treaty of Friendship Commerce and Navigation
FCPA	Foreign Corrupt Practices Act
FDI	Foreign direct investment
FET	Fair and equitable treatment
FPS	Full protection and security
FTA	Free trade agreement
FTC	Free Trade Commission under the North American Free Trade Agreement
GATS	General Agreement on Trade in Service
GATT	General Agreement on Trade and Tariffs
IBA	International Bar Association
ICSID	International Centre for Settlement of Investment Disputes
ICJ	International Court of Justice
ICTR	International Criminal Tribunal for Rwanda
ICTY	International Criminal Tribunal for Former Yugoslavia

IETs	International Environmental Treaties
IIA	International Investment Agreement
IISD	International Institute for Sustainable Development
ILA	International Law Association
ILC	International Law Commission of the United Nations
ILO	International Labour Organization
IMS	International minimum standard
IPRs	Intellectual property rights
ISA	Investor–state arbitration
ISDS	Investor–state dispute settlement
MAI	Multilateral agreement on investment
MEA	Multilateral environmental agreements
MFN	Most-favoured nation
MIT	Multilateral investment treaty
MNE	Multinational enterprise
MOFCOM	Ministry of Commerce of the People's Republic of China
MST	Minimum standard treatment
NAFTA	North American Free Trade Agreement
OECD	Organisation of Economic Co-operation and Development
OHCHR	United Nations Office of the High Commissioner for Human Rights
PCA	Permanent Court of Arbitration
P.R.C.	People's Republic of China
RTA	Regional trade agreement/arrangement
SADC	Southern African Development Community
TBT	Agreement on Technical Barriers to Trade
TEU	Treaty on European Union
TRIPs	Agreement on Trade-Related Intellectual Property Measures
TPP	Trans-Pacific Partnership
TIT	Trilateral investment treaty
TTIP	Trans-Atlantic Trade and Investment Partnership
UDHR	Universal Declaration of Human Rights
UN	United Nations
UNCITRAL	United Nations Commission on International Trade Law
UNCSD	United Nations Conference on Sustainable Development
UNCTAD	United Nations Conference on Trade and Development
UNEP	United Nations Environmental Programme
UNESCAP	United Nations Economic and Social Commission for Asia and the Pacific
UNESCO	United Nations Educational, Scientific and Cultural Organization
UNGA	United Nations General Assembly
UNGC	United Nations Global Compact
UNHRC	United Nations Human Rights Commission
U.K.	United Kingdom of Great Britain and Northern Ireland

U.S.	United States of America
VCLT	Vienna Convention on the Law of Treaties
WCED	World Commission on Environment and Development
WHO	World Health Organization
WSSD	World Summit on Sustainable Development
WTO	World Trade Organization
YBILC	Yearbook of the International Law Commission of the United Nations

Acknowledgements

My idea of writing a book focusing on international investment law and sustainable development was first inspired at a conference convened by the International Institution for Sustainable Development (IISD) in Jakarta, a few years ago. The conference theme was IIA negotiation and developing countries. During the course of a discussion, a negotiator from a Pacific Island country proposed that future IIAs should incorporate a climate change clause, because island countries are extremely prone to be affected by global warming. He argued that the legal discussion of global warming should not be limited to the discourse of international environmental law, but could also take place in the domain of international investment law. This proposal and argument don't seem novel from a purely academic perspective, but when one hears it with one's own ears from an affected group it becomes personal.

I wish to thank the IISD, especially Ms Nathalie Bernasconi-Osterwalder, Mr Howard Mann, the IISD investment law team, and the participating experts of the Jakarta conference, for the inspiration. The IISD investment law team was kind enough to invite me to several ensuing events, from which I have also benefited enormously.

I am immensely indebted to the Centre for Global Cooperation Research, Duisburg, Germany. I was fortunate to be a senior fellow of the Centre, and had a delightful and fruitful academic stay in the inner harbour of Duisburg during 2014 and 2015. The Centre publishes the Global Cooperation Series with Routledge. I am pleased and honoured to contribute this book to the prestigious series. During the preparation and writing, I have benefited greatly from many colleagues of the Centre. I wish to thank Prof. Tobias Debiel, Prof. Dirk Messner, Dr Markus Böckenförde, Dr Rainer Baumann, and the Centre's administrative team. I am grateful to Ms Patricia Rinck and the Centre's publication team for their kind assistance in the preparation and writing of the book. I am also indebted to Prof. Claudia Derichs, Prof. Stephen Brown, Prof. David Carment, Prof. Susan Ericson, Prof. Christian Tams, Dr Salvador Santino F. Regilme, Dr Felix Bethke and other fellows of the Centre for sharing with me their thought-provoking ideas and research experiences.

The writing of this book was a rewarding and pleasant experience, though pressure was always present. The main part of this book was completed while I was Li Ka Shing visiting professor of the Faculty of Law, McGill University, Canada in 2016. McGill enjoys a world-class reputation for its legal studies in many fields, including sustainable development law and international investment law. I benefited greatly from my work in McGill. I wish especially to thank Prof. Andrea K. Bjorklund, Prof. Armand de Mestral, Prof. Kun Fan, Prof. Hoi Kong, Deputy Dean Véronique Bélanger and Ms Des Sitaras. Besides, Ms Nanying Tao, Ms Yueming Yan and Ms Si Chen, PhD candidates of McGill Law, were very helpful and supportive to me and my family. They made our stay in McGill a rewarding and unforgettable one.

Naturally, my appreciation also goes to my home institute, Xiamen University Law School, China. My law school was generous in granting me academic leave for a few months for writing. I especially thank my colleagues at the International Economic Law Institute (IELI) and Xiamen Academy of International Law (Academy). The IELI hosts a top international law faculty in China. My discussions with colleagues were always a rich source of inspiration and knowledge. I serve as a deputy director of the IELI and deputy secretary-general of the Academy's administrative council. While I was writing, my colleagues undertook the administrative work for me. Without going through all their names, I sincerely thank all of them for their constant support.

Special thanks are also due to Prof. Marc Bungenberg of Saarland University, Germany; Prof. Wenhua Shan of Xi'an Jiaotong University, China; Prof. Julien Chaisse of the Chinese University of Hong Kong; and Prof. Yixin Liao of Xiamen University, China, for providing me with insightful advice, the opportunity to present my work, and kind support. I thank Mr Zongyao Li and Ms Xinhui Hong for their helpful assistance as well. I am also indebted to Ms Margaret Farrelly of Routledge for her consistent assistance.

Finally and above all, I am deeply grateful to my family for their unfailing support and complete trust, without which I could not have completed this book project.

Table of cases

Arbitration under UNCITRAL Arbitration Rules

BG Group Plc. v. The Republic of Argentina, UNCITRAL, 2003
Biloune and Marine Drive Complex Ltd v. Ghana Investments Centre and the Government of Ghana, UNCITRAL, 1988
Canfor Corporation v. U.S., Tembec, Inc. et al. v. U.S. and Terminal Forest Products Ltd. v. U.S., UNCITRAL, 2002
Glamis Gold Ltd. v. U.S., UNCITRAL, 2003
International Thunderbird Gaming Corporation v. The United Mexican States, UNCITRAL, 2002
Methanex Corporation v. The United States of America, UNCITRAL, 2001
National Grid plc v. The Argentine Republic, UNCITRAL, 2003
Pope & Talbot Inc. v. The Government of Canada, UNCITRAL, 1999
Saluka Investments B.V. v. The Czech Republic, UNCITRAL, 2001
S.D. Myers Inc. v. Government of Canada, UNCITRAL, 1998
Trinh Vinh Binh v. Vietnam, UNCITRAL, 2004
United Parcel Service of America Inc. v. The Government of Canada, UNCITRAL, 2000

ECHR cases

Case of James and Others v. U.K., ECHR, Application No. 8793/79, 1986
Case of Matos e Silva, Lda and Others v. Portugal ECHR, Application No. 15777/89, 1996
Case of Mellacher and Others v. Austria, ECHR, Application No. 10522/83, 11011/84, 11070/84, 1989
Case of Pressos Compañiá Naviera S.A. and Others v. Belgium, ECHR, Application No. 17849/91, 1995

ICSID arbitration cases

ADC Affiliate Limited and ADC & ADMC Management Limited. v. The Republic of Hungary, ICSID, Case No. ARB/03/16, 2003
ADF Group Inc. v. The United States of America, ICSID, Case No. ARB (AF)/00/1, 2000
Aguas del Tunari, S.A. v. The Republic of Bolivia, ICSID, Case No. ARB/02/3, 2002
Alex Genin, Eastern Credit Limited, Inc.et al. v. The Republic of Estonia, ICSID, Case No. ARB/99/2, 1999

Third, many states and the international community have gradually shifted the development paradigm from stressing economic growth to emphasizing the overall development in economic, environmental and social dimensions. There is a growing consensus that foreign investments should not only contribute to economic growth, but should also contribute to the promotion of the sustainable development of the host states.[6]

Fourth, through the operation of IIAs and the practice of investor–state arbitration (ISA), many states have come to realize that various IIA provisions can unduly limit their regulatory power, which hinders them in taking measures for various public interest purposes.

Last but not the least, IIA-making at the global level is standing at a historical crossroads nowadays. Some states have revised their model BITs for future BIT-making or renegotiation,[7] some have denounced the ICSID Convention and decided to terminate their BITs,[8] some are aggressively engaged in IIA-making,[9] and some have demanded a profound reform of the existing ISDS mechanism.[10] Such a background demonstrates the pressing need to reform the existing IIA system.

The call for making sustainable development-compatible IIAs is further enhanced by the initiation of some high-profile disputes, such as Methanex v. U.S.,[11] Vattenfall v. Germany[12] and Philip Morris v. Australia.[13] In these cases, the host states took regulatory measures for various public interest purposes, such as environmental, public health and national security protection. The foreign investors claimed that these measures violated, among others, the indirect expropriation and FET provisions of the underlying IIAs, and initiated ISA to seek compensation. Despite their different factual backgrounds and applicable IIAs, these cases clearly demonstrate that IIAs and ISA may be used by foreign investors as a "powerful weapon" to challenge host states for taking regulatory measures for sustainable development purposes.

Against such a background, it seems both necessary and important to reform the existing IIAs to be compatible with sustainable development on normative and governance bases. Clearly, without careful drafting, IIAs can frustrate sustainable development objectives and create potential conflicts between the commercial, social and environmental goals.[14] The question that naturally follows is how to reform the existing IIAs and how to improve the IIA-making and IIA-enforcement (i.e. ISA) in the future?

This book aims at exploring the above issues. It not only discusses the normative aspects of IIAs, analyses the status quo and possible improvement of the various sustainable development provisions of IIAs, but also studies how to improve the IIA-making and IIA-enforcing process from the governance perspective.

This book consists of three parts. Part I provides the background information. It briefly introduces the evolution of the concept of sustainable development and its legal status within the international law system, as well as a historical review of the development of IIAs (Chapter 1). Then, the book provides a brief introduction and assessment of the several prominent proposals aimed at making future IIAs more compatible with sustainable development (Chapter 2).

Part II is the main body of the book. It explores the thematic issues from the normative perspective. It first identifies the representative sustainable development provisions in existing IIAs and categorizes them into four types, namely: substantive provisions (Chapter 3), exceptive provisions (Chapter 4), public interest provisions (Chapter 5) and procedural provisions (Chapter 6). Under each type, the book discusses the historical development and status quo of these provisions, and analyses their potential impacts on sustainable development.

Part III, based on the previous parts, analyses why existing IIAs are not sufficiently compatible with sustainable development, and further raises suggestions for improving IIA-making in the future. This part first recommends reconceptualizing IIAs from the governance perspective (Chapter 7), then raises suggestions to help enhance the compatibility of IIAs with sustainable development and to improve the IIA-making democracy (Chapter 8).

The concluding part tries to answer the thematic question: will future IIAs be made more compatible with sustainable development? The answer could be explored from different perspectives. First, from the conceptual perspective, the answer depends primarily on how states perceive the investment–development relationship in IIAs. Second, from the normative perspective, the answer depends largely on whether states will incorporate a larger number and higher quality of sustainable development provisions in IIAs. Third, from the governance perspective, the answer mainly depends on how the major stakeholders of the international investment governance regime, including states, MNEs, arbitrators and non-state actors, can play their respective roles in a more balanced and coordinated way.

Notes

1 See R. Dolzer and C. Schreuer, *Principles of International Investment Law* (2nd edn) (Oxford: Oxford University Press, 2012), at 13–19.
2 UNCTAD, available at http://investmentpolicyhub.unctad.org/IIA (last accessed 10 April 2017).
3 See Martti Koskenniemi and Päivi Leino, "Fragmentation of International Law? Postmodern Anxieties", 15 *Leiden Journal of International Law* 553 (2002), at 560–561.
4 See e.g. Schlemmer-Schulte, "Fragmentation of International Law: The Case of International Finance & Investment Law versus Human Rights Law", 25 *Pacific McGeorge Global Business and Development Law Journal* 409 (2012), at 410.
5 European Commission, "Towards a Comprehensive European International Investment Policy", Communication of 7 July 2010, available at http://trade.ec.europa.eu/doclib/docs/2010/july/tradoc_146307.pdf (last accessed 20 October 2016), at 9.
6 W. Alschner and E. Tuerk, "The Role of International Investment Agreements in Fostering Sustainable Development", in F. Baetens (ed.), *International Investment Law within International Law: Integrationist Perspectives* (Cambridge: Cambridge University Press, 2013), at 217.

7   For instance, the U.S. has revised its model BIT in 2012, available at https://ustr.gov/sites/default/files/BIT%20text%20for%20ACIEP%20Meeting.pdf   (last accessed 10 December 2016). India also issued its Model BIT in 2016, available at www.mygov.in/sites/default/files/master_image/Model%20Text%20for%20the%20Indian%20Bilateral%20Investment%20Treaty.pdf (last accessed 10 December 2016).

8   The three Latin American countries, Bolivia, Equador and Venezuela have denounced the ICSID Convention and determined to terminate their BITs gradually. See e.g. UNCTAD, "Denunciation of the ICSID Convention and BITs: Impact on Investor–State Claims", *IIA Issues Note*, No. 2 (December 2010), available at http://unctad.org/en/Docs/webdiaeia20106_en.pdf (last accessed 10 December 2016).

9   For instance, China is in intense negotiation of BITs and FTAs, especially the current negotiations of a China–U.S. BIT and a China–EU BIT. The conclusion of these BITs among the world's biggest economies will reshape the future global IIA landscape. See e.g. Wenhua Shan and Lu Wang, "The China–EU BIT and the Emerging Global BIT 2.0", 30 (1) *ICSID Review* 260 (2015).

10 European Commission, "Commission proposes new Investment Court System for TTIP and other EU trade and investment negotiation", available at http://europa.eu/rapid/press-release_IP-15-5651_en.htm (last accessed 10 November 2016).

11 Methanex Corporation v. United States of America (*ad hoc* arbitration under UNCITRAL Rules), available at www.italaw.com/cases/683 (20 August 2016).

12 Vattenfall AB, Vattenfall Europe AG, Vattenfall Europe Generation AG v. Federal Republic of Germany (ICSID Case No. ARB/09/6), available at www.italaw.com/cases/1148 (20 August 2016).

13 Philip Morris Asia Limited v. The Commonwealth of Australia (PCA Case No. 2012-12), available at www.italaw.com/cases/851 (20 August 2016).

14 M. W. Gehring and A. Kent, "International Investment Agreements and Sustainable Development: Future Pathways", in S. Alam, J. H. Bhuiyan, T. M. R. Chowdhury and E. J. Techera (eds.), *Routledge Handbook of International Environmental Law* (Abingdon: Routledge, 2013), at 564.

Part I

The sustainable development challenge for IIAs

1 Sustainable development and IIA

The ideal of sustainable development enjoys a long history and has gained a status comparable to that of democracy, freedom and justice: it is universally desired, differently understood, complex in scope, extremely difficult to establish and impossible to do away with.[1] Today, sustainable development has evolved into a comprehensive concept that captures environmental, economic and social dimensions, and has become an unavoidable paradigm underpinning almost all human actions and pervading the environmental, social, political, economic and cultural discourses from the local through to the "global" level by both the public and private sectors.[2]

Sustainable development has been widely recognized in a number of international treaties, especially in international environmental treaties (IETs). In international investment law, sustainable development has also gradually penetrated into modern IIAs, despite the fact that IIAs are originally designed for investment protection. As a matter of fact, an investment–development relationship that is evolutive in nature can be identified in international investment law.

To provide necessary background information, this chapter briefly reviews the evolution and legal status of sustainable development, the historical development of IIAs, as well as the evolutive investment–development relationship in international investment law.

The concept and legal status of sustainable development

The concept of sustainable development is intrinsically evolutive, and is adaptive to the circumstances according to the time, the area or the subjects concerned.[3] Although it originated from international environmental law discourse, today it has evolved from the original meaning of sustainable use of natural resources, to a concept with more anthropocentric and socioeconomic substance.[4] Despite the universal acceptance of this concept, whether and to what extent sustainable development could amount to a legal norm is not a settled issue.

DOI: 10.4324/9781315642840-3

The evolution of the concept of sustainable development

The international community noticed the close relationship between development and environment long ago. The concept of sustainable development was first incorporated in the global development agenda in the Brundtland Report in 1987.[5] This landmark report contains a commonly accepted definition of sustainable development:

> Sustainable development is development that meets the needs of the present without compromising the ability of future generations to meet their own needs. It contains within it two key concepts:

> - the concept of "needs", in particular the essential needs of the world's poor, to which overriding priority should be given; and
> - the idea of limitations imposed by the state of technology and social organization on the environment's ability to meet present and future needs.[6]

Under this definition, sustainable development should be perceived as a process of change in which the exploitation of resources, the direction of investments, the orientation of technological development, and institutional change are all in harmony and enhance both current and future potential to meet human needs and aspirations.[7]

Global efforts for developing an effective legal regime to address sustainable development began in Rio de Janeiro, which marks the point at which sustainable development becomes a primary focus of the international agenda.[8] Through its milestone documents, i.e. the Rio Declaration on Environment and Development (Rio Declaration)[9] and Agenda 21,[10] the United Nations Conference on Environment and Development (UNCED) has made sustainable development a "leading concept of international environmental policy".[11]

Until the 1990s, sustainable development was largely limited to the context of environmental law, aiming chiefly at addressing the potential incompatibility between economic development and environmental protection. Such an observation can be drawn from the Rio Declaration, which states that "In order to achieve sustainable development, environmental protection shall constitute an integral part of the development process and cannot be considered in isolation from it".[12]

Though sustainable development has its origin in the environmental discourse, the scope of this concept is no longer limited to serve the needs of the environment.[13] In 2002, the World Summit on Sustainable Development (WSSD) was held in Johannesburg, South Africa. The main outcome of the WSSD, the Johannesburg Declaration on Sustainable Development (Johannesburg Declaration),[14] overlaps significantly with the Rio Declaration. Yet the main contribution of the WSSD to the sustainable development regime was adding a third pillar to the concept of sustainable development, i.e. along with environmental protection and economic development, social development became a recognized element of sustainable development.[15] The Johannesburg Declaration expressly states that:

> Accordingly, we assume a collective responsibility to advance and strengthen the interdependent and mutually reinforcing pillars of sustainable development – economic development, social development and environmental protection – at the local, national, regional and global levels.[16]

This statement is shared globally, and has been repeatedly cited in many international instruments, such as the 2005 World Summit Outcome.[17]

A more comprehensive understanding of sustainable development has been offered by the International Law Association (ILA) Committee of International Law on Sustainable Development. In 2002, the ILA Committee drafted the New Delhi Declaration of Principles of International Law Relating to Sustainable Development (New Delhi Declaration), which identifies seven related principles:

1 The duty of states to ensure sustainable use of natural resources;
2 The principle of equity and the eradication of poverty;
3 The principle of common but differentiated responsibilities;
4 The principle of the precautionary approach to human health, natural resources and ecosystems;
5 The principle of public participation and access to information and justice;
6 The principle of good governance;
7 The principle of integration and interrelationship, in particular in relation to human rights and social, economic and environmental objectives.[18]

One may observe that the principles identified in the New Delhi Declaration in essence echo the various principles contained in the Rio Declaration and Johannesburg Declaration.[19] Despite the enrichment of the concept of sustainable development, a clear definition of sustainable development remains missing.

Today, despite the universal recognition of sustainable development, the exact content of this concept remains unclear.[20] The concept is often understood as a balancing paradigm. It has been suggested that the essence of this concept is to strike a balance of the different elements thereof, with the goal of the preservation of our ecosystems as the very basis of our existence and the achievement of the best possible world for all of humanity.[21] Indeed, the New Delhi Declaration implies such a balancing paradigm by proposing the principle of integration and interrelationship of the elements. In judicial practice, such a balancing paradigm is also implied. As the ICJ Judge Weeramantry held in his separate opinion in Gabčíkovo-Nagymaros, "there is always the need to weigh considerations of development against environmental considerations, as their underlying juristic bases—the right to development and the right to environmental protection—are important principles of current international law".[22]

Sustainable development as a legal norm

It has been proposed that sustainable development has become an established concept with normative status in international law,[23] and forms a part of modern international law.[24] Yet it is also argued that the status of sustainable development as a legal norm in the international law system remains largely uncertain.[25] Partly for such reasons it has been argued that, although sustainable development has been on the international agenda for decades, difficulties persist in developing an effective regime to address it.[26]

In this respect, reference should be made to Article 38(1) of the ICJ Statute, which provides for sources of international law, according to which the binding sources of international law include international conventions, international customs and general principles of law. A legal norm becomes binding upon states as "hard law" if it forms a part of a treaty, a customary rule or a general principle of law. Thus, the legal status and binding force of sustainable development as a legal norm should be assessed within this system as well.

First, sustainable development has been widely incorporated in an increasing number of international treaties and other legal instruments in the past decades. While many of these treaties are IETs, some are in other fields, such as trade treaties. Some of these treaties are landmarks, such as the UN Convention on Biological Diversity of 1992 (CBD), the UN Framework Convention on Climate Change of 1992 (UNFCCC) and the Paris Agreement of 2015.[27]

The treatification of sustainable development may take two modes. One mode is to incorporate sustainable development in the treaty's preamble, thus making it one of the treaty objectives. For instance, the Agreement Establishing the World Trade Organization (Marrakesh Agreement) provides in its preamble that:

> Recognizing that their relations in the field of trade and economic endeavour should be conducted with a view to raising standards of living, ensuring full employment and a large and steadily growing volume of real income and effective demand, and expanding the production of and trade in goods and services, while allowing for the optimal use of the world's resources in accordance with the objective of sustainable development, seeking both to protect and preserve the environment and to enhance the means for doing so in a manner consistent with their respective needs and concerns at different levels of economic development.

A second mode is to incorporate sustainable development into the treaty's functional provisions, which is often found in IETs. For instance, Article 3(4) of the UNFCCC provides that:

The Parties have a right to, and should, promote sustainable development. Policies and measures to protect the climate system against human-induced change should be appropriate for the specific conditions of each Party and should be integrated with national development programmes, taking into account that economic development is essential for adopting measures to address climate change.

As can be seen, under the UNFCCC provision, promoting sustainable development is not only a right and an obligation of the contracting states in the context of addressing climate change, but the exercise of such a right and obligation should also be in line with the international law principle of common but differentiated responsibilities.[28]

Notwithstanding the treatification of sustainable development, the binding force of sustainable development as a legal norm is uncertain. On one hand, treaty preambles often express the objective and purpose of the treaty, without creating specific rights and obligations for the contracting states, thus their binding force is limited and they are often deemed "incapable of giving rise to valid rules of international law".[29] On the other hand, the incorporation of sustainable development in treaty texts in many cases only constitutes partial integration or sub-principle integration, implying that only some elements of sustainable development are treatified, such as sustainable use of natural resources and the principle of common but differentiated responsibilities, while many more elements are not made into treaty norms.[30] Partial integration limits the application of sustainable development in the international environmental law discourse, despite the social and economic dimensions of sustainable development.

Second, it remains unsettled whether sustainable development can constitute a customary international law rule. Under Article 38 of the ICJ Statute, the formation of a customary rule requires two elements: state practice that is widespread and consistent, and *opinion juris*, i.e. "the assertion of a legal right or the acknowledgment of a legal obligation".[31] The formation of the principle of sustainable development relies largely on UN-led promotional activities, and has been developed through a number of international organization resolutions, declarations, conventions and judicial decisions.[32] Thus, unlike many other customary law rules, the principle of sustainable development is not created by the traditional combination of state practice and *opinio juris* or some variation thereon, which fails to grant it the status of customary law rule.[33]

Third, with regard to general principles of law under Article 38 of the ICJ Statute, much vagueness remains. The determination of general principles of law consists of two ways: first, by recourse to the decisions of international courts and tribunals; and second, in the absence of such decisions, by comparative law. The second way consists of two operations, namely abstracting the principle from the legal rules of national legal systems and verifying the generality of nations that recognize this principle.[34] In this regard, although sustainable development has been mentioned in some international judicial decisions, none of the decisions clearly confirms its legal status as a general principle of law. Rather, sustainable development has only been confirmed as a principle of law within the realm of international environmental law. For instance, in the Arbitration Regarding the Iron Rhine ("Ijzeren Rijn") Railway (Belgium v. Netherlands), the Permanent Court of Arbitration (PCA) tribunal held that,

> Environmental law and the law on development stand not as alternatives but as mutually reinforcing, integral concepts, which require that where development may cause significant harm to the environment there is a duty to prevent, or at least mitigate, such harm. This duty, in the opinion of the Tribunal, has now become a principle of general international law.[35]

To briefly sum up, though sustainable development has been widely treatified, such treaties are mainly IETs. Aside from this, it is unclear whether sustainable development has acquired the legal status of a customary law rule or general principle of law within the meaning of Article 38 of the ICJ Statute.[36] However, given its evolutive nature, further treatification and wide acknowledgement of sustainable development by states and the international community could grant sustainable development the status of customary law rule or general principle of law within the international law system.

The evolution of IIAs in a nutshell

International investment law is evolutive and has a comparatively short history. As R. Dolzer and C. Schreuer have insightfully pointed out, two decades ago the state of the rules of international law pertaining to foreign investment had not yet reached such terminological and professional specialization. Until the early 1990s, this area was characterized by a limited set of rules of general international law and by a number of bilateral treaties, which until then did not in practice lead to a significant legal edifice in the form of disputes or of case law.[37]

IIAs are the major components of modern international investment law. The development of IIAs should be understood in the light of international law relating to the protection of foreign investments. Before the birth of IIAs, foreign investments were regulated mainly by the national law of host states, and foreign investors were treated equally as citizens of the host states in case of expropriation and nationalization.[38] Internationally, foreign investment protection was subject to the customary rules of state responsibility and of the treatment of aliens.[39]

The protection of foreign investors and their investments offered by national laws and customary law rules has limits. At the national level, host states have sovereign power to promulgate, revise and abolish national laws. Change of national law may have unpredictable and profound impacts on foreign investors and investments. During the latter half of the nineteenth century and the first half of the twentieth century, nationalization of foreign investments went rampant in many parts of the world, such as Eastern European states, Latin American states, China, Russia and Mexico.[40] Because nationalization measures are taken by states through legal procedures in accordance with national laws, it is difficult for foreign investors to challenge these measures before the national courts. In Lena Goldfields, for instance, the former Soviet Union tried to justify its uncompensated expropriation of foreign investments relying on national treatment standards.[41]

At the international level, some countries disputed the existence and the contents of the minimum standard treatment of foreign investments, and insisted that foreigners should not be treated more favourably than the nationals of the host states. This can be reflected by the Calvo doctrine raised by some Latin American countries.[42] Though it is possible for home states to exercise diplomatic protection over their investors, this can be practically difficult. The theory underlying the principle of diplomatic protection is that an injury to a state's national is an injury to the state itself, for which it may claim reparation from any responsible state.[43] However, the exercise of diplomatic protection by a state over its nationals is deemed as a right instead of an obligation of the state under international law, and is thus at the discretion of the home state.[44] Even if the home state exercises diplomatic protection over its investor, strict requirements must be fulfilled, i.e. the investor must possess continuous nationality of the home state and have exhausted the local remedies in the host state.[45] A decision of diplomatic protection is ultimately a political one, and the home state may refuse to exercise this right for some non-legal considerations.[46]

The inadequacy of national law and customary international law in protecting foreign investors and investments leaves two options for home states. One is to resort to non-legal mechanisms, especially the use of military force. This option is not feasible nowadays. Prior to World War II, international investments were largely made in the context of colonial expansion.[47] Protection of foreign investments was not often a concern in international agreements,[48] as the non-legal means of military force and diplomacy provided the principal means for protecting foreign investments.[49] Since World War II, the UN Charter prohibits the use of force,[50] except in self-defense[51] and with the authorization of the UN Security Council.[52] These rules render non-legal means for investment protection infeasible.

The other option is to develop a special body of international law for the purpose of protecting foreign investments, which is independent from and external to the national laws of host states. Against such a background, BITs were created by developed countries in response to the uncompensated expropriation of their investments by the newly independent developing countries.[53] Though many pre-existing Friendship, Commerce and Navigation (FCN) treaties of the U.S. include provisions on the treatment of foreign investments, BITs are innovative, as they protect foreign investors and investments from expropriation, and allow foreign investors to directly resort to international arbitration against the host states without necessarily exhausting the local remedies in the host states.[54]

It is often viewed that the making of modern BITs starts from the conclusion of the first BIT between Germany and Pakistan in 1959.[55] In the 1960s, many European countries followed Germany to conclude BITs with developing countries to protect their overseas investments. In 1974, the Declaration on the Establishment of a New International Economic Order was adopted.[56] This Declaration expressly confirms that states have full permanent sovereignty over natural resources, including the right to nationalization or the transfer ownership of foreign investments.[57] To protect their overseas investments, developed countries initiated additional BIT programmes during the 1970s. Since the 1980s, as developing countries began to abandon the hostility towards foreign investments and became active in BIT-making in order to attract foreign investments to boost their national economy, the number of BITs in the world increased drastically.[58]

Though it remains arguable whether and to what extent the presence of BITs is truly helpful in attracting foreign investments,[59] it is agreed that BITs help secure the legal environment for foreign investors, establish mechanisms for dispute resolution and facilitate the entry and exit of capital.[60]

IIA-making at the global level has shown some distinct features. First, the contents and purpose of BITs have undergone changes. Early BITs aimed mainly at investment protection and economic development, while recent BITs also stress market access and investment liberalization. Second, the ideological and North–South paradigm in BIT-making has also faded over time. Early BITs were mainly concluded between developed and developing countries, while an increasing number of BITs nowadays are concluded among the developing countries, and the core provisions of these BITs do not significantly deviate from those concluded with developed countries.[61] Third, since the 1990s, states have also shown an increased interest in concluding FTAs and regional trade agreements (RTAs) in addition to BITs, aiming at achieving deeper trade liberalization and economic integration.[62] The conclusion of the North Atlantic Free Trade Agreement (NAFTA) is a typical example.[63] More recently, some "mega-FTAs" were signed or negotiated, such as the Trans-Pacific Partnership Agreement (TPP)[64] and the Transatlantic Trade and Investment Partnership Agreement (TTIP).[65] Last but not least, it has been argued that the international community should consider concluding a multilateral investment treaty, especially given the inability of the WTO in international investment rule-making, and the failure of the negotiation of an Multilateral Agreement on Investment (MAI) under the auspices of the Organisation for Economic Co-operation and Development (OECD) some twenty years ago.[66]

International investment law, although with a comparatively short history, has undergone and is still experiencing profound changes. It is reasonable to expect that the ongoing development of IIA-making at both bilateral and regional levels will have profound impacts on international investment governance in the future.

The changing investment–development relationship in IIAs.

The relationship between foreign investments and development has been recognized for a long time.[67] Such a relationship can be complex because foreign investments may have both positive and negative impacts on the host states' development. On the positive side, foreign investments can help promote economic development of the host states, since they may not only bring in "a package of assets, including capital, technology, managerial capacities and skills and access to foreign markets", but can also stimulate "technological capacity-building for production, innovation and entrepreneurship within the larger domestic economy through catalyzing backward and forward linkages".[68] On the negative side, foreign investments could harm the host states' development if they are poorly regulated and unreasonably utilized. For instance, certain types of foreign investments may require a minimum level of technology or education in order to learn from foreign companies, engage in their networks, and take up the employment they provide, while the host states are not able to meet such needs of the foreign investments.[69]

An implied positive investment–development relationship can be found in IIAs. The first modern BIT, the 1959 Germany-Pakistan BIT provides in its preamble that "an understanding reached between the two states is likely to promote investment, encourage private industrial and financial enterprise and to increase the prosperity of both the states".[70] Though the term "development" is not used, the term "prosperity" carries the similar meaning of "economic development". Today, it is almost standard treaty language for IIAs to expressly incorporate "economic development" in their preambles.

Such an implied positive investment–development relationship is also present in the ICSID Convention. The *travaux préparatoires* of the ICSID Convention show that the contracting parties did not intend to define the term "investment".[71] Yet, as Article 25 of the ICSID Convention serves as the jurisdictional gateway for access to ICSID arbitration, the understanding of the term is at the forefront of jurisdictional arguments.[72] Thus ICSID tribunals need to decide if a claimed investment constitutes a qualified investment within the meaning of Article 25 and the underlying BIT for jurisdictional purposes. It is at this juncture that the investment–development relationship is conceptualized within the ICSID Convention framework. In Salini v. Morocco,[73] the arbitral tribunal listed four criteria to judge if an investment is a qualified one, which are known as the "Salini criteria", namely substantial commitment, a certain duration, assumption of risk, and a significance for the development of the host state.[74] As indicated in the "Salini criteria", an investment should contribute to the development of the host states under the ICSID Convention.

ICSID practice seems inconsistent with respect to the determination of investment. In some cases, arbitrators broadly interpreted the term "investment", which could damage the positive investment–development relationship enshrined in the ICSID Convention. For instance, in SGS v. Pakistan,[75] the arbitral tribunal broadly interpreted investment to cover the supply contract.[76] In SGS v. Philippines,[77] similar legal and factual issues were raised. Although the tribunal in this case decided to stay the arbitral proceedings, it also broadly interpreted investment in the BIT for jurisdictional purposes.[78] It has been criticized that an effect of such broad interpretation of investment is that "it provides only a weak filtering mechanism to help limit the scope of a BIT's protection to those investments that meaningfully contribute to host states' economic developments".[79]

It should be noted that although a positive investment–development relationship is implied in the ICSID Convention, what is recognized is the economic dimension of development. Such recognition does not reflect the concept of sustainable development in its entirety, as it fails to take into account the environmental and social dimensions of this concept. This negligence is understandable in light of the background of the ICSID Convention and many early IIAs. The ICSID Convention was negotiated between 1955 and 1962, a time of rapid decolonization and of the emergence of newly independent states with great developmental needs, while foreign investments were impeded by fears of political or non-commercial risks of expropriation, breach of government contract, currency transfer restrictions and war and civil disturbance.[80] During this period, the concept of sustainable development has not yet entered the main discourse of international law, and its various dimensions have not been fully acknowledged. Indeed, it would have been practically unreasonable for the new states to prioritize environmental and social protection over economic development in IIA-making.

This situation has undergone some changes in recent decades. There is a growing global consensus that foreign investments should be a key component of any development agenda.[81] Since transnational investment activities often prompt sustainable development concerns, such as environmental and labour rights concerns, IIAs should also be a necessary discourse to address such concerns.[82]

In the international plane, various key international instruments highlight the need and the role of foreign investments in promoting sustainable development. For instance, in Agenda 21, it is stated that

> Sustainable development requires increased investment, for which domestic and external financial resources are needed. Foreign private investment and the return of flight capital, which depend on a healthy investment climate, are an important source of financial resources. Many developing countries have experienced a decade-long situation of negative net transfer of financial resources, during which their financial receipts were exceeded by payments they had to make, in particular for debt-servicing. As a result, domestically mobilized resources had to be transferred abroad instead of being invested locally in order to promote sustainable economic development.[83]

Similar statements have been made in a series of ensuing international events, such as the 2002 World Summit, the G8 and the G20 summits.[84] Recently, during the G20 Ministerial Meeting under China's presidency in July 2016, trade ministers of the world's largest economies agreed on a set of non-binding Guiding Principles for Global Investment and Policymaking, with the purpose to "promote investment for inclusive economic growth and sustainable development".[85] In addition to these statements, several international organizations and NGOs have also put forward their proposals to reform the current IIA system to make it more compatible with sustainable development.[86]

On the national plane, states have realized the relevance and importance of sustainable development in IIA-making. Here, the recent development of China's IIA-making is an illustrative example. China's IIA-making scheme began from the end of the 1970s. This point of time marks the end of the international community's long-time isolation of China and the start of China implementing economic reform and the "open door" policy. Against such a background, BITs were used by China both as a diplomatic tool to engage itself with the world, and as a legal tool to help attract foreign investments to boost its economy. Many early BITs of China only mention economic prosperity.

Since around 2010, sustainable development has entered into the mainstream practice of China's IIA-making, and there is a clear trend that China's IIAs are increasingly environmentally friendly.[87] China's recent BITs clearly recognize sustainable development. Some IIAs expressly set sustainable development as a treaty objective. For instance, the China–Canada BIT recognizes "the need to promote investment based on the principles of sustainable development".[88] Other IIAs do not use the term "sustainable development", but list the key elements thereof. For instance, the China–Japan–Korea TIT states that "these objectives can be achieved without relaxing health, safety and environmental measures of general application".[89]

The enhanced awareness of sustainable development in global IIA-making enriches and reshapes the investment–development relationship enshrined in IIAs. While early IIAs stress economic development in such a relationship, recent IIAs expressly incorporate sustainable development, especially the environmental dimension thereof. To some extent, such a paradigm shift helps transform the investment–development relationship in IIAs from a unidimensional paradigm into a multidimensional one. As the international community now faces profound sustainability challenges, it is likely that sustainable development will gain more attention in future IIA-making and become more pervasive in construing the investment–development relationship in IIAs.

Typical sustainable development provisions in IIAs

Though IIAs assume that the central problem to be solved is the protection of foreign investors and investments from discriminatory actions by the host states,[90] an increasing number of IIAs nowadays incorporate provisions that are designed for, or have an effect on the promotion of sustainable development. These provisions are collectively referred to as sustainable development provisions, for simplicity of discussion. There is no fixed pattern for sustainable development and its elements to be incorporated in IIAs. This book identifies four major types of sustainable development provisions typically seen in modern IIAs.

First, the preambles of IIAs. IIAs may integrate sustainable development or its elements in the preamble. For instance, the 2004 Canadian Model BIT expressly provides that "the execution of the BIT should be conducive to the promotion of sustainable development".[91] Though the 2012 US Model BIT does not expressly refer to the principle of sustainable development, it incorporates the various key elements of this principle, including "improve living standards", and "achieve these objectives in a manner consistent with the protection of health, safety, and the environment, and the promotion of internationally recognized labor rights".[92]

From the treaty-law perspective, the preamble to a treaty consists of statements at the beginning expressing the parties' general purpose and aims in concluding the treaty, as well as the values underlying the treaty.[93] Though it forms an integral part of a treaty, it is different from the operational clauses of the treaty in that it usually does not confer contractual rights or obligations on the contracting parties, though they may reflect rules of customary law.[94] According to the Vienna Convention on Law of Treaties (VCLT), preambles may play an assistive role under several important provisions.[95] For instance, the preamble of a treaty plays an important role in ascertaining and establishing the objective and purpose of the treaty. This is helpful in interpreting the treaty under Article 31, and in determining the violation of the treaty under Article 18 and Article 60.

Because many IIAs incorporate statements relating to sustainable development promotion in the preamble, such statements should be deemed as an object and purpose of the IIAs, which is not necessarily in conflict with economic prosperity and investment protection.[96] In ISA practice, arbitral tribunals often refer to the preambles of IIAs when interpreting the IIA provisions. In Siemens v. Argentina, the ICSID tribunal held that it "shall be guided by the purpose of the Treaty as expressed in its title and preamble", and that:

> The preamble provides that the parties have agreed to the provisions of the Treaty for the purpose of creating favourable conditions for the investments of nationals or companies of one of the two States in the territory of the other State.[97]

Similarly, in Vivendi v. Argentina, the ICSID tribunal held that "As to the object and purpose of the BIT, the tribunal notes the parties' wish, as stated in the preamble …" and that "In interpreting the BIT, we are thus mindful of these objectives".[98]

Second, substantive sustainable development provisions. Substantive provisions have been and still are the core provisions of IIAs. They guarantee certain treatment and protection to foreign investors and investments. A growing number of IIAs incorporate the elements of sustainable development in substantive provisions. These provisions can be further divided into two subtypes. One subtype is affirmative provisions, which require the states to conduct certain acts or to refrain from conducting certain acts for sustainable development purposes. For instance, some IIAs require the contracting states not to degrade their environmental protection level to attract foreign investments; some require contracting states to conduct environmental review when admitting foreign investments.

The other subtype is exceptive provisions, aiming at exempting the contracting states from being held liable for taking certain measures that are otherwise inconsistent with their IIA obligations. The exempted measures are often taken for public interest and sustainable development purposes. Some IIAs incorporate a clause of general exceptions modelled after GATT Article XX (General Exceptions) and GATS Article XVI (General Exceptions). If the measures taken by the state fall within the scope of this clause, the state shall not be held liable for the damage incurred thereby to the foreign investors and investments.

Third, public interest provisions. These provisions are designed for the protection of the public interest, and are often in the form of soft-law rules in IIAs. Soft law falls out of the source of international law as listed in Article 38 of the ICJ Statute, and is not promulgated by authorized law-makers of the contracting states. Therefore, the question of whether soft-law rules should be incorporated in IIAs and what roles they may play has generated controversy and criticism.[99] Despite such debate, some IIAs incorporate soft-law rules, especially corporate social responsibility (CSR) rules. Although the incorporation of soft-law rules in IIAs does not necessarily transform these rules to "hard law" rules, and can hardly impose affirmative obligations on the contracting states and foreign investors, the presence of these rules is helpful in making IIAs more compatible with sustainable development.

Fourth, procedural sustainable development provisions. Early IIAs, especially IIAs of European countries, do not contain comprehensive procedural rules. The procedural rules of these IIAs simply serve the purpose of extending state consent to submit certain types of investment disputes to arbitration, ICSID or *ad hoc*. Rather, in the case of arbitration, the rules governing the arbitral proceedings are provided by the applicable arbitration laws and rules, such as ICSID arbitration rules or UNCITRAL arbitration rules. Recent IIAs, especially American-style IIAs, often contain comprehensive procedural rules dealing with the various aspects of the dispute settlement proceedings. Some of these rules are relevant to sustainable development, such as rules on procedural transparency, the participation of non-disputing contracting states and of non-disputing parties (such as amicus curiae).

Except for the preambles of IIAs, which only have "limited" effectiveness, the other types of sustainable development provisions in IIAs will be discussed in the next part of this book. Before examining these typical IIA provisions, a few points should be mentioned. First, these provisions are frequently seen in IIAs, but they should not be deemed to constitute an exhaustive list of sustainable development provisions in IIAs. In fact, IIAs vary with respect to their sustainable development provisions. Second, when discussing these provisions, this book does not aim at providing a complete and thorough study of them, but only focuses on the aspects or elements of these provisions that may have direct impacts on the promotion of sustainable development. Finally, these provisions are not necessarily mutually exclusive with one another. One type of sustainable development concern can be addressed by several different IIA provisions. For example, the environmental concerns associated with transnational investment activities can be addressed via the clause of general exceptions, the provision of amicus curiae participation and the provision of public interest protection.

Notes

1   W. M. Lafferty, "From Environmental Protection to Sustainable Development: The Challenge of Decoupling through Sectoral Integration", in W. M. Lafferty (ed.) *Governance for Sustainable Development: The Challenge of Adopting Form to Function* (Cheltenham: Edward Elgar, 2004), at 192.
2   V. Barral, "Sustainable Development in International Law: Nature and Operation of an Evolutive Legal Norm", 23 (2) *European Journal of International Law* 377 (2012), at 377.
3   Ibid., at 382.
4   See N. Schrijver, "The Evolution of Sustainable Development in International Law: Inception, Meaning and Status", 329 *Recueil des cours* 217 (2007), at 373.
5   Ibid., at 238.
6   World Commission on Environment and Development, Our Common Future, available at www.un-documents.net/ocf-02.htm#I (last accessed 10 October 2015), at para. 1.
7   K. Ellison, "Rio+20: How the Tension between Developing and Developed Countries Influenced Sustainable Development Efforts", 27 *Pacific McGeorge Global Business and Development Law Journal* 107 (2014), at 111.
8   See P. Birnie, A. Boyle and C. Redgwell, *International Law and the Environment* (3rd edn.) (Oxford: Oxford University Press, 2009), at 53.
9   UNCED, *Rio Declaration on Environment and Development* (UN Doc. A/CONF.151/26 (Vol. I)) (12 August 1992), available at www.un.org/documents/ga/conf151/aconf15126-1annex1.htm.
10 UNCED, *Agenda 21* (3–14 June 1992), available at https://sustainabledevelopment.un.org/outcomedocuments/agenda21.
11 P. Birnie, A. Boyle and C. Redgwell, at 50.
12 The Rio Declaration, at principle 4.
13 See P. Birnie and A. Boyle, *International Law and the Environment* (2nd edn.) (Oxford: Oxford University Press, 2002), at 45.
14 WSSD, *Johannesburg Declaration on Sustainable Development* (UN Doc. A/CONF.199/20) (4 September 2002), available at www.un-documents.net/jburgdec.htm.
15 H. M. Osofsky, "Defining Sustainable Development after Earth Summit 2002", 26 *Loyola Los Angeles International and Comparative Law Review* 111 (2003), at 123.
16 The Johannesburg Declaration, at para. 5.
17 UNGA, *2005 World Summit Outcome* (UN Doc. A/RES/60/1) (24 October 2005), available at www.un.org/womenwatch/ods/A-RES-60-1-E.pdf, at 11–12.
18 ILA, "New Delhi Declaration of Principles of International Law Relating to Sustainable Development", reprinted in 2 (2) *International Environmental Agreements* 211 (2002), at 211–216.

19 See M. Segger, M. W. Gehring and A. Newcombe (eds.), *Sustainable Development in World Investment Law* (Alphen aan den Rijn: Kluwer Law International, 2011), at 7–9.

20 See e.g. D. Tladi, *Sustainable Development in International Law: An Analysis of Key Enviro-economic Instruments* (Cape Town: Pretoria University Law Press, 2007), at 95–97.

21 B. Sjafjell, "Quo Vadis, Europe? The Significance of Sustainable Development as Objective, Principle and Rule of EU Law", in C. M. Bailliet (ed.), *Non-State Actors, Soft Law and Protective Regimes: From the Margins* (Cambridge: Cambridge University Press, 2012), at 254.

22 Case Concerning the Gabčíkovo-Nagymaros Project of 25 September 1997 (Hungary v. Slovakia), Separate Opinion of Vice-President Weeramantry, *I.C.J. Rep.* 7 (1997), at 89.

23 N. Schrijver, "ILA New Delhi Declaration of Principles of International Law Relating to Sustainable Development", 49 (2) *Netherlands International Law Review* (2002), at 299.

24 See Case Concerning the Gabčíkovo-Nagymaros Project of 25 September 1997 (Hungary v. Slovakia), Separate Opinion of Vice-President Weeramantry, *I.C.J. Rep.* 7 (1997), at 92–95.

25 See e.g. C. Voigt, *Sustainable Development as a Principle of International Law: Resolving Conflicts between Climate Measures and WTO Law* (Leiden: Martinus Nijhoff Publishers, 2009), at 161.

26 K. Ellison (2014), at 107.

27 UN Documents, available at www.un-documents.net/k-001303.htm.

28 E. B. Bonanomi, *Sustainable Development in International Law Making and Trade* (Cheltenham: Edward Elgar Publishing, 2015), at 188.

29 V. Barral (2012), at 384.

30 E. B. Bonanomi (2015), at 193.

31 C. Greenwood, "Sources of International Law: An Introduction", available at http://legal.un.org/avl/pdf/ls/greenwood_outline.pdf.

32 V. Barral (2012), at 378.

33 See V. Lowe, "Sustainable Development and Unsustainable Arguments", in A. Boyle and D. Freestone (eds.), *International Law and Sustainable Development* (Oxford: Oxford University Press, 1999), at 34 *et seq.*

34 F. O. Raimondo, *General Principles of Law in the Decisions of International Criminal Courts and Tribunals* (Leiden: Martinus Nijhoff Publishers, 2008), at 45.

35 Award, Arbitration Regarding the Iron Rhine ("Ijzeren Rijn") Railway (Belgium v. Netherlands) (24 May 2005), available at http://legal.un.org/riaa/cases/vol_XXVII/35-125.pdf, at para. 59.

36 See e.g. P. Sands, "International Courts and the Application of the Concept of Sustainable Development", 3 *Max Planck Yearbook of United Nations Law* 389 (1999), at 404–405.

37 R. Dolzer and C. Schreuer, *Principles of International Investment Law* (1st edn.) (Oxford: Oxford University Press, 2008), at 4.

38 See R. Dolzer and C. Schreuer (2012), at 1–3.

39 See S. Hobe, "The Law Relating to Aliens, the International Minimum Standard and State Responsibility", in M. Bungenberg, J. Griebel, S. Hobe and A. Reinisch (eds.), *International Investment Law: A Handbook* (Baden-Baden: Nomos, 2015), at 6–22; A. A. Ghouri, "The Evolution of Bilateral Investment Treaties, Investment

Treaty Arbitration and International Investment Law", 14 (6) *International Arbitration Law Review* 189 (2011), at 191.

40   See A. Newcombe and L. Paradell, *Law and Practice of Investment Treaties* (Alphen aan den Rijn: Kluwer Law International, 2009), at 18–19.

41   See V. V. Veeder, "The Lena Goldfields Arbitration: The Historical Roots of Three Ideas", 47 *International and Comparative Law Quarterly* 747 (1998).

42   K. J. Vandevelde, "A Brief History of International Investment Agreement", 12 (1) *University of California at Davis Journal of International Law and Policy* 156 (2005), at 159–160.

43   J. Dugard, "Articles on Diplomatic Protection", *United Nations Audiovisual Library of International Law*, available at http://legal.un.org/avl/pdf/ha/adp/adp_e.pdf, at 3.

44   Article 2, "Articles on Diplomatic Protection with Commentaries", YBILC, 2006, Vol. 2, Part Two, at 29.

45   Article 44, "Draft Articles on Responsibility of States for Internationally Wrongful Acts with Commentaries", YBILC, 2001, Vol. 2, Part Two, at 120.

46   See e.g. A. Newcombe and L. Paradell (2009), at 5–7.

47   M. Sornarajah, *The International Law on Foreign Investment* (3rd edn.) (Cambridge: Cambridge University Press, 2010), at 19.

48   K. J. Vandevelde (2005), at 158.

49   Ibid., at 161.

50   Article 2, the UN Charter.

51   Article 51, the UN Charter.

52   Article 42, the UN Charter.

53   A. Newcombe and L. Paradell (2009), at 41; K. J. Vandevelde (2005), at 168.

54   K. J. Vandevelde (2005), at 172–173.

55   Available at http://investmentpolicyhub.unctad.org/IIA/country/78/treaty/1732

56   UNGA, Declaration on the Establishment of a New International Economic Order (UN Doc. A/RES/S-6/3201), available at www.un-documents.net/s6r3201.htm.

57   Ibid., at para. 4(d).

58   K. J. Vandevelde (2005), at 178.

59   See e.g. UNCTAD, "The Role of International Investment Agreements in Attracting Foreign Direct Investment to Developing Countries", *UNCTAD Series on International Investment Policies for Development* (2009), available at http://unctad.org/en/Docs/diaeia20095_en.pdf; L. N. S. Poulsen, "The Importance of BITs for Foreign Direct Investment and Political Risk Insurance: Revisiting the Evidence", K. Sauvant (ed.), *Yearbook on International Investment Law and Policy 2009/2010* (New York: Oxford University Press, 2010), at 539–574.

60   S. Rose-Ackerman and J. L. Tobin, "Do BITs Benefit Developing Countries?", in C. A. Rogers and R. P. Alford (eds.), *The Future of Investment Arbitration* (New York: Oxford University Press, 2009), at 134.

61   See R. Dolzer and C. Schreuer (2012), at 158; UNCTAD, *Bilateral Investment Treaties 1995–2006: Trends in Investment Rulemaking* (2007), available at http://unctad.org/en/docs/iteiia20065_en.pdf, at 141.

62   K. J. Vandevelde (2005), at 178.

63   Available at www.nafta-sec-alena.org/Home/Texts-of-the-Agreement/North-American-Free-Trade-Agreement.

64   Available at https://ustr.gov/trade-agreements/free-trade-agreements/trans-pacific-partnership/tpp-full-text.

65   Available at http://ec.europa.eu/trade/policy/in-focus/ttip/.

66 See e.g. A. Åslund, "The World Needs a Multilateral Investment Agreement", *Policy Brief of Peterson Institute for International Economics* (No. PB 13–01), available at https://piie.com/sites/default/files/publications/pb/pb13-1.pdf; B. Ferrarini, *A Multilateral Framework for Investment?*, available at www.cid.harvard.edu/cidtrade/Papers/ferrarini_wti_investment.pdf.

67 See e.g. O. De Schutter, J. Swinnen and J. Wouters (eds.), *Foreign Direct Investment and Human Development: The Law and Economics of International Investment Agreements* (Abingdon: Routledge, 2013), at 1; S. W. Schill, C. Tams and R. Hofmann, "International Investment Law and Development: Friends or Foes?", in S. W. Schill, C. Tams and R. Hofmann (eds.), *International Investment Law and Development: Bridging the Gap* (Cheltenham: Edward Elgar Publishing, 2015), at 3–5.

68 UN Doc. No. TD/378.

69 O. De Schutter, J. Swinnen and J. Wouters (eds.) (2013), at 2.

70 Treaty between the Federal Republic of Germany and Pakistan for the Promotion and Protection of Investments (1959), available at http://investmentpolicy hub.unctad.org/Download/TreatyFile/1387.

71 1 ICSID Reports 28, para 25.

72 R. Dolzer and C. Schreuer (2012), at 245.

73 Salini Costruttori S.p.a. and Italstrade S.p.A. v. Kingdom of Morocco, ICSID Case No. ARB/00/4, available at www.italaw.com/cases/958 (last accessed 20 September 2016).

74 Salini Costruttori S.p.a. and Italstrade S.p.A. v. Kingdom of Morocco (ICSID Case No. ARB/00/4), Decision on Jurisdiction, reprinted in 42 *International Legal Materials* 624 (2003), at 618–624, available at www.italaw.com/sites/default/files/case-documents/ita0738.pdf.

75 SGS Société Générale de Surveillance S.A. v. Islamic Republic of Pakistan (ICSID Case No. ARB/01/13), available at www.italaw.com/cases/1009 (20 September 2016).

76 SGS v. Pakistan, Decision of the Tribunal on Objections to Jurisdiction, available at www.italaw.com/sites/default/files/case-documents/ita0779.pdf, at para. 140.

77 SGS Société Générale de Surveillance S.A. v. Republic of the Philippines (ICSID Case No. ARB/02/6), available at www.italaw.com/cases/1018 (last accessed 20 September 2016).

78 SGS v. Philippines, Decision of the Tribunal on Objections to Jurisdiction, available at www.italaw.com/sites/default/files/case-documents/ita0782.pdf, at para. 112.

79 N. Bernasconi-Osterwalder and L. Johnson (eds.), *International Investment Law and Sustainable Development: Key Cases from 2000 to 2010*, available at www.iisd.org/publications/international-investment-law-and-sustainable-development-key-cases-2000-2010, at 123.

80 A. R. Parra, *The History of ICSID* (Oxford: Oxford University Press, 2012), at. 12.

81 A. Newcombe, "Sustainable Development and Investment Treaty Law", 8 (3) *J. World Inv. & Trade* 357 (2007), at 357.

82 See M. Segger, M. W. Gehring and A. Newcombe (2011), at 9.

83 UNCED, *Agenda 21*, available at https://sustainabledevelopment.un.org/outcome documents/agenda21, at para. 2.23.

84 See M. Segger, M. W. Gehring and A. Newcombe (2011), at 4–5.

85 UNCTAD (2016). UNCTAD facilitates G20 consensus on Guiding Principles for

Global Investment Policymaking, available at http://investmentpolicyhub.unctad.org/News/Hub/Home/508; MOFCOM, Trade Minister Gao Hucheng Attends the G20 Ministerial Meeting Outcome Delivery Meeting, www.mofcom.gov.cn/article/ae/ai/201607/20160701355815.shtml.

86   See Chapter 2.

87   See generally M. Chi, "The 'Greenization' of Chinese BITs: An Empirical Study of the Environmental Provisions in Chinese BITs and its Implications for China's Future BIT-Making", 18 (3) *Journal of International Economic Law* 511 (2015).

88   See Preamble, China–Canada BIT.

89   See Preamble, China–Korea–Japan TIT.

90   IISD Model IIA, at iii.

91   Preamble, the 2004 Canadian Model BIT.

92   Preamble, the 2012 U.S. Model BIT.

93   M. E. Villiger, *Commentary on the 1969 Convention on the Law of Treaties* (Leiden: Martinus Nijhoff, 2009), at 43.

94   See G. Fitzmaurice, "The Law and Procedure of the International Court of Justice 1951–1954", 33 *BYBIL* 229 (1957).

95   M. E. Villiger (2009), at 44.

96   See F. Ortino, "Investment Treaties, Sustainable Development and Reasonableness Review: A Case against Strict Proportionality Balancing", 30 (1) *Leiden Journal of International Law* 71 (2017), at 75–83.

97   *Siemens A.G. v. The Argentine Republic* (ICSID Case No. ARB/02/8), Decision on Jurisdiction of 3 August 2004, available at www.italaw.com/cases/1026, at para. 81.

98   Compañiá de Aguas del Aconquija S.A. and Vivendi Universal v. Argentine Republic (ICSID Case No. ARB/97/3), Award of 20 August 2007, available at www.italaw.com/cases/309, at para. 7.4.4.

99   See A. K. Bjorklund, "Assessing the Effectiveness of Soft Law Instruments in International Investment Law", in A. K. Bjorklund and A. Reinisch (eds.), *International Investment Law and Soft Law* (Cheltenham: Edward Elgar, 2013), at 51–53.

2   Assessment of the existing models and proposals

IIAs are concluded primarily for investment protection and promotion. They can be insufficiently compatible with sustainable development. As the international community today faces unprecedented sustainability challenges, there is a growing call to reform the current IIA system to address sustainable development concerns associated with transnational investment activities. Since the new millennium, state governments, academics and ISA practitioners have started to reflect on the IIA system. A number of model IIAs and proposals or suggestions have been raised by major international organizations and NGOs to reform the existing IIAs to be compatible with sustainable development, or, in a slightly different term, to make "balanced IIAs". These models and proposals discuss the interrelation between IIAs and sustainable development, and provide insights for reforming the current IIA and ISDS systems. This chapter analyses and compares the major models and proposals as well as their implications for future global IIA-making.

IISD Model IIA (2004)

The International Institute of Sustainable Development (IISD) observed that the existing IIAs are not sufficiently helpful in addressing sustainable development challenges because "they largely assume that the central problem to be solved is the protection of foreign investors from discriminatory actions by the host state", and that the issues that need to be addressed in IIAs have inevitably increased.[1]

The IISD issued the Model International Investment Agreement for the Promotion of Sustainable Development (IISD Model IIA) in 2004 to serve as a template for states in IIA-making.[2] The IISD Model IIA is probably the earliest comprehensive model designed with sustainable development as a core value of IIA. Its main purpose is to "increase long-term foreign investment that supports sustainable development".[3] It highlights the need to achieve balance between investor rights, development objectives and protection of public goods, in a manner that is legitimate, transparent and accountable.[4]

Upholding the ideal of promoting sustainable development through IIAs, the IISD Model IIA "redefines" the existing IIA paradigm. It contains several parts,

DOI: 10.4324/9781315642840-4

including general provisions; foreign investor rights and standards of treatment; foreign investor obligations; host state rights and obligations; home state rights and obligations; relation to other agreements, dispute settlement, institutional provisions, exceptions and final provisions. While some rules of this Model routinely appear in many IIAs, some are quite innovative and rarely seen in existing IIAs.

The distinct feature of the IISD Model IIA is the engagement of a broader range of stakeholders of transnational investment activities, especially foreign investors and home states. This Model not only aims at protecting foreign investors, but also directly imposing obligations on the investors to ensure that their investments are consistent with sustainable development and do not harm local environment and communities. It suggests that specific codes of practice for CSR be incorporated in IIAs by reference.[5] It also requires the home state to undertake the responsibility to regulate its overseas investors and take liability for the failure to do so.[6]

The IISD Model IIA, through including non-state stakeholders in the IIA framework, represents a bold deviation from the existing IIAs in structure, content and objective. It helps transform IIAs from legal instruments for protecting and promoting foreign investments into a discourse for promoting sustainable development as well.

The UNCTAD Policy Framework (2012 and 2015)

The United Nations Conference on Trade and Development (UNCTAD) stands in the forefront of promoting sustainable development, especially from a developing country perspective. In 2012, the UNCTAD issued the Investment Policy Framework for Sustainable Development (UNCTAD Policy Framework).[7] The Framework not only provides suggestions for IIA-making, but contains a set of "designed criteria" for investment policies that aim to mainstream sustainable development in investment policymaking, while confirming the basic principles of sound development-oriented investment policies in a balanced approach.[8]

The UNCTAD Policy Framework raises several advices for IIA-making that may help address sustainable development concerns associated with transnational investment activities. First, given the fact that existing IIAs only obligate host states to protect foreign investments, the Framework proposes that IIAs should incorporate concrete commitments to promote and facilitate investment for sustainable development. Second, as most IIAs provide for state obligations but are silent on investor obligations, the Framework proposes that IIAs should balance state commitments with investor obligations. Third, as the nature of an IIA is to obligate host states to grant a certain standard of treatment and protection to foreign investors and investments, and to limit the regulatory power of the states, the Framework proposes that IIAs should ensure an appropriate balance between protection commitments and regulatory space for development. Fourth, as most IIAs allow foreign investors to directly pursue relief against host states through ISA, which may cause excessive liability and procedural costs, the

Framework proposes that IIAs should be able to shield host states from unjustified liabilities and high procedural costs.[9]

The UNCTAD Policy Framework contains both strategic guidelines and concrete suggestions for drafting IIAs compatible with sustainable development. It features several unique "balancing paradigms", including the balance among investors, host states and home states, and the balance between substantive and procedural aspects. The concrete suggestions for IIA-drafting are the following:

- including a scope and definition clause that excludes portfolio, short-term and speculative investments from IIA coverage;
- formulating a fair and equitable treatment (FET) clause as an exhaustive list of state obligations;
- clarifying the distinction between legitimate regulatory activity and regulatory takings (indirect expropriation) giving rise to compensation;
- limiting the full protection and security (FPS) provision to "physical" security only and specifying that protection shall be commensurate with the country's level of development;
- limiting the scope of a transfer of funds clause by providing an exhaustive list of covered payments and including exceptions in case of serious balance-of-payment difficulties;
- including exceptions to protect human rights, health, core labour standards and the environment;
- excluding the ISDS clause or making it the last resort for foreign investors;
- establishing an institutional set-up that makes the IIA adaptable to changing development contexts and major unanticipated developments.[10]

In 2015, a revised version of the UNCTAD Policy Framework was released in light of the emergence of a "new generation" of investment policies.[11] The revised Framework recognizes the marginalization of sustainable development in global investment policies, and proposes that sustainable development be highlighted in investment policymaking and IIA-making in the future. The mission states that:

> "New generation" investment policies place inclusive growth and sustainable development at the heart of efforts to attract and benefit from investment. Sustainable development issues – including environmental, social and poverty alleviation concerns – as well as investor responsibility in these areas, are not "new" in and by themselves. However, to date, the myriad of solutions and options developed over the years to address sustainable development concerns have not been part and parcel of mainstream investment policymaking, and the international consensus on sustainable development is not reflected in it. "New generation" investment policies aim to systematically integrate sustainable development and operationalize it in concrete measures and mechanisms at the national and international level, and at the level of policymaking and implementation.[12]

The revised Framework outlines a three-level strategy for investment policy-making, including state development strategy-making at unilateral level, IIA provision-designing at bilateral and regional level, and investment policy consensus building at multilateral level.[13]

With special regard to IIA-making, the revised Framework states that "Addressing sustainable development challenges through the detailed design of provisions in investment agreements principally implies four areas of evolution in treaty-making practice".[14] Following this line, four different suggestions are proposed:

- incorporating concrete commitments to promote and facilitate investment for sustainable development;
- balancing state commitments with investor obligations and promoting responsible investment;
- ensuring an appropriate balance between protection commitments and regulatory space for development;
- reforming the ISDS system.[15]

Compared with the old Framework, the revised Framework appears to be more practical and timely regarding how to make IIAs more compatible with sustainable development. Particularly, the three-step strategy of investment policymaking at national, regional and international levels will have far-reaching impacts in the future.

The SADC Model BIT (2012)

In 2012, the South African Development Community (SADC) proposed its model BIT.[16] A major purpose of this BIT is to promote sustainable development of the SADC through foreign investment governance. The preamble of this model BIT, in several paragraphs, clearly incorporates sustainable development. Particularly, this model BIT aims at "seeking an overall balance of the rights and obligations among the state parties, the investors, and the investments". According to the official commentary of the SADC Model BIT, the need for a "balanced" BIT is a result of the reflection of the existing ISDS system and ISA case law. The purpose is to better reconcile the interests of foreign investors and the development objectives of the host states. The major tool for realizing such a purpose is to "preclude unintended expansive interpretation of substantive provisions in favour of investors on the basis of the intent to protect investors expressed in the preamble".[17]

Compared with the existing IIAs, a main feature of the SADC Model BIT lies in that it incorporates a provision entitled "objective", which clarifies what has been stated in the treaty preamble. This provision provides that the main objective of this BIT is to encourage and increase investments "that support the sustainable development of each Party, and in particular the Host State where an investment is to be located". Here, it is of interest to note that this provision, by taking into consideration the situation that almost all states of the region are developing countries, sends out a clear message that sustainable development is of paramount importance in IIA-making for developing countries, despite their dire need for attracting foreign investments.

In addition, the SADC Model BIT also contains a specific provision entitled "Right of States to Regulate".[18] This provision makes clear that in accordance with customary international law and general principles of international law, the host state retains the right to take regulatory or other measures to ensure that development is consistent with the goals and principles of sustainable development and other legitimate social and economic policy objectives.

The Commonwealth Guide (2012)

In August 2012, the Commonwealth Secretariat published its IIA-making guide, mainly for the developing state members of the Commonwealth. The guide is entitled "Integrating Sustainable Development into International Investment Agreements: A Guide for Developing Countries" (Commonwealth Guide).[19]

The Commonwealth Guide, at the outset, recognizes that traditional IIAs focus exclusively on investment protection but do not otherwise address development. It also observes that the link between investment and development is "inconclusive", meaning that such links can be either positive or negative. Whether and to what extent foreign investments can promote host states' development depends on a wide range of factors.[20] While acknowledging such an inconclusive link, the Commonwealth Guide aims primarily at illustrating the various ways in which traditional IIAs can be modified to contribute to sustainable development.

Given that states may have different interpretations of sustainable development, the Commonwealth Guide first adopts a working interpretation of this term. Instead of focusing purely on economic growth or environmental sustainability, this Guide employs a holistic and comprehensive notion of development that encompasses a wide range of considerations, such as environmental protection, human health and welfare, human rights and the rights of indigenous peoples.[21] As can be seen, such understanding substantively echoes the three main aspects of sustainable development.

The Commonwealth Guide surveys several major substantive and procedural provisions of selected IIAs, and discusses their relevance with sustainable development. On such a basis, the Guide puts forward various mechanisms that may be used by negotiators in IIA-making, which include the following:

- encouraging investment;
- protecting the regulatory flexibility of host states to achieve development goals;
- partnerships with the investor's home states to support sustainable development;
- sustainability assessments;

- a grievance procedure;
- standards for investors;
- developing domestic measures and enforcement mechanisms for promoting sustainable development in the host and home states;
- counterclaims by states in ISA and limitations on investor access.[22]

Also, as the Commonwealth Guide is prepared mainly for negotiators of developing state members, it also discusses issues that are not directly linked with IIAs but related to the IIA-making of development countries, such as negotiation capacity-building, international cooperation and domestic law preparation.

In general, the Commonwealth Guide provides a comprehensive analysis of the typical IIA provisions that may be relevant to sustainable development. These provisions cover a wide range, including not only substantive and procedural provisions frequently incorporated in existing IIAs, but also "new" ones designed for sustainable development promotion in recent IIAs, such as environmental and labour rights provisions.

The OECD Survey (2014)

In 2014, the OECD published a report entitled Investment Treaty Law, Sustainable Development and Responsible Business Conduct: A Fact Finding Survey (the OECD Survey), based on the result of its comprehensive survey of over two thousand IIAs and over one thousand treaty-based ISA cases.[23]

As a first step, the OECD Survey identifies four major types of sustainable development elements associated with transnational investment activities, i.e. environment protection, labour rights, anti-corruption and human rights. It further observes that these elements received different degrees of attention in IIA-making at different times. To be more specific, environmental provisions appeared in IIAs in 1985, labour rights provisions in 1990, anti-corruption provisions in 2000 and human rights provisions in 2002.[24] The Survey confirms that the major inadequacy of existing IIAs in addressing sustainable development concerns lies in two aspects. On one side, IIAs only create rights but not responsibilities for foreign investors regarding their contributions to sustainable development. On the other side, IIAs may unduly limit the host states' ability to enact public policies needed to promote sustainable development and responsible business conduct.[25]

Being the second step, the OECD Survey identifies nine types of treaty languages referring to sustainable development in IIAs, including:

- preamble;
- preserving policy space;
- not lowering standards;
- taking measures to protect public welfare;
- commitment to cooperate on sustainable development matters;
- establishing a relation between sustainable development and ISDS;

- maintaining or implementing internationally recognized standards;
- establishing commitments to act in the fight against corruption;
- encouraging the respect of sustainable development standards.[26]

Being the third step, while based on the examination of the treaty languages in IIAs and their application in ISA, the OECD Survey draws several observations and makes some suggestions. First, countries may hold different attitudes to sustainable development in IIAs. In general, while sustainable development provisions frequently appear in the IIAs of some developed countries, they are seldom included in IIAs of developing countries.[27] Second, recent IIAs appear friendlier towards sustainable development because they incorporate more sustainable development provisions. Third, in some treaty-based ISA cases, arbitral tribunals discussed the identified sustainable development elements and referred to international treaties relating to sustainable development.[28]

Finally, two proposals are raised, namely updating the IIA stock that incorporate sustainable development provisions, and making sure that ISDS mechanisms and treaty provisions are well designed to enable the arbitral tribunals to take into account sustainable development issues in ISDS proceedings.[29]

Strictly speaking, these proposals stay largely at policy level, and cannot directly serve as IIA-making suggestions. However, by highlighting the four substantive sustainable development provisions of IIAs, the OECD Survey illustrates the fields where further IIA-making efforts should be made to promote sustainable development.

The EU's proposal of an investment court system (2015)

One of the most notable recent developments in the field of international investment law is probably the EU's IIA-making. The conclusion of the Treaty of Lisbon amending the Treaty on European Union and the Treaty establishing the European Community (Lisbon Treaty) in 2007 significantly changed the constitutional structure of the EU. And the inclusion of FDI in the Common Commercial Policy (CCP) in the Lisbon Treaty is perhaps "the largest change".[30] The Lisbon Treaty grants the EU exclusive foreign direct investment (FDI) competence, although FDI is not defined in the Treaty of Functioning of the European Union (TFEU).[31] As a result, while different interpretations of FDI could be produced, the EU has nonetheless acquired exclusive competence to conclude IIAs.[32] Formerly, however, the EU only had shared competence in international investment matters with its member states.[33]

Against such a background, the EU started to negotiate a series of IIAs. During the negotiation of the TTIP, the EU raised a proposal for an investment court system in 2015.[34] According to the EU, the key challenge for the reformed investment policy is the need to ensure that the goal of protecting and encouraging investment does not affect the ability of the EU and its member states to continue to pursue public policy objectives.[35] The EU wants to replace the existing ISDS mechanism in the TTIP and in all ongoing and future EU trade and investment negotiations with this court system, first at bilateral level, then at multilateral level.

Being the first step, the EU seeks the establishment of the bilateral investment court system to "safeguard the right to regulate and create a court-like system with an appeal mechanism based on clearly defined rules, with qualified judges and transparent proceedings". Being the second step, while in parallel to the TTIP negotiations and in future EU trade and investment negotiations, the EU will start to work together with other countries on setting up a permanent International Investment Court.[36]

The EU's proposal of an investment court system represents a profound deviation from the existing ISDS system. This system boasts several major features and improvements:

- A public Investment Court System composed of a first-instance Tribunal and an Appeal Tribunal would be set up.
- Judgments would be made by publicly appointed judges with high qualifications, comparable to those required for the members of permanent international courts such as the International Court of Justice and the WTO Appellate Body.
- The new Appeal Tribunal would be operating on similar principles to the WTO Appellate Body.
- The ability of investors to take a case before the Tribunal would be precisely defined and limited to cases such as targeted discrimination on the base of gender, race or religion, or nationality, expropriation without compensation, or denial of justice.
- Governments' right to regulate would be enshrined and guaranteed in the provisions of the trade and investment agreements.[37]

As the TTIP negotiation has not been completed, it is unclear whether and to what extent the EU's proposal will be incorporated in the treaty. Nevertheless, already in the making of the EU–Canada Comprehensive Economic and Trade Agreement (CETA)[38] and the EU–Vietnam FTA,[39] the EU has tried to realize its proposal. Both of these agreements include an investment dispute tribunal system that is similar to the EU's proposed investment court system in many aspects. Also, aside from the detailed procedure rules, the system enshrined in these agreements provides a two-tiered dispute settlement mechanism, including a first-instance tribunal procedure and an appeal tribunal procedure.[40]

Though the EU's proposal was not raised for sustainable development considerations, it may have profound impacts on the compatibility of future EU IIAs with sustainable development. Essentially, this proposal deals with two key aspects of the international investment governance regime, i.e. investment dispute settlement and preservation of host states' regulatory power. As discussed earlier, these two aspects are among the major grounds that render the existing IIAs insufficient in addressing sustainable development concerns. The EU's proposal can be helpful in remedying such insufficiency. The establishment of an appeal system may help reduce the inconsistency of ISDS decisions (awards or judgements); the compulsory publishing of the judgments would lead to a higher level of procedural transparency; and the enhanced restriction on the investors' ability in initiating arbitration against the host states would better preserve the regulatory power of the host states.

Comparison and conclusion

The model IIAs and reform proposals are raised by different international organizations or NGOs from different perspectives and with different focuses. To some extent, they represent the plausible efforts and remarkable achievements of the international community in reforming the current IIA system to be more compatible with sustainable development. A few observations can be drawn by comparing and reviewing these models and proposals.

First, despite their differences, these models and proposals share the consensus that the current IIA system is not sufficiently compatible with sustainable development, and that the chief reason is that the existing IIAs are primarily concluded for the purpose of investment protection. Though many IIAs incorporate sustainable development in their preambles, this is symbolic because treaty preambles only have limited effectiveness in practice.

Second, these models and proposals try to reform the current IIA system by striking a better balance between preserving state regulatory power and protecting foreign investments from different perspectives. Some proposals present a comprehensive approach of IIA-making, such as the IISD Model IIA, the SADC Model BIT and the Commonwealth Guide; others focus on certain aspects of IIA-making, such as the EU's proposal. Methodologically, while some proposals aim at providing model IIA provisions, such as the IISD Model IIA, others only highlight certain policy considerations for IIA negotiators, such as the UNCTAD Framework, the OECD Survey and the Commonwealth Guide.

Third, many of these models and proposals include suggestions on redesigning IIA provisions and stressing the regulatory impacts of these provisions. Regarding substantive provisions, they exclude certain state regulatory acts from the ambit of the expropriation and fair and equitable treatment (FET) clauses, or list these acts in the exception clauses. Regarding procedural provisions, they aim at restricting foreign investors' ability in initiating arbitration against the host states.

Fourth, though all model IIAs and proposals stress the importance of sustainable development, they vary with regard to the understanding of sustainable development. Some proposals adopt a narrow and traditional understanding, focusing mainly on the issue of environmental protection; others take a broader understanding, trying to address a wide range of sustainable development concerns, such as labour and human rights protection, legitimacy of the ISDS, and CSR.

Finally, it should also be noted that these models and proposals have varied policy goals, which may limit their practical effects. For instance, the OECD

Survey puts more emphasis on the need to regulate the behaviour of foreign investors; the SADC Model BIT sets its focus on the preservation of policy-making flexibility and the regulatory power of the host states. Such difference is understandable and makes sense considering that the OECD is a "club" of developed countries that host the majority of the world's MNEs (investors), but the SADC is composed of developing and least-developed countries that are trying to attract more foreign investments for national economic development.

Up to the present, it is largely unclear whether and how states would follow these models and proposals in IIA-making. Thus, it remains difficult to accurately assess how these proposals would impact global IIA-making. Yet one thing is clear: all of these models and proposals will be beneficial in making the IIAs more compatible with sustainable development. It would not be surprising that states adopt or refer to these models and proposals in IIA-making.

Notes

1　See IISD, *Model International Investment Agreement for the Promotion of Sustainable Development* (2004), available at www.iisd.org/publications/model-internationalinvestment-agreement-promotion-sustainable-development, at iii.
2　Ibid.
3　The IISD Model IIA, at 3.
4　The IISD Model IIA, at 4.
5　The IISD Model IIA, at 16.
6　The IISD Model IIA, at 24.
7　See UNCTAD, *Investment Policy Framework for Sustainable Development* (2012), available at http://unctad.org/en/PublicationsLibrary/diaepcb2012d5_en.pdf.
8　UNCTAD, "Towards a New Generation of International Investment Policies: UNCTAD's Fresh Approach to Multilateral Investment Policy-Making", *IIA Issue Note*, No. 5, July 2013, at 9.
9　UNCTAD Policy Framework (2012), at 39–41.
10　UNCTAD Policy Framework (2012), at 44–45.
11　See UNCTAD, *Investment Policy Framework for Sustainable Development* (2015), available at http://unctad.org/en/PublicationsLibrary/diaepcb2015d5_en.pdf.
12　UNCTAD Policy Framework (2015), at 14.
13　UNCTAD Policy Framework (2015), at 69.
14　UNCTAD Policy Framework (2015), at 74.
15　UNCTAD Policy Framework (2015), at 74–76.
16　SADC, "SADC Model Bilateral Investment Treaty Template with Commentary", available at www.iisd.org/itn/wp-content/uploads/2012/10/sadc-model-bit-template-final.pdf.
17　SADC Model BIT with Commentary, at 7.
18　Article 21, the SADC Model BIT.
19　Commonwealth Secretariat (prepared by J. A. Van Duzer, P. Simons and G. Mayeda), *Integrating Sustainable Development into International Investment Agreements: A Guide for Developing Countries* (2012), available at www.iisd.org/pdf/2012/6th_annual_forum_commonwealth_guide.pdf.
20　The Commonwealth Guide, at 25–27.

21   The Commonwealth Guide, at 30.
22   The Commonwealth Guide, at 32–35.
23   K. Gordon, J. Pohl and M. Bouchard, *Investment Treaty Law, Sustainable Development and Responsible Business Conduct: A Fact Finding Survey* (OECD Working Papers on International Investment 2014/01), OECD Publishing.
24   See the OECD Survey, at 11.
25   The OECD Survey, at 5.
26   The OECD Survey, at 15–17.
27   The OECD Survey, at 11–12.
28   The OECD Survey, at 25.
29   The OECD Survey, at 25–26.
30   M. Bungenberg, "Going Global? The EU Common Commercial Policy after Lisbon", in C. Herrmann and J. P. Terhechte (eds.), *European Yearbook of International Economic Law* (2010), at 151.
31   Articles 206 and 207, the Treaty of Functioning of the European Union (TFEU).
32   W. Shan and S. Zhang, "The Treaty of Lisbon: Halfway towards a Common Investment Policy", 21 (4) *European Journal of International Law* (2011), at 1060–1065.
33   See W. Shan, "Towards a Common European Community Policy on Investment Issues", 2(3) *Journal of World Investment* (2001), at 603.
34   European Commission, Concept Paper (Investment in TTIP and Beyond – the Path for Reform), available at http://trade.ec.europa.eu/doclib/docs/2015/may/tradoc_153408.PDF.
35   Ibid., at 1.
36   European Commission, EU Finalizes Proposal for Investment Protection and Court System for TTIP (12 November 2015), available at http://trade.ec.europa.eu/doclib/press/index.cfm?id=1396.
37   European Commission, Commission Proposes New Investment Court System for TTIP and Other EU Trade and Investment Negotiations (16 September 2015), available at http://europa.eu/rapid/press-release_IP-15-5651_en.htm.
38   CETA, available at http://ec.europa.eu/trade/policy/in-focus/ceta/.
39   EU–Vietnam FTA, available at http://trade.ec.europa.eu/doclib/press/index.cfm?id=1437.
40   CETA, at Chapter 8 (Investment), Section F (Resolution of investment disputes between investors and states); EU–Vietnam FTA, at Chapter 8 (Trade in Service, Investment and E-Commerce), Chapter II (Investment), Section 3 (Resolution of Investment Disputes).

Part II

Core sustainable development provisions in IIAs

3 Substantive provisions

As with many other international agreements, IIAs limit the sovereign power of the contracting states. In particular, IIAs limit the contracting states to subject foreign investors and investments to their domestic law system. As suggested by R. Dolzer, the main clauses typically included in modern IIAs operate in ways to define and narrow the types of domestic administrative regulation to which foreign investors must subject themselves.[1]

Typical substantive sustainable development provisions of IIAs include expropriation and FET clauses. First, as these clauses restrict state regulatory power, they potentially limit states' ability in taking measures for sustainable development goals. Second, as the application of these clauses in ISA practice exposes state conduct – including legislative, judicial and administrative conduct – to the external scrutiny of private and international arbitral tribunals, they may have significant impacts on the states' expectations of the boundary of their conduct in investment governance. Third, FET as a general clause is apt to act as a gateway for the integration of external principles into the investment process, such as the principle of equity.[2] And the FET standard is also an expression of the principle of the rule of law in the context of IIAs.[3] These principles are typical elements of sustainable development as well.

Without studying the expropriation and FET clauses comprehensively, this chapter focuses on some specific elements of these clauses, aiming at analysing how these elements, especially the application thereof in ISA, may restrain states from pursuing sustainable development goals.

The restraining effect of an (indirect) expropriation clause

Expropriation has been a major public international law issue throughout the twentieth century. The rules of international law governing the expropriation of alien property have long been of central concern to foreign investors.[4] As IIAs are designed primarily for the protection of foreign investors and investments, it is almost a standard practice for IIAs to incorporate an expropriation clause. Because such a clause targets the exercise of state regulatory power, it may have a profound restraining effect on the states, which could impede the states in pursuing sustainable development goals.

DOI: 10.4324/9781315642840-6

The incorporation of an indirect expropriation clause in IIAs

A definition of expropriation can be found in customary international law, with "taking of property" as the core meaning.[5] Expropriation can be in both direct and indirect forms. Most IIAs deal with both forms of expropriation.

Direct expropriation means a mandatory legal transfer of the title to the property or its outright physical seizure, normally benefiting the state itself or a state-mandated third party.[6] In this case, the state has an open, deliberate and unequivocal intent of expropriation, as reflected in a formal law or decree or physical act.[7] Direct expropriation has been popular among states in Latin American, Asian, African and Eastern European regions after World War II, as many newly independent states relied on the nationalization of foreign investments to lay down the foundation of a new economic and social order.[8] For example, after its establishment in 1949, the People's Republic of China (P.R.C.) started an unprecedented nationalization movement targeted at foreign investments in the name of "socialist transformation of capitalist industry and commerce", which finally eliminated foreign investments in China and pushed China's national economy to the edge of collapse.[9] Even today, direct expropriation has not disappeared. In 2009, Venezuela passed a law authorizing its government to take over oil-service contractors. Relying on this law, the Venezuelan President ordered the seizure of oil installations and engaged in the direct expropriation of foreign-owned facilities in a wide range of industries. This has given rise to many ICSID arbitration cases.[10] Direct expropriation is an extreme way of taking of private properties, thus it is unambiguous and easily identifiable and is generally prohibited under international law.

Today, indirect expropriation has become the predominant form of expropriation.[11] Indirect expropriation involves total or near-total deprivation of an investment without a formal transfer of title or outright seizure of the property, but would effectuate the loss of management, use or control, or a significant depreciation in the value of the investment.[12] Thus, interference with an alien's property may amount to expropriation even when no explicit attempt is made to affect the legal title to the property, and even though the respondent state may specifically disclaim any such intention.[13]

In IIAs, it is frequently seen that various terminologies are used as equivalents or subcategories of indirect expropriation, such as creeping, constructive, disguised, consequential, regulatory, virtual, de facto expropriation,[14] or measures equivalent to expropriation, measures tantamount to expropriation, measures having an effect equivalent to expropriation.[15] These terms are different in the strict sense, but such difference is not significant in defining indirect expropriation.

Based on state practice, doctrine and arbitral awards, the UNCTAD has concluded that indirect expropriations are characterized by several cumulative elements: an act attributable to the state; interference with property rights or other protected legal interests, of such degree that the relevant rights or interests lose all or most of their value, or the owner is deprived of control over the investment, even though the owner retains the legal title or remains in physical possession.[16]

The establishment of an indirect expropriation depends on a case-by-case and fact-based analysis of the various factors relating to the measure in question, typically including, (i) the economic impact of the measure; (ii) the extent to which the measure interferes with distinct, reasonable investment-backed expectations; and (iii) the nature, purpose and character of the measure.[17]

Because indirect expropriation is becoming increasingly widespread, IIAs incorporate clauses to protect foreign investments from indirect expropriatory measures of the host states. By and large, there are two major modes of expropriation clauses. One mode can be described as "simple clause", referring to IIA provisions that deal with both direct and indirect expropriation in an integrated manner. A typical example of such a clause would read like NAFTA Article 1110 (1): "No Party may directly or indirectly nationalize or expropriate an investment of an investor of another Party in its territory or take a measure tantamount to nationalization or expropriation of such an investment ('expropriation')". Under this NAFTA clause, the term nationalization or expropriation covers both direct and indirect forms of expropriation. As suggested, the terms "indirectly nationalize or expropriate" and "a measure tantamount to nationalization or expropriation" plainly aim at government behaviour beyond traditional expropriatory acts such as government occupation of an investor's property, or forced transfer of title.[18]

The other mode of indirect expropriation clause can be described as a "comprehensive clause", meaning that in addition to the expropriation clause, the IIA also includes one or more provisions that further clarify the expropriation clause. Typically, some IIAs contain an annex to the expropriation clause that defines indirect expropriation in a clearer way. For instance, Article 6 of the 2012 U.S. Model BIT (expropriation and compensation) lays down the general expropriation rule, stating that "Neither Party may expropriate or nationalize a covered investment either directly or indirectly through measures equivalent to expropriation or nationalization". In addition to Article 6, Annex B of this BIT contains further rules relating to expropriation. This Annex clearly identifies indirect expropriation:

Annex B
Expropriation

3   Article 6 (1) addresses two situations. The first is direct expropriation, where an investment is nationalized or otherwise directly expropriated through formal transfer of title or outright seizure.
4   The second situation addressed by Article 6 is indirect expropriation, where an action or series of actions by a Party has an effect equivalent to direct expropriation without formal transfer of title or outright seizure.

The annex in the 2012 U.S. Model BIT is a typical and popular model in IIA-making. Similar provisions can be found in many other IIAs, such as the 2004

Canadian Model BIT,[19] the China–Canada BIT,[20] the TPP,[21] the CETA, the CAFTA,[22] and the ASEAN Comprehensive Investment Agreement.[23]

Both forms of expropriation clause are widely adopted. Their difference is more formal than substantive. Essentially, both forms impose a general ban on the expropriation of foreign investments. The words "no party may" expressly show their prohibitive nature. Thus, although expropriation remains possible under international law, it would be illegal and unacceptable unless certain legality requirements are satisfied. As discussed *infra*, though such a ban contributes greatly to the protection of foreign investments, it may also bring about profound restraining effects on state regulatory power if the legality requirements are made too strict.

The strict legality requirements for expropriation

Expropriation clauses aim at protecting foreign investments from being hurt by the expropriatory acts of the host states. To achieve this goal, these clauses often contain varying requirements for lawful expropriation, though they do not prohibit expropriation in an overall manner. Debates over the legality requirements are long-lasting and abundant.

That states have the right to expropriate foreign investments in their territories has long been recognized in international law. For instance, it is expressly recognized in the United Nations General Assembly (UNGA) Resolution 1803 of 1962, entitled "Permanent Sovereignty over Natural Resources" (Resolution 1803).[24] This resolution provides in relevant part that

> Nationalization, expropriation or requisitioning shall be based on grounds or reasons of public utility, security or the national interest which are recognized as overriding purely individual or private interests, both domestic and foreign. In such cases the owner shall be paid appropriate compensation, in accordance with the rules in force in the State taking such measures in the exercise of its sovereignty and in accordance with international law. In any case where the question of compensation gives rise to a controversy, the national jurisdiction of the State taking such measures shall be exhausted. However, upon agreement by sovereign States and other parties concerned, settlement of the dispute should be made through arbitration or international adjudication.[25]

Though Resolution 1803 allows states to expropriate foreign investments, it imposes two legality requirements for expropriation. First, the purpose of expropriation should be for "public utility, security or the national interest which are recognized as overriding purely individual or private interests". Second, foreign investors shall be entitled to "appropriate compensation".

The legality requirements are not static. The two requirements in Resolution 1803 have been immensely enriched and enunciated over the past decades. Today, much higher legality requirements have been widely adopted in IIAs. As suggested by some commentators, expropriation is illegal under international law unless several requirements are satisfied, including public purpose, due process, non-discrimination and compensation.[26] The expropriation clause of NAFTA Chapter Eleven is typical:

a) for a public purpose;
b) on a non-discriminatory basis;
c) in accordance with due process of law and Article 1105 (1) [minimum standard of treatment]; and
d) on payment of compensation in accordance with paragraphs 2 through 6 (the standard of compensation).[27]

Along with the evolution of the legality requirements, there exists a high level of normative convergence of the expropriation provisions of IIAs globally. Nowadays, provisions similar or even identical to the NAFTA one are widely incorporated in many other IIAs, such as the 2004 Canadian Model BIT,[28] the 2012 U.S. Model BIT,[29] the China–Canada BIT,[30] the investment chapters of the CETA,[31] the TPP[32] and the CAFTA,[33] the ASEAN Comprehensive Investment Agreement,[34] and the 2016 Indian Model BIT.[35]

The evolution of the compensation standard of expropriation can be an illustrative example in explaining the normative convergence of the expropriation clauses of IIAs. Developed states opine that customary international law requires "adequate, prompt and effective compensation" for expropriation, which is also known as the "Hull formula". There are some alternative expressions of this formula in IIAs. For instance, under the investment chapter of the TPP, "adequate" is replaced by "equivalent to the fair market value of the expropriated investment immediately before the expropriation took place"; "prompt" is replaced by "paid without delay"; and "effective" is replaced by "fully realizable and freely transferable".[36] Because the "Hull formula" sets up a high compensation standard, it has been rejected by developing states, many of which deny the customary international law status of this formula and are only willing to make "appropriate compensation".[37]

Notwithstanding the disagreement over the "Hull formula", recent IIA-making practice seems to suggest that the key elements of this formula are shared by developing countries. As suggested by the UNCTAD, "one of the most salient trends among recent BITs is that most agreements include language that has the effect of applying the standard of prompt, adequate and effective compensation".[38] For instance, though China has been an opponent of the "Hull formula", China's BIT-making has experienced a "Westernization" or "Americanization" process in recent decades as a result of its economic policy shift.[39] A key symbol of this process is the incorporation of the "Hull formula" into China's new generations of BITs.[40]

A consequence of the normative convergence of the expropriation clauses in IIAs is that, today, most IIAs incorporate the strict legality requirements, including the "Hull formula". Consequently, states find it increasingly difficult to take regulatory measures. Such measures are likely to be seen as acts of indirect expropriation, and in ISA practice it is frequently seen that foreign investors sue the host states, citing indirect expropriation as the legal ground. In this sense, the strict legality requirements for expropriation in IIAs can heavily restrain states' regulatory power.

The difficulty in differentiating state police powers from indirect expropriation

Despite the lack of a uniform definition of state police powers, such powers are generally accepted as a matter of customary international law.[41] State police powers can be understood both broadly and narrowly. A narrow understanding limits the "public purpose" of state regulatory measures to the restricted fundamental state functions of custody, security and protection.[42] Such powers cover the following state acts that are traditionally limited to (a) forfeiture or a fine to punish or suppress crime; (b) seizure of property by way of taxation; (c) legislation restricting the use of property, including planning, environment, safety, health and the concomitant restrictions to property rights; and (d) defense against external threats, destruction of property of neutrals as a consequence of military operations, and the taking of enemy property as part payment of reparation for the consequences of an illegal war.[43] Clearly, if the narrow understanding is adopted in IIA-making, almost all potential indirect expropriation could be deemed as the exercise of state regulatory power.[44] This would heavily restrict state regulatory power.

On the contrary, the broad understanding of state police powers implies that such powers must be understood as encompassing a state's full regulatory dimension, as modern states may go well beyond their fundamental functions of custody, security and protection.[45] Because states today shoulder heavier and broader public governance duties, the broad understanding would preserve broader regulatory flexibility and policy space for the states in fulfilling their duties. Therefore, when a state adopts regulatory measures under its normal function to protect the environment, human health, national safety or other legitimate public welfare objectives, the state should be deemed as exercising its police powers, and the measures should not be seen as indirect expropriation not giving rise to an obligation of compensation.[46] In this aspect, H. Mann and K. von Moltke have argued that,

> Under the traditional international law concept of the exercise of police powers, when a state acted in a non-discriminatory manner to protect public goods such as its environment, the health of its people or other public welfare interests, such actions were understood to fall outside the scope of what was meant by expropriation … Such acts are simply not covered by the concept of expropriation, were not a taking of property, and no compensation was payable as a matter of international law.[47]

In the international sphere, there is no consensus about the exact scope of state police powers. This results in normative and practical difficulty in distinguishing state police powers and compensable expropriation.[48] For instance, the tribunal in Saluka v. Czech held that,

> [i]nternational law has yet to identify in a comprehensive and definitive fashion precisely what regulations are considered "permissible" and "commonly accepted" as falling within the police or regulatory power of States and, thus, non-compensable.[49]

It is unsurprising to see that in case of indirect expropriation, the host state will refuse to acknowledge the expropriatory nature of the measure and will not offer compensation to the aggrieved investor; and in case of a dispute, it will be the task of arbitral tribunals to determine whether the conduct constitutes an expropriation.[50]

The difficulty in distinguishing indirect expropriation from the exercise of state police powers may put states in a difficult situation. On the one hand, states constantly need to take regulatory measures for a wide range of public purposes as required by domestic or international law. States' maintenance of regulatory power is an essential element of their permanent sovereignty over their economies, and nothing in the IIA language purports to undermine such sovereignty.[51] On the other hand, foreign investments should be protected under national and international law as well. Thus, state police powers should be reasonably restricted and must not be abused. On this issue, the tribunal in ADC v. Hungary held that,

> A sovereign state possesses the inherent right to regulate its domestic affairs, the exercise of such right is not unlimited and must have its boundaries … the rule of law, which includes treaty obligations, provides such boundaries. Therefore, when a State enters into a bilateral investment treaty like the one in this case, it becomes bound by it and the investment-protection obligations it undertook therein must be honoured rather than be ignored by a later argument of the State's right to regulate.[52]

Though ISA case law seems to show that state police powers shall be reasonably restricted, arbitrators are somewhat reluctant to produce any general rule to define such powers or to draw a clear line for the state to lawfully exercise police powers. In some cases, arbitrators simply refused to consider the sensitivity of the sustainable development-related claims, but inclined to regard such claims no differently from "general" expropriation claims. For instance, in Santa Elena v. Costa Rica, the ICSID tribunal held that, "Expropriatory environmental measures—no matter how laudable and beneficial to society as a whole—are, in this respect, similar to any other expropriation measures that a state may take in order to implement its policies: where property is expropriated, even for environmental purposes, whether domestic or international, the state's obligation to pay compensation remains".[53]

The difficulty or reluctance of arbitrators in differentiating state police powers and indirect expropriation gives rise to a high level of uncertainty for states taking regulatory measures. This gives rise to the restraining effects of the indirect expropriation provisions on state regulatory power.

The ambiguous "public purpose" test in making expropriation determinations

A key requirement to justify a non-compensable indirect expropriation under many IIAs is that the state regulatory measure should be taken for public purposes. This requirement has long been recognized as part of customary international law, and has been widely codified in IIAs.[54] In IIA-making, various slightly different terminologies are used to convey the meaning of public purpose, such as public welfare purpose, public interest, public order and social interest, public benefit, national interest, or public purpose related to internal needs.[55] It is sometimes seen that IIAs include a non-exhaustive list of typical public purposes, such as the protection of public health, safety and the environment.

The public purpose requirement of expropriation has a significant relationship with sustainable development. Public purpose, whether narrowly or broadly construed, often encompasses the main elements of sustainable development, such as the protection of the environment, public health and national security. Despite the frequent use of this term, few IIAs provide a clear definition or the determinant thereof. A limited number of IIAs contain a restrictive explanation of this requirement. For instance, some IIAs provide that public policy should be understood as a concept of public international law and shall be interpreted in accordance with international law, thus differentiating it from the concept of public purpose in domestic law.[56] In contrast, some other IIAs provide that public purpose should be understood as compatible with the concept of public purpose in the domestic law.[57]

In international investment law, there is lacking a wide consensus as to the distinction of acceptable and unacceptable public purposes.[58] Such a vacuum, compounded by the almost unavoidable information asymmetry between host states and foreign investors in investment policymaking, makes it easy for states in claiming that there exists a public purpose underlying a regulatory measure, while foreign investors may find it much harder to deny the existence of such a public purpose. Because states are the designers and implementers of regulatory measures, and they enjoy inherent rights in regulating domestic affairs as sovereigns, it is likely that the public purpose requirement could be abused by states. In several cases, the ECHR held that,

> The decision to enact laws expropriating property will commonly involve consideration of political, economic and social issues on which opinions within a democratic society may reasonably differ widely. The Court, finding it natural that the margin of appreciation available to the legislature in

implementing social and economic policies should be a wide one, will respect the legislature's judgment as to what is "in the public interest" unless that judgment be manifestly without reasonable foundation. In other words, although the Court cannot substitute its own assessment for that of the national authorities, it is bound to review the contested measures under Article 1 of Protocol No. 1 (P1-1) and, in so doing, to make an inquiry into the facts with reference to which the national authorities acted.[59]

ICSID tribunals have also demonstrated some reluctance to question the determination of host states of what they considered to be in their public interest.[60] For instance, the tribunal in Goetz v. Burundi held that,

In the absence of an error of fact or law, of an abuse of power or of a clear misunderstanding of the issue, it is not the Tribunal's role to substitute its own judgement for the discretion of the government of Burundi of what are "imperatives of public need […] or of national interest".[61]

States' determination of public purpose is often not conclusive in cases of a dispute relating to indirect expropriation. In ISA practice, it is often necessary for arbitrators to ascertain whether a public purpose truly exists on a case-by-case basis. In this connection, it has been established in case law that a mere declaration or reference to a public purpose by a state is not enough to meet the public purpose requirement in IIAs. In ADC v. Hungary, for instance, the Cypriot claimants entered into a contract with a Hungarian state agency in renovating and constructing two airport terminals for Hungary in 1995. The claimants completed the construction in 1998 and operated the airport until 2001. Hungary issued a decree in December 2001, resulting in the takeover of all the activities in relation to the airport from the claimants. The claimants claimed for compensation on the ground of indirect expropriation. Hungary argued that there was a public purpose for the expropriation. According to the Expropriation Act of Hungary, "real estate properties may be expropriated for the purpose of transportation".[62] The Hungarian transport legislation and the decree constituted "important elements of the harmonization of the Government's transport strategy, laws and regulations with EU law in preparation of Hungary's accession to the EU in May 2004".[63]

The ICSID tribunal held that to meet the public purpose requirement of the applicable BIT, there must be "a genuine interest of the public" involved, holding that,

In the Tribunal's opinion, a treaty requirement for "public interest" requires some genuine interest of the public. If mere reference to "public interest" can magically put such interest into existence and therefore satisfy this requirement, then this requirement would be rendered meaningless since the Tribunal can imagine no situation where this requirement would not have been met.[64]

In light of the factual background of ADC v. Hungary, the tribunal did not go further to elaborate on what should be deemed as the "genuine interest of the public". A commentator, after analysing the issue of public purpose in a series of cases, has suggested that there is no recognizable distinction in international investment law between acceptable and unacceptable public purposes, and that international investment law does not contain a hierarchy under which public purposes that are recognized by all states are legitimate, whilst those only invoked by some states are not.[65] In light of the broad regulatory right states may possess under international law, "almost any purpose if a state regards it as in its public interest".[66]

Therefore, despite the recognition of the public purpose requirement in IIAs, ISA jurisprudence seems to suggest that states still keep a high level of autonomy and broad policy space in taking regulatory measures for a wide range of public purposes under international investment law. However, this does not necessarily mean that state regulatory power is not restricted under this requirement. First, since few IIAs clarify the term "public purpose", arbitrators have a broad discretion in determining whether a state regulatory measure is taken for public purposes on a case-by-case basis with all relevant circumstances taken into consideration. Second, public purpose is merely one of the requirements for lawful expropriation, the restraining effect of this requirement will be assessed in combination with the assessment of other requirements.

The restraining effect of FET clause

The concept of FET is not new but has appeared in international documents for some time.[67] The origin of FET clauses seems to date back to the Charter for an International Trade Organization (ITO Charter) and the FCN treaties of the U.S. Over the years, the FET standard and its variations, such as "just and equitable treatment" or "equitable and reasonable treatment", have become an indispensable constituent provision of modern IIAs.[68] Today, the FET standard is deemed as the "most significant substantive protection" contained in IIAs today,[69] which effectively embodies the cardinal principle of the rule of law.[70]

Viewed as a yardstick for the exercise of state administrative, judicial or legislative powers vis-à-vis foreign investors, the FET standard redefines acceptable restraints on state sovereignty whilst ringing in changes to the legal framework governing investments in the states.[71] Similar to indirect expropriation clauses, FET clauses also aim at the exercise of state regulatory power, and may have profound restraining effects on states' ability in taking regulatory measures for sustainable development goals as well.

The diversified formulations of FET clauses in IIAs

In IIA-making, there is no uniform model of FET clauses, despite the proliferation of FET clauses in IIAs.[72] A small number of IIAs do not contain an FET clause. Such silence may well indicate that the contracting states are unwilling to subject their regulatory measures to external review under the FET standard. However, despite the absence of an FET clause in IIA, the international minimum standard of treatment (MST) still exists in customary international law, thus the remaining issue is whether an investor would be able to enforce the IMS treatment of aliens, especially through ISDS, which will depend on the breadth of the treaty's ISDS clause.[73]

Today, the majority of IIAs contain an FET clause. Roughly speaking, an FET clause can be either conditional or autonomous in nature. A conditional FET clause is one that is linked to other international or national law standards, and is widely used by countries like the U.S., the U.K. and France; while an autonomous FET clause only requires the contracting states to grant FET to foreign investors, without imposing any external qualification onto the FET.[74]

Conditional FET clauses can be further divided into several subgroups, depending on the external standards to which they are linked. First, an FET clause linked to general international law. A typical clause could read something like, "Investments or returns of investors of either Contracting Party in the territory of the other Contracting Party shall be accorded fair and equitable treatment in accordance with international law …"[75] or "Each Party shall at all times accord to covered investments fair and equitable treatment and full protection and security, and shall in no case accord treatment less favorable than that required by international law".[76] Here, the term "international law" should be understood as a general one, meaning that all applicable sources of international law should be considered to decide what treatment foreign investors should enjoy.[77]

Second, an FET clause linked to customary international law. Such a clause may merely refer to customary international law or to other relevant standards under customary international law, especially the MST of aliens, and full protection and security; or it may simply provide that the FET does not go beyond customary international law. Such a type of FET clause is especially popular in IIAs in the U.S. and Canada.[78] For instance, Article 5(1) of the 2012 U.S. Model BIT provides that "Each Party shall accord to covered investments treatment in accordance with customary international law, including fair and equitable treatment and full protection and security", and Article 5 (2) of this BIT further provides that "The concepts of 'fair and equitable treatment' and 'full protection and security' do not require treatment in addition to or beyond that which is required by that standard, and do not create additional substantive rights". It should be noted that an FET clause linked to the MST may be open to controversies. Apart from the controversy of whether an MST exists in international law, a further question relates to the content of the MST.[79]

Third, an FET clause linked to domestic law and regulations. IIAs incorporating such FET clauses are rare. A typical example reads as, "Each party shall ensure fair and equitable treatment of investments of investors of the other party under and subject to national laws and regulations".[80] The effectiveness of such an FET clause is doubted. While an FET clause is designed to offer to foreign investors a level of protection that is independent of the host state's domestic law,[81] the dependency of FET on the domestic law actually voids this basic idea of having an independent international standard against which the behaviour of the host state can be assessed.[82]

Autonomous FET standards are widely adopted in European countries, such as Germany, Switzerland and Sweden.[83] A typical example reads, "All investments made by investors of one Contracting Party shall enjoy a fair and equitable treatment in the territory of the other Contracting Party".[84] Such a clause often gives rise to debate regarding whether the FET standard is a treaty-based treatment that is independent from customary international law. While it is undeniable that there is a certain degree of interaction and overlap with other standards, it is widely accepted that FET is an autonomous standard, unless a clear indication to the contrary is made in the IIAs.[85]

To briefly sum up, as FET clauses in IIAs are diversified and many are linked to external standards under international law, their contents are relatively imprecise. According to an UNCTAD study, while there seems to exist a broad consensus that some types of improper and discreditable state conduct would constitute a violation of the FET standard – such as defeating foreign investors' legitimate expectations, denial of justice and due process and manifest arbitrariness in decision-making – profound controversies exist with regard to other types of state conduct, such as transparency and consistency of decisions.[86] In light of this, the contents of the FET standard should not be ascertained in the abstract, but should be decided on a state-specific and case-by-case basis. As held by the ICSID tribunal in Waste Management v. U.S., "Evidently the standard [FET] is to some extent a flexible one which must be adapted to the circum-stances of each case".[87]

The protection of legitimate expectation and the FET standard

Prior to the new millennium, there were no publicly available arbitral awards applied to the FET standard; investors since then have alleged breach of FET in almost every claim brought under an IIA.[88] Thus, remarkably swiftly, FET clauses have risen to prominence in ISA practice. Besides, FET claims raised by investors also seem to have a good record of success in ISA practice.[89] In ISA, investors may raise FET claims either solely or in combination with expropriation claims to increase the chances of compensation.

State regulatory measures can profoundly influence the legitimate expect-ations of investors. In ISA practice, it is often seen that legitimate expectation claims arise in situations where the investors suffered losses due to the changes of the regulatory measures of the host states taken for public purpose. In this connection, legitimate expectation determination is closely related with the host states' pursuit of sustainable development goals.

Protection of investors' legitimate expectations has been identified in ISA practice as a key element of the FET standard.[90] Especially in long-term invest-ment projects, the legitimate expectation of foreign investors should be protected, since investors would lose bargaining power against the host states substantially once the investments have been made. The ICSID tribunal in Tecmed v. Mexico is the first in clearly spelling out that the FET standard encompasses protection of legitimate expectations of foreign investors.[91] In this case, Tecmed, a Spanish company, invested in Mexico in a project related to land, buildings and other assets. Due to Mexico's refusal to renew the licence, Tecmed alleged that the project was lost and that Mexico had violated the provisions of the Mexico–Spain BIT, including expropriation, FET and full protection and security. With regard to legitimate expectation, the tribunal held that,

> The Arbitral Tribunal considers that this provision of the Agreement, in light of the good faith principle established by international law, requires the Contracting Parties to provide to international investments treatment that does not affect the basic expectations that were taken into account by the foreign investor to make the investment. The foreign investor expects the host State to act in a consistent manner, free from ambiguity and totally transparently in its relations with the foreign investor, so that it may know beforehand any and all rules and regulations that will govern its investments, as well as the goals of the relevant policies and administrative practices or directives, to be able to plan its investment and comply with such regulations. Any and all State actions conforming to such criteria should relate not only to the guidelines, directives or requirements issued, or the resolutions approved thereunder, but also to the goals underlying such regulations. The foreign investor also expects the host State to act consistently, i.e. without arbitrarily revoking any pre-existing decisions or permits issued by the State that were relied upon by the investor to assume its commitments as well as to plan and launch its commercial and business activities. The investor also expects the State to use the legal instruments that govern the actions of the investor or the investment in conformity with the function usually assigned to such instruments, and not to deprive the investor of its investment without the required compensation.[92]

In the context of NAFTA arbitration, a definition of legitimate expectation under FET has been put forward by the Thunderbird v. Mexico tribunal,[93] stating that,

> The concept of "legitimate expectations" relates, within the context of the NAFTA framework, to a situation where a Contracting Party's conduct creates reasonable and justifiable expectations on the part of an investor (or investment) to act in reliance on said conduct, such that a failure by the NAFTA Party to honour those expectations could cause the investor (or investment) to suffer damages [sic].[94]

The legitimate expectation principle enunciated by the Tecmed v. Mexico tribunal is deemed as a comprehensive illustration of the elements now firmly established in the FET standard.[95] It has been accepted in many subsequent ISA cases, such as CMS v. Argentina and Enron v. Argentina, where the tribunals similarly held that the FET standard include the requirement of a "stable framework for the investment".[96] In other ISA cases, such as Occidental v. Ecuador[97] and PSEG v. Turkey,[98] the tribunals have gone even further to suggest that any adverse change in the business or legal framework of the host state may give rise to a breach of the FET standard, because the investors' legitimate expectations of predictability and stability are thereby undermined.[99]

The heavy reliance on the legitimate expectation by arbitral tribunals has generated controversy. For instance, it has been argued that "the Tecmed 'standard' is actually not a standard at all; it is rather a description of perfect public regulation in a perfect world, to which all states should aspire but very few (if any) will ever attain".[100] In MTD v. Chile,[101] the ICSID Annulment Committee held that the tribunal's apparent reliance on the foreign investor's expectations as the source of the host state's obligations in Tecmed is "questionable".[102] Similarly, as suggested by the UNCTAD, overreliance on the legitimate expectation test in making FET decisions is unjustified, since this practice would potentially prevent the host state from introducing any legitimate regulatory change, and from undertaking a necessary regulatory reform. It ignores the fact that foreign investors should legitimately expect regulations to change over time as an aspect of the normal operation of legal and policy processes of the economy they operate in.[103]

Realizing that the legitimate expectation principle may not be fully convincing, some arbitral tribunals require further qualifying elements to this principle. A typical example is Duke Energy v. Ecuador,[104] which involved several contracts entered into between the disputants for electrical power generation in Ecuador. Regarding the issue of legitimate expectation, the tribunal held that,

> The stability of the legal and business environment is directly linked to the investor's justified expectations. The Tribunal acknowledges that such expectations are an important element of fair and equitable treatment. At the same time, it is mindful of their limitations. To be protected, the investor's expectations must be legitimate and reasonable at the time when the investor makes the investment. The assessment of the reasonableness or legitimacy must take into account all circumstances, including not only the facts surrounding the investment, but also the political, socioeconomic, cultural and historical conditions prevailing in the host State. In addition, such expectations must arise from the conditions that the State offered the investor and the latter must have relied upon them when deciding to invest.[105]

As can be seen, the arbitral tribunal, recognizing the importance of legitimate expectation in making FET decisions, raised two further requirements. First, not only the facts surrounding the investment should be considered, but the political, socioeconomic, cultural and historical conditions prevailing in the host state should also be considered. Second, specific commitment of the host state should be considered. These qualifying requirements have been accepted by other tribunals expressly or impliedly. For instance, in CMS v. Argentina, the arbitral tribunal stressed the requirement of specific commitments in making FET decisions, holding that,

> It is not a question of whether the legal framework might need to be frozen as it can always evolve and be adapted to changing circumstances, but neither is it a question of whether the framework can be dispensed with altogether when specific commitments to the contrary have been made. The law of foreign investment and its protection has been developed with the specific objective of avoiding such adverse legal effects.[106]

In several other cases, the arbitral tribunals found that the investors should have been aware of the general regulatory environmental of the host states, which should be taken into account in making FET decisions. Such a requirement, namely the presumption of the knowledge of the host state, can play an important role in making FET decisions in disputes involving politically unstable and economically transitional states. For instance, in Genin v. Estonia,[107] the tribunal gave particular consideration to the political situation of Estonia, holding that,

> The Tribunal considers it imperative to recall the particular context in which the dispute arose, namely, that of a renascent independent state, coming rapidly to grips with the reality of modern financial, commercial and banking practices and the emergence of state institutions responsible for overseeing and regulating areas of activity perhaps previously unknown. This is the context in which Claimants knowingly chose to invest in an Estonian financial institution, EIB.[108]

It should be noted that some of these qualifying requirements have been incorporated in recent IIAs. For instance, Article 8.10.4 of the investment chapter of the CETA provides that,

> When applying the above fair and equitable treatment obligation, a Tribunal may take into account whether a Party made a specific representation to an investor to induce a covered investment, that created a legitimate expectation, and upon which the investor relied in deciding to make or maintain the covered investment, but that the Party subsequently frustrated.

To conclude, two major observations can be drawn. First, the legitimate expectation element in the FET standard can potentially restrict state regulatory power, since it implies that adverse changes of the legal and business environment of the host state can be deemed as a violation of the FET standard. Second, ISA practices relating to the legitimate expectation element under the FET standard are inconsistent and evolutionary. While some tribunals, such as the one in

Tecmed v. Mexico, seemed to view this element as the decisive component of the FET standard, others, such as the tribunal in Duke Energy v. Ecuador, have gradually posed limits and qualifications to this test.[109] Such evolution has profound implications. Because qualifying requirements actually raise the threshold to prove FET violation, they help preserve state regulatory power by screening certain regulatory measures from being held as FET violation.

The "balance paradigms" of indirect expropriation and FET clauses

While indirect expropriation and FET clauses protect foreign investors and investments, they also restrict host states' power of taking regulatory measures and even raise concerns over the sovereignty of the host states at a more fundamental level.[110] Such restraining effects have become an unavoidable governance obstacle for states when pursuing sustainable development goals. Whether and to what extent the restraining effects can be alleviated depends largely on how IIA drafters strike a balance between states' obligation of protecting foreign investors and their right to take regulatory measures. To help alleviate such restraining effects, some IIAs incorporate different types of "balance provisions", which can be roughly categorized into four types.

The element-listing paradigm

A major type of the "balancing provisions" is one that incorporates certain criteria to help determine the occurrence of indirect expropriation. For instance, the investment chapter of the CETA provides that,

> The determination of whether a measure or series of measures of a Party, in a specific fact situation, constitutes an indirect expropriation requires a case-by-case, fact-based inquiry that takes into consideration, among other factors:
>
> a) the economic impact of the measure or series of measures, although the sole fact that a measure or series of measures of a Party has an adverse effect on the economic value of an investment does not establish that an indirect expropriation has occurred;
> b) the duration of the measure or series of measures of a Party;
> c) the extent to which the measure or series of measures interferes with distinct, reasonable investment-backed expectations; and
> d) the character of the measure or series of measures, notably their object, context and intent.[111]

These criteria inquire into the different aspects of state regulatory measures, combining both subjective and objective considerations. Although they are not exhaustive and may need further clarification, they do provide helpful guidance, especially for arbitrators, in determining whether a state regulatory measure constitutes an indirect expropriation act. Similar criteria can be found in the 2012 U.S. Model BIT,[112] and the ASEAN Comprehensive Investment Agreement.[113]

Some IIAs also incorporate a list of the contents of the FET standard. Such a list can be merely indicative; it can also be exhaustive. For instance, Article 5(2)(a) of the 2012 U.S. Model BIT contains a descriptive list of the FET standard, providing that the standard "includes the obligation not to deny justice in criminal, civil, or administrative adjudicatory proceedings in accordance with the principle of due process embodied in the principal legal systems of the world".

A recent development is that the investment chapter of the CETA incorporates an exhaustive list of FET standards, which is uncommon in IIA-making. Article 8.10 of the CETA provides the following,

Treatment of investors and of covered investments

1 Each Party shall accord in its territory to covered investments of the other Party and to investors with respect to their covered investments fair and equitable treatment and full protection and security in accordance with paragraphs 2 through 6.

2 A Party breaches the obligation of fair and equitable treatment referenced in paragraph 1 if a measure or series of measures constitutes:

   a) denial of justice in criminal, civil or administrative proceedings;
   b) fundamental breach of due process, including a fundamental breach of transparency, in judicial and administrative proceedings;
   c) manifest arbitrariness;
   d) targeted discrimination on manifestly wrongful grounds, such as gender, race or religious belief;
   e) abusive treatment of investors, such as coercion, duress and harassment; or
   f) a breach of any further elements of the fair and equitable treatment obligation adopted by the Parties in accordance with paragraph 3 of this Article [*regular review of the contents of the FET standard by the contracting parties*].

The FET clause in the CETA investment chapter has several distinct features. First, unlike many IIAs, it delinks FET from any external standards, especially the ambiguous international law standard. Second, it limits the FET standard to an exhaustive list of situations. This provision not only implies that this FET standard should be deemed an "autonomous" standard, but more importantly, it also helps remedy the ambiguity of the FET standards and restrict the arbitrators' interpretation discretion.

The carved-in exception paradigm

The second major type of "balancing provision" is "carved-in exception" in expropriation provisions. Such exception excludes some types of state regulatory measures from the application of the expropriation provision. Typical measures that fall within this exception are those taken for public purposes, such as environmental protection, public health and safety. Under this exception, even if a state regulatory measure incurs property loss to foreign investors, it shall not be deemed to constitute an indirect expropriation act and the host state shall not be held liable to compensate the foreign investors.

A typical "carved-in exception" of an expropriation provision can be found in Annex B of the 2012 U.S. Model BIT, which provides that, "Except in rare circumstances, non-discriminatory regulatory actions by a Party that are designed and applied to protect legitimate public welfare objectives, such as public health, safety, and the environment, do not constitute indirect expropriations".[114] It is commonly seen that the indirect expropriation provision of IIAs incorporates a "carved-in exception". Depending on the specific needs and situations of the contracting states, the list of exempted regulatory measures in the "carved-in exception" may be different. For instance, the "carved-in exception" in the Korea–U.S. FTA not only covers the listed measures in the 2012 U.S. Model BIT, but also extends to state regulatory measures for the purpose of stabilizing real estate price.[115] Similarly, the China–Canada BIT excludes the issuance of compulsory licences granted in relation to intellectual property rights (IPRs) from the scope of indirect expropriation.[116] This exception ensures that IPRs holders will not be able to challenge the compulsory licence taken by the host states as an indirect expropriation of their IPRs. Besides, it is also seen that some IIAs phased out tax measures from the realm of indirect expropriation. For instance, under the 2012 U.S. Model BIT, a foreign investor cannot proceed with its expropriation claim in relation to the tax measure taken by a contracting state, unless the tax authorities of the two contracting states come to an agreement that the measure in question amounts to expropriation.[117]

The carved-in exception provision may cover a wide range of state regulatory measures for public purposes. This can be a helpful tool for states in pursuing sustainable development goals without being excessively restrained by the indirect expropriation clause. To successfully invoke such an exception, several requirements should be met. First, the regulatory measures in question should be non-discriminatory; second, the measures must be taken for public purpose; and third, such an exception can only be applied in "rare circumstances". The determination of the satisfaction of these requirements is a fact-intensive and measure-sensitive process, which should be made on a case-by-case basis with all attending circumstances taken into consideration.

The mitigation paradigm

The third major type of "balancing provision", the mitigating test, is slightly less aggressive than the previous ones. Its purpose is not to exclude state regulatory measures for public purposes from the realm of indirect expropriation, but to deem these measures as a mitigation factor when considering the compensation for expropriation. For instance, the 2016 Indian Model BIT provides the following,

> Mitigating Factors under Article 5.6 (compensation for expropriation) include
> …
> j) any other relevant considerations regarding the need to balance the public interest and the interests of the investment.[118]

Under this BIT, state regulatory measures may be held as an act of indirect expropriation, and foreign investors are allowed to claim compensation for such measures. Yet, the actual amount of compensation may be mitigated if the state measures in question are taken for public purposes. However, notwithstanding its helpful role in preserving state regulatory power, such provision fails to draw a clear line between state regulatory measures and indirect expropriation. Thus, whether and to what extent it can truly alleviate the restraining effects of the indirect expropriation provision will be subject to the determination of arbitrators on a case-by-case basis.

The differentiation paradigm

Some, though few, IIAs provide that the FET standard should not be deemed as a fixed set of standards that apply to both or all contracting states of the IIAs in the same manner. Rather, FET violations should be determined on a state-specific basis, i.e. the FET standard may be understood differently in light of the developmental level of different IIA contracting states. For instance, Article 14 (3) of the 2007 Investment Agreement for the COMESA Common Investment Area provides that,

> For greater certainty, Member States understand that different Member States have different forms of administrative, legislative and judicial systems and that Member States at different levels of development may not achieve the same standards at the same time. Paragraphs 1 and 2 of this Article [*prohibition of the denial of justice and affirmation of the minimum standard of treatment of aliens*] do not establish a single international standard in this context.

This FET clause clearly recognizes the different levels of development of the contracting states. At least in theory, it implies that regulatory measures of a contracting state that is deemed as a violation of the FET clause may be deemed as a non-violating measure were they taken by a different contracting state. As this clause does not elaborate how such a difference should be ascertained in practice, it is unclear how it will be applied and what legal consequences this would bring about.

Conclusion

Indirect expropriation and FET clauses are key components of IIAs. An indirect expropriation clause generally prohibits state regulatory measures that would amount to the taking of foreign investments; and an FET clause requires the host states to maintain the stability of the legal and business regime in force. Both clauses target the scope of state regulatory power and the manner in which such power is exercised. By subjecting a wide range of state regulatory measures – including state legislative, administrative and judicial conduct – to the external review under international law standards, these clauses serve the purpose of protecting foreign investors and investments and ensure that certain rule-of-law standards are followed by the host states.

Though these clauses help protect foreign investors and investments, they also have profound restraining effects on state regulatory power. Because state regulatory measures would inevitably affect foreign investments in one form or another, these clauses may impede states' efforts in pursuing legitimate sustainable development goals.

Besides, in ISA practice, when making indirect expropriation and FET determinations, arbitrators need to take into account a wide range of factors on a case-by-case and fact-inquiring basis. However, it seems that arbitrators often fail to take into account the sensitivity of sustainable development elements in making these determinations. The absence of an environmental and social perspective in interpreting indirect expropriation and FET clauses is criticized by some commentators.[119] In addition, serious concerns have also been voiced that the restraining effect of investment protection regimes on host states threatens the ability of these states to pursue sustainable development policies.[120]

To respond to the restraining effects of indirect expropriation and FET clauses, it is necessary to strike a proper balance between the two conflicting aims: protecting foreign investments, and preserving state regulatory power for public purposes. There is no uniform model to strike an ideal balance in IIA-making. A brief study of some typical IIAs shows that states resort to several types of "balancing paradigms" in IIA-making, each with its pros and cons. In practice, these balancing paradigms will be subject to interpretation by arbitrators. Therefore, whether and to what extent they can truly help alleviate the restraining effects of the indirect expropriation and FET clauses remain uncertain, and should be assessed on a case-by-case basis.

Notes

1   R. Dolzer, "The Impact of International Investment Treaties on Domestic Administrative Law", 37 *NYU Journal of International Law and Politics* 953 (2007), at 953.
2   R. Kläger, *Fair and Equitable Treatment in International Investment Law* (Cambridge: Cambridge University Press, 2011), at 203–205.
3   See e.g. S. W. Schill, "Fair and Equitable Treatment under Investment Treaties as an Embodiment of the Rule of Law", 3 (5) *Transnational Dispute Management* (2006).

4 A. Reinisch, "Expropriation", in P. Muchlinski, F. Ortino and C. Schreuer (eds.), *The Oxford Handbook of International Investment Law* (Oxford: Oxford University Press, 2008), at 410.

5 See e.g. Harvard Law School, Draft Convention on the International Responsibility of States for Injuries to Aliens (1961), Article 10 (3)(a).

6 UNCTAD, "Expropriation", in *UNCTAD Series of Issues of International Investment Agreements II* (2012), available at http://unctad.org/en/Docs/unctaddiaeia 2011d7_en.pdf.

7 UNCTAD, "Expropriation", at 6–7.

8 L. Henkin, "International Law: Politics, Values and Functions", 216 *Recueil des cours* (1989), at 195.

9 N. Gallagher and W. Shan, *Chinese Investment Treaties: Policies and Practice* (Oxford: Oxford University Press, 2009), at 4–5.

10 P. D. Isakoff, "Defining the Scope of Indirect Expropriation for International Investments", 3 (2) *Global Business Law Review* 189 (2013), at 192.

11 See A. Reinisch, "Expropriation", in P. Muchlinski, F. Ortino and C. Schreuer (eds.), *Oxford Handbook on International Investment Law* (Oxford: Oxford University Press, 2008), at 409.

12 UNCTAD, "Expropriation", at 4–7.

13 G. C. Christie, "What Constitutes a Taking of Property under International Law", 38 *BYBIL* 307 (1963), at 309.

14 UNCTAD, "Expropriation", at 11.

15 L. Y. Fortier and S. L. Drymer, "Indirect Expropriation in the Law of International Investment: I know It When I See It, or Caveat Investor", 19 (2) *ICSID Review* 293 (2004), at 297.

16 UNCTAD (2012), "Expropriation", at 12.

17 OECD, *International Investment Law: A Changing Landscape* (Paris: OECD Publishing, 2005), at 54; UNCTAD (2012), Expropriation, at 62–63.

18 J. R. Marlles, "Public Purpose, Private Losses: Regulatory Expropriation and Environmental Regulation in International Investment Law", 16 (2) *Journal of Transnational Law and Policy* 275 (2006), at 279.

19 Annex B 13 (1), the 2004 Canadian Model BIT.

20 Annex B.10, the China–Canada BIT.

21 Annex 9-B, the TPP.

22 Annex 10-C, the CAFTA.

23 Article 15 and Annex 2, the 2009 ASEAN Comprehensive Investment Agreement.

24 Available at www.un.org/ga/search/view_doc.asp?symbol=A/RES/1803%28XVII%29

25 Article 4, UNGA Resolution 1803.

26 L. Yves Fortier and Stephen L. Drymer (2004), at 295–296.

27 Article 1110 (1), the NAFTA.

28 Annex B 13 (1), the 2004 Canadian Model BIT.

29 Annex B 13 (1), the 2004 Canadian Model BIT.

30 Article 10 and Annex B.10, the China–Canada BIT.

31 Article 8.12, CETA.

32 Article 9.8 and Annex 9-B, the TPP.

33 Article 10.7 and Annex 10-C, the CAFTA.

34 Article 15 and Annex 2, the 2009 ASEAN Comprehensive Investment Agreement.

35 Article 5, the 2016 Indian Model BIT, available at www.mygov.in/sites/default/files/master_image/Model%20Text%20for%20the%20Indian%20Bilateral%20Investment%20Treaty.pdf.
36 Article 9.8, the TPP.
37 See e.g. P. Peters, "Recent Developments in Expropriation Clauses in Asian Investment Treaties", in K. S. Sil, M. C. W. Pinto and J. J. G. Syatauw (eds.), 5 *Asian Yearbook of International Law* 1995 (The Netherlands: Kluwer Law International, 1997), at 70–90.
38 UNCTAD, *Bilateral Investment Treaties 1995–2006: Trends in Investment Rulemaking* (United Nations: New York and Geneva), 2007, at 48.
39 See generally Y. Ji, "Voluntary 'Westernization' of the Expropriation Rules in Chinese BITS and its Implication: An Empirical Study", 12 (1) *Journal World Investment and Trade* 79 (2011).
40 See ibid.
41 See e.g. J. E. Viñuales, "Sovereignty in Foreign Investment Law", in Z. Douglas, J. Pauwelyn and J. E. Viñuales (eds.), *The Foundations of International Investment Law: Bringing Theory into Practice* (Oxford: Oxford University Press, 2014), at 329.
42 See e.g. S. Baughen, "Expropriation and Environmental Regulation: The Lessons of NAFTA Chapter Eleven", 18 *Journal of Environmental Law* 207 (2006), at 211.
43 See I. Brownlie, *Principles of Public International Law* (7th edn.) (Oxford: Oxford University Press, 2008), at 532.
44 B. Mostafa, "The Sole Effects Doctrine, Police Powers and Indirect Expropriation under International Law", 15 *Australian International Law Journal* 267 (2008), at 273–274.
45 UNCTAD, "Expropriation" (2012), at 79.
46 See L. Dhooge, "The Revenge of the Trail Smelter: Environmental Regulation as Expropriation Pursuant to the North American Free Trade Agreement", 38 *American Business Law Journal* 475 (2001), at 525; L. Y. Fortier and S. L. Drymer (2004), at 298; Peter D. Isakoff (2013), at 192–193; J. R. Marlles, "Public Purpose, Private Losses: Regulatory Expropriation and Environmental Regulation in International Investment Law", 16 (2) *J. Transnat'l L. & Policy* 275 (2007), at 277.
47 H. Mann and K. von Moltke, "Protecting Investor Rights and the Public Good: Assessing NAFTA's Chapter 11", available at www.iisd.org/sites/default/files/publications/investment_ilsd_background_en.pdf, at 16.
48 L. Y. Fortier and S. L. Drymer (2004), at 299.
49 Saluka Investments B.V. v. The Czech Republic (UNCITRAL Rules), Partial Award of 17 March 2006, available at www.italaw.com/sites/default/files/case-documents/ita0740.pdf, at 53.
50 UNCTAD, "Expropriation", at 12.
51 See V. Lowe, "Regulation or Expropriation", 1 (3) *Transnational Dispute Management* (2004), at 4.
52 ADC Affiliate Limited and ADC and ADMC Management Limited v. The Republic of Hungary (ICSID Case No. ARB/03/16), Award of 2 October 2006, available at www.italaw.com/documents/ADCvHungaryAward.pdf, at para. 423.
53 Compañia del Desarrollo de Santa Elena S.A. v. Republic of Costa Rica (ICSID Case No. ARB/96/1), Final Award of 17 February 2000, available at http://italaw.com/documents/santaelena_award.pdf, at para. 72.
54 See e.g. A. Reinisch, "Legality of Expropriations", in A. Reinisch (ed.), *Standards of Investment Protection* (Oxford: Oxford University Press, 2008), at 178–186; P. Malanczuk, *Akehurst's Modern Introduction to International Law* (7th edn) (London:

Routledge, 1997), at 235; K. Hobér, *Investment Arbitration in Eastern Europe: In Search of a Definition of Expropriation* (New York: Juris Publishing, 2007), at 38.

55 UNCTAD, "Expropriation" (2012), at. 29.

56 See e.g. Article 10.10, the 2008 Peru–Singapore FTA; Article 811, the 2008 Canada–Columbia FTA.

57 See, e.g. Article IX (2), the 2009 Belgium/Luxembourg–Colombia BIT.

58 B. Mostafa (2008), at 277.

59 See e.g. James and Others v. United Kingdom (Application No. 8793/79), European Court of Human Rights, Judgment (21 February 1986), at para. 46; also cited in Pressos Compania Naviera S.A. and Others v. Belgium (Application No. 17849/91), Judgment (20 November 1995), at para. 37.

60 A. Reinisch (2008), at 183.

61 Antoine Goetz et consorts v. République du Burundi (ICSID Case No. ARB/95/3), Decision on Liability (2 September 1998), at para. 126.

62 ADC v. Hungary, Award of 2 October 2006, at para. 418.

63 ADC v. Hungary, Award of 2 October 2006, at para. 392.

64 ADC v. Hungary, Award of 2 October 2006, at para. 432.

65 B. Mostafa (2008), at 277–278.

66 Ibid., at 278.

67 C. Schreuer, "Fair and Equitable Treatment in Arbitral Practice", 6 (3) *Journal World Investment and Trade* 357 (2005), at 357.

68 See generally R. Dolzer and C. Schreuer (2012), at 351–353; J. Bonnitcha, *Substantive Protection under Investment Treaties: A Legal and Economic Analysis* (Cambridge: Cambridge University Press, 2014), at 143–144.

69 R. Dolzer and C. Schreuer (2012), at 130; A. Newcombe and L. Paradell, *Law and Practice of Investment Treaties* (The Netherlands: Kluwer Law International, 2009), at 255.

70 S. Schill, "Fair and Equitable Treatment under Investment Treaties as an Embodiment of the Rule of Law", 3 (5) *Transnational Dispute Management* (2006), at 4.

71 J. Haynes, "The Evolving Nature of the Fair and Equitable Treatment (FET) Standard: Challenging its Increasing Pervasiveness in Light of Developing Countries' Concerns – The Case for Regulatory Rebalancing", 14 *Journal World Investment and Trade* 114 (2013), at 117.

72 R. Kläger (2011), at 14.

73 UNCTAD, "Fair and Equitable Treatment", *UNCTAD Series on Issues in International Investment Agreements II* (2012), Doc. Number: UNCTAD/DIAE/IA/2011/5, at 18–19.

74 See generally R. Dolzer, "The Impact of International Investment Treaties on Domestic Administrative Law", 37 *NYU Journal of International Law and Politics* 953 (2007), at 961.

75 Article 3 (2), 2004 Croatia–Oman BIT.

76 Article 2 (3)(a), 1999 Bahrain–United States BIT.

77 J. Haynes (2013), at 122.

78 R. Kläger (2011), at 18.

79 I. Brownlie, *Principles of Public International Law* (7th edn.) (Cambridge: Cambridge University Press, 2008), at 525–526.

80 See Article IV, the 1997 CARICOM–Cuba BIT.

81 See e.g. R. Dolzer and M. Stevens, *Bilateral Investment Treaties* (The Hague: Nijhoff, 1995), at 58.

82   R. Kläger (2011), at 21.
83   See R. Dolzer (2007), at 961.
84   Article 3, 2009 Belgium–Luxembourg Economic Union–Tajikistan BIT.
85   See e.g. I. Tudor, *The Fair and Equitable Treatment Standard in International Law of Foreign Investment* (Oxford: Oxford University Press, 2008), at 182–202; C. Schreuer, "Fair and Equitable Treatment in Arbitral Practice", 6 (3) *Journal World Investment and Trade* 57 (2005), at 364.
86   UNCTAD, "Fair and Equitable Treatment", *UNCTAD Series on Issues in International Investment Agreements II* (2012), Doc. Number: UNCTAD/DIAE/IA/2011/5, at 62–63.
87   Waste Management, Inc. v. United Mexican States (ICSID Case No. ARB(AF)/00/3), Award (30 April 2004), available at www.italaw.com/sites/default/files/case-documents/ita0900.pdf, at para. 99.
88   J. Bonnitcha (2014), at 144.
89   See R. Dolzer and C. Schreuer (2012), at 130; M. Paparinskis, *International Minimum Standard and Fair and Equitable Treatment* (Oxford: Oxford University Press, 2013), at 4.
90   UNCTAD, "Fair and Equitable Treatment", *UNCTAD Series on Issues in International Investment Agreements II* (2012), Doc. Number: UNCTAD/DIAE/IA/2011/5, at 63.
91   Técnicas Medioambientales Tecmed, S.A. v. The United Mexican States (ICSID Case No. ARB (AF)/00/2), available at www.italaw.com/cases/1087.
92   Técnicas Medioambientales Tecmed, S.A. v. The United Mexican States (ICSID Case No. ARB (AF)/00/2), Award (29 May 2003), available at www.italaw.com/sites/default/files/case-documents/ita0854.pdf, at para. 154.
93   International Thunderbird Gaming Corporation v. The United Mexican States (*ad hoc* arbitration under the UNCITRAL Arbitration Rules), available at www.italaw.com/cases/571.
94   International Thunderbird Gaming Corporation v. The United Mexican States (*ad hoc* arbitration under the UNCITRAL Arbitration Rules), Award (26 January 2006), available at www.italaw.com/sites/default/files/case-documents/ita0431.pdf, at para. 147.
95   G. Sacerdoti, P. Acconci, M. Valenti and A. De Luca (eds.), *General Interests of Host States in International Investment Law* (Cambridge: Cambridge University Press, 2014), at 39.
96   UNCTAD, "Fair and Equitable Treatment" (2012), at 66.
97   Occidental Petroleum Corporation and Occidental Exploration and Production Company v. The Republic of Ecuador (ICSID Case No. ARB/06/11), available at www.italaw.com/cases/767.
98   PSEG Global, Inc., The North American Coal Corporation, and Konya Ingin Electrik Üretim ve Ticaret Limited Sirketi v. Republic of Turkey (ICSID Case No. ARB/02/5), available at www.italaw.com/cases/880.
99   UNCTAD, "Fair and Equitable Treatment" (2012), at 66–67.
100   Z. Douglas, "Nothing If Not Critical for Investment Treaty Arbitration: *Occidental, Eureko* and *Methanex*", 22 (1) *Arbitration International* 27 (2006), at 28.
101   MTD Equity Sdn. Bhd. and MTD Chile S.A. v. Chile (ICSID Case No. ARB/01/7), available at www.italaw.com/cases/717.
102   See MTD Equity Sdn. Bhd. and MTD Chile S.A. v. Chile (ICSID Case No. ARB/01/7), Decision on Annulment (21 March 2007), available at www.italaw.com/sites/default/files/case-documents/ita0546.pdf, at paras. 66–78.

103 UNCTAD, "Fair and Equitable Treatment" (2012), at 67.
104 Duke Energy Electroquil Partners and Electroquil S.A. v. Republic of Ecuador (ICSID Case No. ARB/04/19), available at www.italaw.com/cases/356.
105 Duke Energy Electroquil Partners and Electroquil S.A. v. Republic of Ecuador (ICSID Case No. ARB/04/19), Award (18 August 2008), available at www.italaw.com/sites/default/files/case-documents/ita0256.pdf, at para. 340.
106 CMS Gas Transmission Company v. The Republic of Argentina (ICSID Case No. ARB/01/8), Award (12 May 2005), available at www.italaw.com/sites/default/files/case-documents/ita0184.pdf, at para. 277.
107 Alex Genin, Eastern Credit Limited, Inc. and A.S. Baltoil v. The Republic of Estonia (ICSID Case No. ARB/99/2), available at www.italaw.com/cases/484.
108 Alex Genin, Eastern Credit Limited, Inc. and A.S. Baltoil v. The Republic of Estonia (ICSID Case No. ARB/99/2), Award (25 June 2001), available at www.italaw.com/sites/default/files/case-documents/ita0359.pdf, at para. 348.
109 M. Potesta, "Legitimate Expectations in Investment Treaty Law: Understanding the Roots and the Limits of a Controversial Concept", 28 (1) *ICSID Review* 88 (2013), at 100.
110 See e.g. I. Pupolizio, "The Right to an Unchanging World – Indirect Expropriation in International Investment Agreements and State Sovereignty", 10 (2) *Vienna Journal of International Constitutional Law* 143 (2016), at 143–162.
111 Paragraph 2, Annex 8-A, Chapter 8, the CETA.
112 Paragraph 5 (a), Annex B, the 2012 U.S. Model BIT.
113 Paragraph 3, Annex 2, the ASEAN Comprehensive Investment Agreement.
114 Paragraph 4 (b), Annex B, the 2012 U.S. Model BIT.
115 Annex 11-B, the Korea–U.S. FTA.
116 Article 10 (2), the China–Canada BIT.
117 Article 21 (2), the 2012 U.S. Model BIT.
118 Article 5.7, the 2016 Indian Model BIT.
119 See e.g. A. Kulick, *Global Public Interest in International Investment Law* (Cambridge: Cambridge University Press, 2012), at 262–263.
120 See e.g. M. Sornarajah, *The International Law on Foreign Investment* (2nd edn) (Cambridge: Cambridge University Press, 2004), at 259 *et seq.*; O. Chung, "The Lopsided International Investment Law Regime and its Effects on the Future of Investor–State Arbitration", 47 *Virginia Journal of International Law* 953 (2007), at 963; R. Kläger (2011), at 205.

4   Exceptive provisions

In recent years, there has emerged a proliferation of various types of clauses of exceptions in IIAs. Some IIAs, especially recent ones, incorporate exceptive provisions to address various kinds of public interest concerns, such as the protection of national security interests, the preservation and protection of life (including the physical environment that makes life possible), the regulation of the economy and the preservation of the diversity of cultures.[1] Exceptive provisions may help address sustainable development concerns associated with transnational investment activities. Because they may exempt the host states from liability for taking IIA-inconsistent measures for public purposes,[2] they can play an assistive role in enabling states in pursuing sustainable development goals. There are different types of exceptive provisions in IIAs, depending on their subject matter and forms. This chapter focuses on the two major types of exceptions increasingly commonly seen in IIAs, namely the clause of general exceptions and the clause of security exception.

Clause of general exceptions

The clause of general exceptions is typically known in WTO/GATT law. It serves the purpose of preserving policy freedom for WTO members in taking trade regulatory measures that are otherwise inconsistent with their WTO obligations. Nowadays, such a clause has also been incorporated in IIAs with a similar purpose. Up to the present, there has been no ISA case in which a clause of general exceptions has been applied. For the purpose of the present study, a brief discussion of the transplantation of GATT Article XX to IIAs is necessary at the outset. The application of this clause and the potential impacts on state regulatory power will also be discussed.

The GATT Article XX general exceptions

The WTO is committed to an open, non-discriminatory and equitable multi-lateral trading system on the one hand, and to the promotion of sustainable development on the other hand.[3] As an important step to achieve these seemingly conflicting goals, the drafters of the GATT and the GATS inserted a

DOI: 10.4324/9781315642840-7

clause of general exceptions in the trade agreements.[4] As ruled by the WTO Appellate Body (AB), the main purpose of these exceptions is to ensure that WTO members are not precluded from adopting measures that pursue policy objectives that the members agree are legitimate and important.[5] In principle, the clause of general exceptions conforms to the WTO's policy goal of promoting sustainable development in global trade governance.

The making of GATT Article XX can be traced back to the 1927 International Agreement for the Suppression of Import and Export Prohibitions and Restrictions. Subsequently, the drafters of the ITO Charter incorporated the same general exceptions during negotiations of the Charter. The current GATT Article XX is based on a clause proposed by the U.S., with necessary revisions of the chapeau made.[6] GATT Article XX provides the following:

Article XX
General Exceptions

Subject to the requirement that such measures are not applied in a manner which would constitute a means of arbitrary or unjustifiable discrimination between countries where the same conditions prevail, or a disguised restriction on international trade, nothing in this Agreement shall be construed to prevent the adoption or enforcement by any contracting party of measures:

a) necessary to protect public morals;
b) necessary to protect human, animal or plant life or health;
c) relating to the importations or exportations of gold or silver;
d) necessary to secure compliance with laws or regulations which are not inconsistent with the provisions of this Agreement, including those relating to customs enforcement, the enforcement of monopolies operated under paragraph 4 of Article II and Article XVII, the protection of patents, trademarks and copyrights, and the prevention of deceptive practices;
e) relating to the products of prison labour;
f) imposed for the protection of national treasures of artistic, historic or archaeological value;
g) relating to the conservation of exhaustible natural resources if such measures are made effective in conjunction with restrictions on domestic production or consumption;
h) undertaken in pursuance of obligations under any intergovernmental commodity agreement which conforms to criteria submitted to the CONTRACTING PARTIES and not disapproved by them or which is itself so submitted and not so disapproved;
i) involving restrictions on exports of domestic materials necessary to ensure essential quantities of such materials to a domestic processing industry during periods when the domestic price of such materials is held below the world price as part of a governmental stabilization plan; Pro-

vided that such restrictions shall not operate to increase the exports of or the protection afforded to such domestic industry, and shall not depart from the provisions of this Agreement relating to non-discrimination;

j) essential to the acquisition or distribution of products in general or local short supply; Provided that any such measures shall be consistent with the principle that all contracting parties are entitled to an equitable share of the international supply of such products, and that any such measures, which are inconsistent with the other provisions of the Agreement shall be discontinued as soon as the conditions giving rise to them have ceased to exist. The CONTRACTING PARTIES shall review the need for this sub-paragraph not later than 30 June 1960.

As can be seen, the GATT clause of general exceptions includes a chapeau and various specific types of exceptions that cover a wide range of public purposes, such as the protection of public morals (para. a), human, animal or plant life or health (para. b), human rights (para. e), cultural heritage (para. f) and environment and natural resources (para. g). This clause does not necessarily constitute an exhaustive list of all legitimate non-trade objectives that a state may pursue.[7] Besides, the words "nothing in this Agreement" in the chapeau imply that the exceptions in Article XX apply to all of the obligations in the GATT 1994.[8] Essentially, under this exception, WTO members may justify trade measures inconsistent with their WTO obligations, if such measures fall under one or more of the listed exceptions.

The high-threshold requirements for invoking WTO exceptions

GATT Article XX exceptions have been frequently invoked in WTO/GATT disputes, especially the environmental exception under paragraphs (b) and (g).[9] The threshold requirements for the application of these exceptions have been gradually established through GATT/WTO case law.

In general, the threshold for the application of GATT Article XX exceptions is very high.[10] WTO case law has established a two-tiered test in assessing whether an exception can be successfully invoked.[11] A classic enumeration of the two-tiered test can be found in the AB report of *US–Gasoline*, stating the following:

In order that the justifying protection of Article XX may be extended to it, the measure at issue must not only come under one or another of the particular exceptions – paragraphs (a) to (j) – listed under Article XX; it must also satisfy the requirements imposed by the opening clauses of Article XX. The analysis is, in other words, two-tiered: first, provisional justification by reason of characterization of the measure under [one of the exceptions]; second, further appraisal of the same measure under the introductory clauses of Article XX.[12]

Taking the invocation of the environmental exception embedded in GATT Article XX (g) for example, the panel and the AB of the Dispute Settlement Body (DSB) must conduct the first-tier test, that is, to determine whether the trade measure in question falls under this exception. This actually necessitates a three-tiered test as the exception requires the attendance of several extra elements, namely (i) is the measure concerned with the conservation of exhaustible natural resources? (ii) Is the measure one "relating to" the conservation? And (iii) is the measure made effective in conjunction with restrictions on domestic production or consumption?[13]

If the above test is satisfied, the DSB panel or the AB would proceed to conduct the second-tier test to determine whether the requirements laid down in the chapeau of this Article are satisfied.[14] As the WTO upholds the notion of free trade, the chapeau is animated by the principle that while the exceptions of Article XX may be invoked as a matter of legal right, they should not be so applied as to frustrate or defeat the legal obligations of the holder of the right under the substantive rules of the GATT.[15] Under the chapeau, three enquires will be examined and decided, namely (i) whether the measure in question is a means of unjustifiable discrimination? Or (ii) whether the measure in question is a means of arbitrary discrimination? And (iii) if the answer to either of the above enquiries is negative, it should be examined whether the measure is a disguised restriction on international trade.[16]

Indeed, the issue of the application of GATT Article XX exceptions has been and remains a difficult and contentious one in the field of international trade law.[17] Yet, the existing empirical study on this issue shows that the threshold requirements for invoking these exceptions are extremely high, which makes it almost impossible for states to successfully invoke the exceptions to defend their trade regulatory measures for public purposes. According to a study of Public Citizen, an NGO, up to August 2015 there have been 43 WTO cases in which GATT Article XX has been invoked by a respondent member seeking to defend a challenged measure, and in one WTO case GATS Article XIV has been invoked. The result is – in only one out of these 44 WTO cases, namely, *EC–Asbestos* – that it was held that all conditions for application of a GATT or GATS general exception had been satisfied; while all other 43 cases failed to satisfy at least one of the threshold requirements.[18] Similarly, another empirical study focusing more specifically on the application of GATT Article XX (g) exception (environmental exception) reveals that there are a total of nine WTO and GATT cases in which GATT Article XX (g) has been invoked, but in no case has the invocation been successful, due largely to the failure to meet the high threshold of this exception.[19]

The creation and inclusion of the exceptions in GATT Article XX indicate that the WTO has taken the policies and interests that are outside the realm of trade liberalization, such as the environment, seriously.[20] However, the extremely high-threshold requirements for invoking the GATT exceptions should not be neglected. For such reasons, the criticism has been raised that the interpretation of the GATT exceptions is rigid and flawed and is likely to invite trouble for global trade governance,[21] and that the WTO has shown a strong bias in favour of free trade over environmental protection and other public interests.[22]

The incorporation and application of the general exceptions in IIAs

The use of general exceptions in IIAs is not common, as the majority of states do not have general exceptions to investment obligations.[23] In recent years, however, there has emerged a growing consensus for states to incorporate a GATT-style clause of general exceptions in IIAs.[24] Such a clause may cover a wide range of exceptions, such as environmental, public health, and public morals protection. Though the exception clauses of the GATT and of the IIAs bear important differences, "their structure and language is inspired by international trade law treaty practice".[25]

The incorporation of GATT-style general exceptions in IIAs

Some states are active in incorporating a GATT-style clause of general exceptions in IIAs. For instance, it has been suggested that "Canada is unique amongst OECD states in including GATT Article XX-like general exceptions in its BITs."[26] Not only does the 2004 Canadian Model BIT incorporate a GATT-style clause,[27] but many Canadian BITs currently in force also incorporate a clause of general exceptions.[28]

Various other states have also shown an increasing interest in making their IIAs more balanced through incorporating general exceptions. Australia holds a somewhat unique view on the international investment regime and has been sceptical with respect to ISA.[29] The scepticism became strong after Philip Morris initiated an arbitration to challenge Australia's plain-packaging Act, enacted for public health purposes.[30] According to the Australian government, incorporation of a GATT-style clause of general exceptions in IIAs is a sensible way to improve the existing IIA system.[31] China also shows a similar preference for general exceptions in its recent IIA-making. All Chinese BITs concluded after 2010 included a clause of general exceptions.[32]

There are two main reasons to explain the necessity and desirability of inserting a clause of general exceptions in IIAs. First and foremost, it is believed that such a clause can make IIAs more balanced with respect to the rights and obligations of the host states. As mentioned, this clause may exempt the host states from the liability incurred by IIA-inconsistent regulatory measures taken for public purposes. It thus helps preserve state regulatory power.

Second, incorporation of a GATT-style clause of general exceptions in IIAs can also be justified by the recent convergence of international trade and investment laws.[33] Though it is traditionally opined that these two branches of laws have developed along separate tracks, there appears to be an emerging trend of convergence of them as a result of globalization.[34] The incorporation of general exceptions in some IIAs *mutatis mutandis*;[35] the overlap of the jurisdictions of ISA tribunals and WTO panels and the AB;[36] and the cross reference of international investment and trade disputes jurisprudence[37] are convincing proof of such convergence.

Today, an increasing number of IIAs incorporate a GATT-style clause of general exceptions, although their total number remains small, and the wordings of these clauses are not necessarily the same. Such differences may demonstrate the different states' policy priorities. For instance, a typical clause of general exceptions can be found in the 2016 Indian Model BIT, which provides that,

Article 16
General Exceptions

16.1. Nothing in this Treaty precludes the Host State from taking actions or measures of general applicability which it considers necessary with respect to the following, including:

a) protecting public morals or maintaining public order;
b) ensuring the integrity and stability of its financial system, banks and financial institutions;
c) remedying serious balance-of-payments problems, exchange rate difficulties and external financial difficulties or threat thereof;
d) ensuring public health and safety;
e) protecting and conserving the environment including all living and non-living natural resources;
f) improving working conditions;
g) securing compliance with the Law for the prevention of deceptive and fraudulent practices or to deal with the effects of a default on a contract;
h) protecting privacy of individuals in relation to the processing and dissemination of personal data and the protection of confidentiality of individual records and accounts; or
i) protecting national treasures or monuments of artistic, cultural, historic or archaeological value.

16.2. Nothing in this Treaty shall bind either Party to protect Investments made with capital or assets derived from illegal activities.
16.3. Nothing in this Treaty shall apply to any Measure taken by a local body or authority at the district, block or village level in the case of India. For avoidance of doubt, a local body or authority shall include the Municipal Corporation, district level officers, *Gram Panchayats* and *Gram Sabha*.

This clause covers a wide range of exceptions, many of which are a clear reflection of the elements of sustainable development, such as the protection of the public moral, public health and safety, environmental protection, and labour rights. Some of these exceptions are the same as those contained in GATT Article XX.

In comparison, the 2004 Canadian Model BIT incorporates a more comprehensive clause of general exceptions,[38] which not only covers the exceptions in the 2016 Indian Model BIT in principle, but also extends to some other exceptions, such as the protection of cultural industries.[39]

Cross reference between trade and investment laws in ISA

Given that only a limited number of IIAs contain general exceptions and that there is no reported ISA case in which these exceptions are invoked, it remains unclear how the exceptions will be interpreted and applied in practice and what real effects they may have in protecting state regulatory power. Such a situation necessitates a cross reference to the WTO jurisprudence relating to the application of GATT Article XX exceptions.

Several reasons can justify the cross reference between WTO and ISA jurisprudence. First, both trade and investment disputes explore the legality of state regulatory measures while applying international law standards. Second, as mentioned, GATT Article XX and the clause of general exceptions in IIAs share the same origin, similar contents and almost identical structure. Third, the emerging convergence of international trade and investment laws suggests that cross-referencing between the WTO and ISA jurisprudence is reasonable and necessary. In fact, in some ISA cases, the arbitrators clearly referred to the GATT jurisprudence when interpreting the exception clause in IIAs.

For instance, in Continental Casualty v. Argentina, when deciding whether the economic emergency in Argentina towards the end of 2001 was covered by the security exception clause of the Argentina–U.S. BIT, Argentina submitted that the term "necessary" in Art. XI of the BIT must be interpreted in line with GATT and WTO case law.[40] The tribunal also found it necessary to refer to GATT and WTO case law, holding that,

> Since the text of Art. XI derives from the parallel model clause of the U.S. FCN treaties and these treaties in turn reflect the formulation of Art. XX of GATT 1947, the Tribunal finds it more appropriate to refer to the GATT and WTO case law which has extensively dealt with the concept and requirements of necessity in the context of economic measures derogating to the obligations contained in GATT, rather than to refer to the requirement of necessity under customary international law.[41]

A clause of general exceptions in IIAs has only been applied in a very limited number of ISA cases. Though difficulty in applying these exceptions has not been sufficiently elaborated in ISA case law, one may reasonable expect that the chances for successful invocation of these exceptions are slim. First – as suggested by ISA case law – when interpreting IIA provisions, due weight should be given to the objective and purpose of IIAs, i.e. protection and promotion of foreign investments.[42] Such interpretation often leads to a "pro-investor bias" in ISA. Second, WTO/GATT case law imposes an extremely high threshold for the invocation of the general exceptions, making it almost impossible for WTO members to successfully defend its regulatory measures that rely on these exceptions. When ISA tribunals refer to GATT and WTO jurisprudence for cross reference, it is likely that similar high-threshold requirements will be applied.

In Canfor Corporation v. U.S. and Terminal Forest Products Ltd. v. U.S., the tribunal, while referring to GATT case law, has shown a principled position of interpreting the general exceptions in the IIA in a narrow way, holding that,

> The second concerns the manner in which exceptions in international instruments are to be interpreted. The present Tribunal subscribes to the view expressed by the GATT Panel in Canada – Import Restrictions on Ice Cream and Yoghurt: "The Panel … noted, as had previous panels, that exceptions were to be interpreted narrowly and considered that this argued against flexible interpretation of Article XI:2(c)(i)".[43]

As can be seen, successful invocation of the clause of general exceptions in IIAs may be quite difficult. Thus, it remains to be seen how a GATT-style clause of general exceptions in IIAs will be applied in the future and how effective it will be in helping states preserve regulatory rights in practice.

Security exception

States routinely restrict trade and other economic relations for security reasons.[44] Such restrictions may be implemented in both domestic and international planes. In the national plane, states may restrict transnational investment activities within their territories, citing security reasons. The dispute in Ralls Corp. v. The Committee on Foreign Investment in the United States (CFIUS), in which a Chinese investor challenged the CFIUS national security review, is a typical example of such case.[45] In the international sphere, a security exception is probably one of the most commonly seen exceptions in modern IIAs.[46] It has also been invoked in some ISA cases.[47] Especially, as discussed *infra*, in a series of ICSID cases, the arbitral tribunals had to interpret and apply the security exception in the Argentina–U.S. BIT. Similar to general exceptions, a security exception serves the purpose of preserving policy space for states in taking regulatory measures that are otherwise inconsistent with their IIA obligations to address certain emergencies to protect the essential security interests of the states.

Security exception under GATT Article XXI

Historically, the making of the national security exception in international trade agreements can also be traced back to the making of the ITO Charter. At the behest of the U.S., the Havana Conference on Trade and Employment incorp-orated into the proposed ITO Charter a general exception.[48] Under this general exception, nothing in the ITO Charter was to be construed to prevent a member state from taking any action which it considered necessary for the protection of its essential security interests, where such action related to fissionable materials, to traffic in implements of war, to traffic in goods or services for supplying a military establishment, or taken in time of war or other emergency in inter-national relations.[49]

A security exception is incorporated in Article XXI of the GATT 1947. It is thus of interest to briefly discuss this Article, which provides that,

Article XXI
Security Exceptions

Nothing in this Agreement shall be construed

3.1   to require any contracting party to furnish any information the dis-closure of which it considers contrary to its essential security interests; or

3.2   to prevent any contracting party from taking any action which it considers necessary for the protection of its essential security interests:

i)   relating to fissionable materials or the materials from which they are derived;

ii)   relating to the traffic in arms, ammunition and implements of war and to such traffic in other goods and materials as is carried on directly or indirectly for the purpose of supplying a military establishment;

iii)   taken in time of war or other emergency in international relations; or

3.3   to prevent any contracting party from taking any action in pursuance of its obligations under the United Nations Charter for the main-tenance of international peace and security.

While there is no compelling need to discuss GATT Article XXI in detail for the purpose of the present study, several observations can be drawn. First, this exception covers a wide range of circumstances both nationally and inter-nationally, in which a state may invoke the security exception. Second, the wording "nothing in this agreement" shows that the exception may be applied to all obligations under GATT 1994. Third, the words "it considers necessary" implies that the exception is of a self-judging nature, under which the con-tracting states are allowed to decide whether a circumstance would endanger their essential security interests in their own judgement.

The self-judging nature of the security exception in GATT Article XXI is probably one of the most contentious issues pertaining to the interpretation and application of this exception. During the negotiation of the ITO Charter, the preparatory committee held that in designing the security exception, "there must be some latitude [for the contracting states] here for security measures" and that the application of this exception "is really a question of balance". In addition, a number of states also took the position that they should be the sole judge in assessing and deciding what is necessary in their essential security interests and that no external juridical review of such decisions should be allowed.[50]

With regard to the practical impact of the self-judging nature of the security exception, academic opinion seems split.[51] Those who take a textual, historical or prudential viewpoint favour the self-judging nature, arguing that the words "it considers" indicates that no WTO member, nor group of members, and no WTO panel or other adjudicatory body, has any right to determine whether a measure taken by a member satisfies the requirements.[52] Those who are against the self-judging nature of this exception tend to argue that the security exception as a treaty term must be interpreted in good faith as required by the VCLT.[53]

GATT Article XXI exception has only been invoked marginally. In GATT dispute settlement history, there has been only one case where the contracting parties have considered measures justified under Article XXI (b)(ii), and eight cases where measures taken under Article XXI (b)(iii) – although this sub-paragraph has not always been explicitly invoked –were considered; issues arising under the remaining paragraphs of Article XXI have never been examined.[54] In WTO dispute settlement history, the security exception has never been applied. It has been pointed out by commentators that states have generally demonstrated significant levels of self-restraint in challenging other states' security measures, as they probably have doubted the appropriateness and effectiveness of the GATT and WTO dispute settlement mechanism to settle political and security matters.[55] Thus, unlike the established WTO and GATT case law of the application of the general exceptions, jurisprudence with regard to the application of the security exception seems hardly sufficient or helpful.

Incorporation of security exception in IIAs

Differently than general exceptions in IIAs, security exception has been incorporated in IIAs since early times, even before the negotiation of the ITO Charter. Security exceptions appear regularly in the BITs of states that play a major role in the international financial system, such as the U.S., Germany, India, the Belgian–Luxembourg Union and Canada.[56] There is a close link between the security exception in IIAs and that in GATT Article XXI. Such linkage is recognized in ISA case law. The ICSID tribunal in Continental Casualty v. Argentina pointed out that the security exception of the Argentina–U.S. BIT actually derived from the parallel model clause of the U.S. FCN treaties, and that these treaties in turn reflect the formulation of Art. XX of GATT 1947.[57]

State practices vary on the incorporation of a security exception in IIA-making. According to an OECD report, some states, such as the U.S., have been consistent in favouring the insertion of a security exception in IIAs; some have never inserted a national security exception in their IIAs; while some have been inconsistent in this practice.[58] Besides, a security exception in IIAs may take different forms. Some IIAs incorporate it as a standalone provision;[59] some IIAs absorb it as one paragraph of the clause of general exceptions;[60] and some IIAs contain both a security exception provision and a protocol or annex providing further clarification thereof.[61] Such formal differences do not have material impact on the application of the security exception.

As mentioned, the U.S. has consistently favoured the incorporation of a security exception in IIAs. As early as in the post-war period, the U.S. had included a security exception in its FCN treaties, which are believed to be the "predecessor" of modern BITs. When the U.S. inaugurated its BIT programme in 1977, it continued including a security exception in BITs, which followed very closely the language in the FCN treaties.[62] The security exception in the 2012 U.S. Model BIT is a typical one, which provides that,

Article 18
Essential Security

Nothing in this Treaty shall be construed:

1   to require a Party to furnish or allow access to any information the disclosure of which it determines to be contrary to its essential security interests; or
2   to preclude a Party from applying measures that it considers necessary for the fulfillment of its obligations with respect to the maintenance or restoration of international peace or security, or the protection of its own essential security interests.

Two main aspects predominate the effectiveness of a security exception, namely whether the exception is self-judging in nature, and whether the exception is broad in coverage. These aspects can be ascertained from the wordings and interpretation of the security exception.

It should also be mentioned that as the wrongfulness of a state act can be precluded by necessity under customary international law,[63] a state is always entitled to invoke the security exception in case of necessity, even if the applicable IIA does not have a clause of security exception.[64] Here, a line should be drawn between a security exception in an IIA and one under customary international law. If an IIA contains a security exception, it should be applied as a primary rule *lex specialis* vis-à-vis customary international law as a supplementary rule.[65] In this sense, a security exception in an IIA not only reaffirms the state's preservation of its regulatory rights to protect its essential security interests, but also provides an extra layer of protection to the state in conjunction with and in addition to customary international law.

The self-judging nature of the security exception in IIAs

Whether a security exception in an IIA is self-judging in nature essentially decides the margin of appreciation the contracting states may have when invoking this exception. Not all security exceptions are self-judging. In the case of non-self-judging security exceptions, the contracting states do not enjoy unilateral power in deciding if there exists a circumstance that warrants the invocation of the security exception. Their decision may be subject to the external review by international adjudicators.

In treaty practice, the phrases "it considers" or "it determines" used in a security exception of an IIA are a strong indication of the self-judging nature of the exception, although the lack of these terms does not necessarily mean that the arbitrators may fully replace the contracting states in assessing a situation and the measures to remedy it.[66]

A self-judging security exception in an IIA not only grants the contracting states unilateral power in deciding if and what situation would warrant the invocation of such exception, but it also represents a situation in which the state regards its national security as more important than the protection of foreign investors. When two interests collide, the state's national security interests would prevail.[67] In this sense, a self-judging security exception helps the states preserve the right to unilaterally declare their IIA obligations non-binding if they determine that their essential security interests are at stake according to their own judgement.[68] The only obligation that the states need to abide by is the international law principle of carrying out their treaty obligations in "good faith".[69] However, it has also been pointed out that because it is practically difficult to judge in an objective manner whether a state has invoked the security exception in "good faith", such an exception may provide an easy way for the state to escape from its treaty obligations.[70]

The security exception in the 2012 U.S. Model BIT is a typical self-judging one. Such an exception is favoured by many other states, especially developed states. For instance, the OECD report reveals that all of the surveyed clauses of security exception have an explicitly self-judging character.[71] The OECD Guidelines for Recipient Country Investment Policies Relating to National Security also clearly confirms that "essential security concerns are self-judging" and that "OECD investment instruments recognize that each country has a right to determine what is necessary to protect its national security".[72]

The coverage of the security exception in IIAs

The coverage of a security exception is a major determinant of the practical effectiveness of the exception. As different states may have a different understanding and priority of national security, different terms are used to define the coverage of a security exception in IIAs. For instance, the security exception in the 2012 U.S. Model BIT can be applied to two major situations, namely, "the protection of essential security interests" and "the maintenance or restoration of international peace or security". The term "essential security interests" seems to be commonly used in IIAs. Other terms that are also frequently seen in IIAs include, *inter alia*, "public interests", "public order", "national interests" and "extreme emergency". These terms reflect different policy aims of the contracting states and may be interpreted to have different coverage.[73]

Despite the literal difference of these terms, the crucial question is whether a term is concrete enough to clarify its scope and meaning. On this issue, the UNCTAD has observed that terms such as "extreme emergency", "strategic industry" or "international peace and security" appear narrower than terms such as "public interests", "public order" or "essential security interests".[74] These terms need to be interpreted in ISA in accordance with the VCLT. As mentioned earlier, some of these terms, especially "essential security interests" in the security exception of the Argentina–U.S. BIT have been interpreted by ICSID tribunals in a series of ISA cases.

Finally but equally importantly, it should be noted that a large number of security exceptions in IIAs are actually adapted from standard templates found in various Model BITs.[75] Despite the convenience of this IIA-making method, the transplantation of an exception from a model IIA invites potential perils. A model IIA is heavily unilateral-oriented in the sense that it is driven and designed by the interests of the drafting state. It has been suggested that "model BITs are often a by-product of extensive bureaucratic analysis and refinement by legal and business communities, making it ripe for the domestic ratification process",[76] and that these prototypes "serve as a way for powerful states to frame acceptable norms in the orientation and content of investment treaties".[77] In addition, since IIA provisions are often moderated and adapted from model IIAs and lack preparatory work, interpretation of these provisions could be difficult by arbitrators who are not necessarily familiar with the model IIAs and have no IIA-making experiences.[78] Consequently, it would not be surprising that inconsistent interpretations of a security exception are produced by different tribunals, which could lead to conflicting decisions.[79]

The Argentine financial crisis and the security exception

The existing ISA case law relating to the application of the security exception has been essentially built on the experience of a series of ICSID cases consequential to the Argentine financial crisis that occurred between 2001 and 2002. Relying on the Argentina–U.S. BIT, a number of U.S. investors sued Argentina for compensation, and Argentina invoked the security exception in this BIT in defence.

Before discussing in detail how the ICSID arbitrators interpreted and applied the security exception, it is helpful to briefly review the factual background of the Argentine financial crisis. Prior to the financial crisis, Argentina faced a deep economic recession, large levels of debt, and twin deficits in the fiscal and current accounts. To restore its competitiveness, Argentina enacted domestic deflation and improved its solvency by increasing its fiscal accounts. These measures failed to produce the expected results, and Argentina was unable to devalue its currency without breaking the convertibility law. The rapid outflow of dollar deposits finally triggered the financial crisis. To respond, Argentina enacted emergency measures to control the outflow of deposits, which led to a monetary crunch and a collapse of the fixed exchange rate regime, and, further, led to a collapse of economic activity and widespread social unrest.[80]

Argentina's emergent measures seriously hurt foreign investors. In the years that followed the financial crisis, a number of ISA cases were initiated against Argentina, including Enron v. Argentina,[81] CMS v. Argentina,[82] LG&E v. Argentina,[83] Sempra v. Argentina,[84] Continental Casualty v. Argentina,[85] Metalpar v. Argentina,[86] Suez v. Argentina,[87] Total v. Argentina,[88] Impregilo v. Argentina,[89] El Paso v. Argentina,[90] BG v. Argentina[91] and National Grid v. Argentina[92].

The factual and legal backgrounds of these cases are quite similar. While most of them are ICSID cases, some are *ad hoc* arbitration cases under UNCITRAL Arbitration Rules. In these cases, the U.S. investors claimed, *inter alia*, that Argentina's regulatory measures constituted an act of indirect expropriation and/or a violation of the FET under the Argentina–U.S. BIT. In response, Argentina invoked the security exception embedded in Article XI of the BIT (clause of non-precluded measures) to defend itself.[93] The security exception provides that,

> This Treaty shall not preclude the application by either Party of measures necessary for the maintenance of public order, the fulfilment of its obligations with respect to the maintenance or restoration of international peace or security, or the protection of its own essential security interests.

Judging from its wording, this security exception can only be invoked in three circumstances, namely (i) the maintenance of public order; (ii) the maintenance or restoration of international peace or security; and (iii) the protection of the state's essential security interests. It is also uncertain whether this exception is self-judging, since it does not use the indicative term "it considers necessary". These issues appeared to be outstanding.

Firstly, in these cases the tribunals faced a common legal question, i.e. whether the financial crisis could be covered by the "essential security interests" of the security exception. Some commentators proposed that an expansive interpretation of the term "essential security interests" is necessary on several grounds: (i) It seems that the plain language of the exception does not foreclose such an interpretation.[94] (ii) The term "essential security interests" appears broad and potentially ambiguous, and there is no uniform definition at the global level.[95] (iii) In an ever more globalized world, the kinds of exceptional circumstances covered by the security exception are all too common, such as financial crises, terrorist threats and public health emergencies.[96] Therefore, essential security interests should be comprehensive and cover not only external military security, but also internal political, social and economic security.

Other commentators took into account the U.S. treaty practice with regard to the making of the security exception, and observed that financial crises could not fall within the scope of "essential security interests". For instance, K. Vandevelde has put forward the following argument,

> The history of the exception suggests that the drafters did not contemplate its application to economic crises. During the ITO Charter negotiations, the United States proposed an elaborate exception in which the circumstances to which the exception applied were specified in greater detail. The various circumstances, such as trade in fissionable materials or trade in armaments, all appear to have been related to military security. After the Havana conference, the United States simplified the exception in its FCN treaties by removing the various qualifying conditions, but I have seen no evidence that the purpose of this change was to broaden its application to include economic crises.[97]

On this issue, the tribunals in these cases shared the consensus that economic crisis in general could be covered by the "essential security interests" of a state. For instance, the tribunal in CMS v. Argentina held that,

> If the concept of essential security interests were to be limited to immediate political and national security concerns, particularly of an international character, and were to exclude other interests, for example, major economic emergencies, it could well result in an unbalanced understanding of article 11 [of the Argentina–U.S. BIT].[98]

Such interpretation of "essential security interests" implies that a security exception similar to the one in the 2012 U.S. Model BIT can be invoked in a wide range of circumstances. This is helpful in preserving state regulatory power in coping with various types of emergency circumstances.

Notwithstanding the consensus, what makes a difference in these cases lies mainly in that the tribunals had different findings with regard to the severity of the financial crisis. In short, in Enron v. Argentina, CMS v. Argentina and Sempra v. Argentina, the tribunals held that the financial crisis was not sufficiently severe to invoke the security exception, holding that only "an economic crisis imperiling a state's existence and its independence would be of a sufficient scale to fulfil the requirements of the security exception". In contrast, in LG&E v. Argentina, the tribunal had the opposite finding, holding that the financial crisis was severe enough to "threaten the total collapse of the Government and the Argentine State" and allowed the invocation of the security exception.[99] In Continental Casualty v. Argentina, the tribunal also allowed the invocation of the security exception, holding that the protection of "essential security interests" does not require the "total collapse" of the country or a "catastrophic situation" in order to be recognized.[100]

Secondly, the disputants also disagreed on whether the security exception is self-judging in nature. As mentioned, the security exception clause has no indicative words of "it considers" or "it determines". Although there is a strong evidence to show that the U.S. and Argentina intended the security exception of the BIT to be self-judging and subject only to a good-faith review, the states failed to expressly manifest that intent in the text of the treaty.[101] On this issue, the tribunals were unanimous in finding that the security exception of the Argentina–U.S. BIT is not self-judging in nature, on different legal grounds.[102] Such a result seems to suggest that if states wish to make the security exception in their IIA a self-judging one, they should make such intent unequivocally clear, preferably by using the terms of "it considers" or "it determines".

As discussed, despite the fact that these cases were based on the same BIT and similar factual backgrounds, the tribunals reached different and even contradictory conclusions.[103] The inconsistency of the awards in these cases, according to some commentators, can be deemed a result of the tribunals' different understandings of the bargain that lies behind the Argentina–U.S. BIT and the risk-allocation function of the security exception in the BIT.[104] Such inconsistency not only casts doubt onto the function and practical effectiveness of the security exception in IIAs in preserving state regulatory power, but may also give rise to concerns over the legitimacy of ISA at a more profound level.[105] The arguments presented and the jurisprudence established in these cases may shed helpful light upon and provide necessary references for future cases involving the security exception.

Conclusion

Modern IIAs often incorporate one or more types of exceptive provisions, as a general or special exception. Despite their formal differences, these provisions play two major functions. First, they play an "exemptive role". Successful invocation of the exceptions could preclude the wrongfulness of the regulatory measures taken by a state that are inconsistent with its IIA obligations, and that the state should not be held liable for compensation.

Second, they also play a "supplementary role". Exceptions in IIAs are not the only legal grounds for a state to be exempted from its IIA obligations. Under customary international law, the wrongfulness of a state's conduct may also be precluded in various circumstances, such as *force majeure*, necessity, and compliance with peremptory norms.[106] In light of this, exceptions in IIAs may provide "extra or supplementary protection" to the states in the sense that they may cover a broader scope of circumstances or provide lower invocation requirements than those in customary international law.

The exemptive and supplementary functions of exceptive provisions can be helpful to states in pursuing sustainable development goals. Many exceptions are designed to defend some main sustainable development values. For instance, general exceptions in IIAs serve the purpose of protecting the environment, preservation and sustainable use of natural resources, which are *ipso facto* core elements of sustainable development. As exceptions help preserve state regulatory power, states potentially gain more autonomy in taking measures for sustainable development purposes.

Despite the potential helpful role of the exceptive provisions in IIAs, the invocation threshold of the exceptions remain high. Exceptions have been invoked in a limited number of ISA cases to date, which were rarely successful. Existing ISA case law suggests that expropriation and FET provisions remain the most frequently invoked provisions in ISA involving state regulatory measures. In these cases, the arbitrators often do not distinguish claims that are sensitive to sustainable development from the "general" claims. The difficulty in invoking exceptions in IIAs seems to suggest that the practical effectiveness of the exceptions is weak. Thus, it remains difficult, if possible, for states to defend their regulatory measures relying on the exceptive clauses in IIAs

Notes

1 K. J. Vandevelde, "Rebalancing through Exceptions", 17 (2) *Lewis and Clark Law Review* 449 (2013), at 450.
2 G. K. Foster, "Investors, States, and Stakeholders: Power Asymmetries in International Investment and the Stabilizing Potential of Investment Treaties", 17 (2) *Lewis and Clark Law Review* 361 (2013), at 376–377.
3 See Preamble, The (Marrakesh) Ministerial Decision on Trade and Environment (15 April 1994), Doc. No.: GATT/MTN.TNC/MIN(94)/1/Rev.1.
4 The clause of general exceptions is contained in GATT Article XX and GATS Article XIV.
5 AB Report, US–Shrimp, at para. 121.
6 See generally P. Ala'i, "Free Trade or Sustainable Development? An Analysis of the WTO Appellate Body's Shift to a More Balanced Approach to Trade Liberalization", 14 (4) *American University International Law Review* 1129 (1999), at 1131–1136.
7 AB Report, US–Shrimp, at para. 121.
8 See AB Report, US–Gasoline, at para. 24.
9 See e.g. P. Ala'i (1999); S. Gaines, "The WTO's Reading of the GATT Article XX Chapeau: A Disguised Restriction on Environmental Measures", 22 (4) *University of Pennsylvania Journal of International Economic Law* 739 (2001); N. Bernasconi-Osterwalder *et al.*, *Environment and Trade: A Guide to WTO Jurisprudence* (London: Earthscan, 2005).
10 See e.g. Bin Gu, Mineral Export Restraints and Sustainable Development – Are Rare Earths Testing the WTO's Loopholes?, 14 (4) *Journal of International Economic Law* 765, 787–789 (2011).
11 See e.g. AB Report, China–Raw Materials, para. 354, p. 140; Peter Van den Bossche, *The Law and Policy of the World Trade Organization: Text, Cases and Materials* (2nd edn.) (Cambridge: Cambridge University Press, 2008), at 620.
12 US–Gasoline, AB Report, DSR 1996, at 20–21.

13 See P. Van den Bossche (2008), at 634; S. Charnovitz, "The WTO's Environmental Progress", 10 (3) *Journal of International Economic Law* 685 (2007), at 699.

14 US–Shrimp, AB Report, at para. 156

15 US–Gasoline, AB Report, DSR 1996, at 21.

16 See WTO Secretariat, "GATT/WTO Dispute Settlement Practice Relating to GATT Article XX, Paragraphs (b), (d) and (g)", WT/CTE/W/203, at 22.

17 See F. Fontanelli, "Necessity Killed the GATT – Art XX GATT and the Misleading Rhetoric about 'Weighing and Balancing'", 5 (2) *European Journal of Legal Studies* 36 (2012), at 36–56.

18 Public Citizen, "Only One of 44 Attempts to Use the GATT Article XX/GATS Article XIV 'General Exception' Has Ever Succeeded: Replicating the WTO Exception Construct Will Not Provide for an Effective TPP General Exception", available at www.citizen.org/documents/general-exception.pdf, at 1–2.

19 See Manjiao Chi, "'Exhaustible Natural Resources' in WTO Law: GATT Article XX (g) Disputes and their Implications", 48 (5) *Journal of World Trade* 939 (2014).

20 P. Ala'i (1999), at 1131.

21 See S. Gaines (2001), at 746.

22 See e.g. K. Kilovesi, *The WTO Dispute Settlement System: Challenges of the Environment, Legitimacy and Fragmentation* (The Netherlands: Kluwer Law International, 2011), at 82–90; R. Howse, "Adjudicative Legitimacy and Treaty Interpretation in International Trade Law: The Early Years of WTO Jurisprudence", in J. H. H. Weiler, *The EU, the WTO, and the NAFTA: Towards a Common Law of International Trade?* (Oxford: Oxford University Press, 2010), at 43; J. Pauwelyn, "Recent Books on Trade and Environment: GATT Phantoms Still Haunt the WTO", 15 (3) *European Journal of International Law* 595 (2004), at 585–591.

23 A. Newcombe, *General Exceptions in International Investment Agreements*, available at www.biicl.org/files/3866_andrew_newcombe.pdf, at 2.

24 K. J. Vandevelde (2013), at 449–450.

25 A. Newcombe, *General Exceptions in International Investment Agreements*, available at www.biicl.org/files/3866_andrew_newcombe.pdf, at 5.

26 Ibid., at 3.

27 Article 10, the 2004 Canadian Model BIT.

28 M. Chi (2015), at 520.

29 See S. Lestor, Improving Investment Treaties through General Exceptions Provisions: The Australian Example, www.cato.org/publications/commentary/improving-investment-treaties-through-general-exceptions-provisions.

30 Philip Morris Asia Limited v. The Commonwealth of Australia (UNCITRAL, PCA Case No. 2012-12), available at www.italaw.com/cases/851.

31 See S. Lestor, "Improving Investment Treaties through General Exceptions Provisions: The Australian Example", www.cato.org/publications/commentary/improving-investment-treaties-through-general-exceptions-provisions.

32 M. Chi (2015), at 520.

33 M. Chi (2015), at 519–520; S. Lestor, Improving Investment Treaties through General Exceptions Provisions: The Australian Example, available at www.cato.org/publications/commentary/improving-investment-treaties-through-general-except ions-provisions.

34 See e.g. A. K. Bjorklund, "Convergence or Complementarity?", 12 (1) *Santa Clara Journal of International Law* 65 (2014), at 69–70; R. P. Alford, "The Convergence of International Trade and Investment Arbitration", 12 (1) *Santa Clara Journal of*

International Law 35 (2014), at 37; J. A. Huerta-Goldman, A. Romanetti and F. X. Stirnimann (eds.), *WTO Litigation, Investment Arbitration and Commercial Arbitration* (The Netherlands: Kluwer Law International, 2013).

35   See A. K. Bjorklund (2014), at 70; R. P. Alford (2014), at 55; A. Newcombe, *General Exceptions in International Investment Agreements*, available at www.biicl. org/files/3866_andrew_newcombe.pdf.

36   See e.g. B. E. Allen and Tommaso Soave, "Jurisdictional Overlap in WTO Dispute Settlement and Investment Arbitration", 30 (1) *Arbitration International* 1 (2014).

37   See J. Kurtz, "The Use and Abuse of WTO Law in Investor–State Arbitration: Competition and Its Discontents", 20 (3) *European Journal of International Law* 749 (2009).

38   Article 10, the 2004 Canadian Model BIT.

39   Article 10 (5), the 2004 Canadian Model BIT.

40   *Continental Casualty Company v. The Argentine Republic* (ICSID Case No. ARB/03/9), Award of 5 September 2008, available at www.italaw.com/sites/default/ files/case-documents/ita0228.pdf, at para. 85.

41   Ibid., at para. 192.

42   See e.g. A. Newcombe, *General Exceptions in International Investment Agreements*, available at www.biicl.org/files/3866_andrew_newcombe.pdf, at 6.

43   *Canfor Corporation v. U.S., Tembec, Inc. et al. v. U.S. & Terminal Forest Products Ltd. v. U.S.* (under UNCITRAL Rules), Decision on Preliminary Question, available at www.italaw.com/sites/default/files/case-documents/ita0122.pdf, at para. 187.

44   R. P. Alford, "The Self-Judging WTO Security Exception", 3 *Utah Law Review* 697 (2011), at 700.

45   See generally J. Wang, "Ralls Corp. v. CFIUS: A New Look at Foreign Direct Investments to the US", *Columbia Journal of Transnational Law Bulletin* 30 (2016).

46   K. J. Vandevelde (2013), at 449.

47   See W. W. Burke-White and A. von Staten, "Investment Protection in Extraordinary Times: The Interpretation and Application of Non-Precluded Measures Provisions in Bilateral Investment Treaties", 48 (2) *Virginia Journal of International Law* 308 (2008), at 319–320.

48   Ibid., at 451–452.

49   Ibid., at 451–452.

50   WTO, *WTO Analytical Index* (3rd edn.) (Cambridge: Cambridge University Press, 2012), at 601–602.

51   See generally R. P. Alford (2011), at 706–707.

52   See e.g. R. P. Alford (2011), at 706; R. Bhala, "National Security and International Trade Law: What the GATT Says and What the United States Does", 19 *University of Pennsylvania Journal of International Law* 263 (2014), at 268–269; A. Emmerson, "Conceptualizing Security Exceptions: Legal Doctrine or Political Excuse", 11 *Journal of International Economic Law* 135 (2010), at 142–143.

53   See e.g. R. P. Alford (2011), at 706; D. Akande and S. Williams, "International Adjudication on National Security Issues: What Role for the WTO?", 43 *Virginia Journal of International Law* 365 (2003), at 390–396; S. Rose-Ackerman and B. Billa, "Treaties and National Security", 40 *International Law and Policy*, 437 (2008), at 467.

54   Group of Negotiations on Goods (GATT), "Article XXI, Note by the Secretariat", MTN.GNG/NG7/W/16 (18 August 1987), available at www.wto.org/gatt_docs/ English/SULPDF/92020251.pdf, at 5–8.

55 T. Cottier and P. Delimatsis, "Article XIV bis GATS: Security Exceptions", in R. Wolfrum, P. T. Stoll and C. Feinäugle (eds.), *Max Planck Commentaries on World Trade Law – Trade in Services* (Leiden/Boston: Martinus Nijhoff Publishers, 2008), at 331.

56 W. W. Burke-White and A. von Staten (2008), at 313.

57 Continental Casualty Company v. The Argentine Republic (ICSID Case No. ARB/03/9), Award of 5 September 2008, available at www.italaw.com/sites/default/files/case-documents/ita0228.pdf, at para. 192.

58 OECD, *International Investment Perspectives: Freedom of Investment in a Changing World* (Paris: OECD, 2007), at 98.

59 See e.g. the 2012 U.S. Model BIT.

60 See e.g. the 2004 Canadian Model BIT.

61 See e.g. the Panama–U.S. BIT.

62 See K. J. Vandevelde (2013), at 452; W. W. Burke-White and A.s von Staten (2008), at 312.

63 See Article 25, Chapter V, Responsibility of States for Internationally Wrongful Acts, A/RES/56/83, adopted by the UNGA on 12 December 2001, available at www.un.org/ga/search/view_doc.asp?symbol=A/RES/56/83.

64 UNCTAD, at 71.

65 W. J. Moon, "Essential Security Interests in International Investment Agreements", 15 (2) *Journal of International Economic Law* 481 (2012), at 485. However, for opposing arguments, refer to, e.g. J. Alvarez and K. Khamsi, "The Argentine Crisis and Foreign Investors: A Glimpse into the Heart of the Investment Regime", in K. Sauvant (ed.), *Yearbook of International Investment Law and Policy 2008–2009* (New York: Oxford University Press, 2009), at 427–440.

66 See W. W. Burke-White and A. von Staten (2008), at 371.

67 K. J. Vandevelde (2013), at 456.

68 S. W. Schill and R. Briese, "'If the State Considers': Self-Judging Clauses in International Dispute Settlement", 13 *Max Planck Yearbook of United Nations Law* 61 (2009), at 64.

69 Article 26, the VCLT.

70 UNCTAD, "The Protection of National Security in IIAs" (UNCTAD/DIAE/IA/2008/5), at 91–92.

71 See generally OECD, *International Investment Perspectives: Freedom of Investment in a Changing World* (Paris: OECD, 2007), at 94

72 OECD Guidelines for Recipient Country Investment Policies Relating to National Security, available at www.oecd.org/investment/investment-policy/43384486.pdf, at para. 3.

73 See W. W. Burke-White and A. von Staten (2008), at 336.

74 UNCTAD, "The Protection of National Security in IIAs" (UNCTAD/DIAE/IA/2008/5), at 121–125.

75 J. Kurtz, "Adjudging the Exceptional at International Investment Law: Security, Public Order, and Financial Crisis", 59 *International and Comparative Law Quarterly* 325 (2010), at 328.

76 K. S. Gudgeon, "United States Bilateral Investment Treaties: Comments on their Origin, Purposes, and General Treatment Standards", 4 *International Tax and Business Lawyer* 105 (1986), at 105–106.

77 W. J. Moon, "Essential Security Interests in International Investment Agreements", 15 (2) *Journal of International Economic Law* 481 (2012), at 490.

78   See C. McLachlan, "Investment Treaties and General International Law", 57 *International and Comparative Law Quarterly* 361 (2008), at 372.
79   See K. Connolly, "Say What You Mean: Improved Drafting Resources as a Means for Increasing the Consistency of Interpretation of Bilateral Investment Treaties", 40 *Vanderbilt Journal of Transnational Law* 1597 (2009), at 1579.
80   See M. Kiguel, "Argentina's 2001 Economic and Financial Crisis: Lessons for Europe", available at www.brookings.edu/wp-content/uploads/2016/06/11_argentina_kiguel.pdf, at 1.
81   Enron Corporation and Ponderosa Assets, L.P. v. Argentine Republic (ICSID Case No. ARB/01/3), available at www.italaw.com/cases/401.
82   CMS Gas Transmission Company v. The Republic of Argentina (ICSID Case No. ARB/01/8), available at www.italaw.com/cases/288.
83   LG&E Energy Corp., LG&E Capital Corp., and LG&E International, Inc. v. Argentine Republic (ICSID Case No. ARB/02/1), available at www.italaw.com/cases/621.
84   Sempra Energy International v. The Argentine Republic (ICSID Case No. ARB/02/16), available at www.italaw.com/cases/1002.
85   Continental Casualty Company v. The Argentine Republic (ICSID Case No. ARB/03/9), available at www.italaw.com/cases/329.
86   Metalpar S.A. and Buen Aire S.A. v. The Argentine Republic (ICSID Case No. ARB/03/5), available at www.italaw.com/cases/680.
87   Suez, Sociedad General de Aguas de Barcelona, S.A. and Vivendi Universal, S.A. v. Argentine Republic (ICSID Case No. ARB/03/19), available at www.italaw.com/cases/1057.
88   Total S.A. v. The Argentine Republic (ICSID Case No. ARB/04/01), available at www.italaw.com/cases/1105.
89   Impregilo S.p.A. v. Argentine Republic (ICSID Case No. ARB/07/17), available at www.italaw.com/cases/554.
90   El Paso Energy International Company v. The Argentine Republic (ICSID Case No. ARB/03/15), available at www.italaw.com/cases/documents/383.
91   BG Group Plc. v. The Republic of Argentina (under UNCITRAL Arbitration Rules), available at www.italaw.com/cases/143.
92   National Grid plc. v. The Argentine Republic (under UNCITRAL Arbitration Rules), available at www.italaw.com/cases/732.
93   See generally C. Binder, "Necessity Exceptions, the Argentine Crisis and Legitimacy Concerns", in T. Treves, F. Seatzu and S. Trevisanut (eds.), *Foreign Investment, International Law and Common Concerns* (Abingdon: Routledge, 2014) at 73; J. Alvarez and K. Khamsi, "The Argentine Crisis and Foreign Investors: A Glimpse into the Heart of the Investment Regime", in K. Sauvant (ed.), *Yearbook of International Investment Law and Policy 2008–2009* (New York: Oxford University Press, 2009), at 379–380; L. Reed, "Scorecard of Investment Treaty Cases against Argentina Since 2001", available at http://kluwerarbitrationblog.com/2009/03/02/scorecard-of-investment-treaty-cases-against-argentina-since-2001/.
94   See e.g. J. Alvarez and K. Khamsi (2009), M. C. H. Thjoernelund, "State of Necessity as an Exemption from State Responsibility of Investment", in A. von Bogdandy and R. Wolfrum (eds.), 13 *Max Plank Yearbook of United Nations Law* 423 (2009); K. J. Vandevelde (2013); C. C. Galvez, "Necessity, Investor Rights, and State Sovereignty for NAFTA Investment Arbitration", 46 (1) *Cornell International Law Journal* 143 (2013); D. A. Desierto, "Necessity and Supplementary Means of

Interpretation for Non-Precluded Measures in Bilateral Investment Treaties", 31 (3) *University of Pennsylvania Journal of International Law* 827 (2014).

95   UNCTAD, "The Protection of National Security in IIAs" (UNCTAD/ DIAE/IA/2008/5), at 7.

96   W. W. Burke-White and A. von Staten (2008), at 314.

97   K. J. Vandevelde (2013), at 456.

98   CMS Gas Transmission Company v. The Argentine Republic (ICSID Case No. ARB/01/08), Award of 12 May 2005, available at www.italaw.com/sites/default/ files/case-documents/ita0184.pdf, at para. 360.

99   See UNCTAD, "The Protection of National Security in IIAs" (UNCTAD/DIAE/ IA/2008/5), at 9–10.

100   Continental Casualty Company v. The Argentine Republic (ICSID Case No. ARB/03/9), Award of 5 September 2008, available at www.italaw.com/sites/default/ files/case-documents/ita0228.pdf, at para. 180.

101   See W. W. Burke-White and A. von Staten (2008), at 338.

102   See ibid., at 394–395.

103   See J. Alvarez and K. Khamsi (2009), at 380.

104   See W. W. Burke-White and A. von Staten (2008), at 393–394.

105   See generally S. D. Franck, "The Legitimacy Crisis in Investment Treaty Arbitration: Privatizing Public International Law through Inconsistent Decisions", 73 (4) *Fordham Law Review* 1521 (2005).

106   See Chapter V, Responsibility of States for Internationally Wrongful Acts, A/RES/56/83, adopted by the UNGA on 12 December 2001, available at www.un. org/ga/search/view_doc.asp?symbol=A/RES/56/83.

5 Public interest provisions

Sustainable development inherently links and substantively overlaps with public interest. The principle of integration and interrelationship, in particular in relation to human rights and social, economic and environmental objectives, is a key constituent principle of sustainable development. Though international law traditionally deals with interstate relations, the development of international law seems to prelude that public interest has become an important consideration in international law-making and enforcement. In the field of international investment law, an increasing number of IIAs incorporate provisions on the protection of public interest, such as the environment, human rights and public health. These provisions are collectively referred to as public interest provisions. This chapter discusses some major types of public interest provisions, covering environmental, human/labour rights, CSR and general public interest provisions. It also explores briefly how arbitrators deal with public-interest-sensitive investment disputes in ISA practice.

Public interest and soft-law rules in IIAs

The term "public interest" and its variations, such as "global public interest", "common concerns", "general interest" and "public purpose", are frequently used in general international law, including international investment law.[1] These terms are often used without being clearly defined, but the central theme remains that the common interest of the general public and the international community as a whole should be respected and protected under, and by, international law. In a sense, this trend is a reflection on and deviation from traditional international law. Even some general international rules that are regarded as binding the international community as a whole were not created to protect general interests (i.e. interests going beyond individual parties), but only the interests of each party, or of all parties combined.[2] This situation is undergoing a gradual change. An increasing number of international law instruments are made to protect the interest of the global community including future generations, such as IETs.[3]

In the field of international investment law, there also appears a growing consensus that public interest elements, such as environmental and human rights protection, should be taken into account in IIA-making and ISA practice.[4] Up

DOI: 10.4324/9781315642840-8

to the present, no IIA contains a provision entitled "public interest provision" or provides a clear definition of the term "public interest". However, this does not mean that IIAs and public interest are completely isolated from each other. An increasing number of IIAs nowadays incorporate various types of provisions catering for the protection of various types of public interest. Besides, in ISA practice, public-interest-sensitive disputes also frequently appear. In some cases, arbitrators do take public interest factors into consideration for different purposes.

Public interest provisions in IIAs are often in the form of soft law rules, which is not necessarily binding on the contracting states and foreign investors. The term "soft law" is difficult to be uniformly defined and can be perceived from different perspectives.[5] It is generally agreed that soft law refers to norms that are neither law nor mere political or moral statements, but lie somewhere in between, and that it plays some role in the making, interpretation and development of international law.[6]

With regard to the contents of soft law, opinions seem split. Some scholars include both legal and non-legal norms in the definition, while others restrict the term to legal norms, usually created by treaty, which are vague with respect to their content or weak with respect to the requirements of the obligation.[7] As soft law may cover non-legal norms, the exploration of soft law is likely to go beyond the "safe bounds" defined by Article 38 of the ICJ statute.[8]

Soft law may play an indispensable and significant role in global governance. It provides for flexibility and expertise, and can evolve without the political pressures that hinder cooperation among states, thus allowing states to work towards convergence and harmonization without binding obligations.[9] Specifically, in international investment law, soft law may fulfil three major functions: interpreting ambiguous provisions included in international treaties, filling gaps in existing international investment law, and supporting legal findings arising from other sources of investment law.[10]

Environmental, public health and safety provisions

Provisions relating to the protection of the environment, public health and safety, are a typical type of public interest provision (collectively referred to as "environmental provisions") in modern IIAs. Traditionally, states may be unwilling to incorporate such provisions in IIAs. First, international investment law and international environmental law are deemed to develop along separate tracks, and environmental issues are typically addressed through IETs, not IIAs. Second, some developing states see themselves in fierce competition for foreign investments, and incorporation of environmental provisions in IIAs seems to weaken their institutional attractiveness.[11] Third, as the negotiations of IIAs are often limited to issues of investment protection, it would be uneconomical to put environmental issues on the agenda.[12] In light of the above difficulties, it seems hard for states to agree to incorporate environmental provisions in IIAs as hard law. The fact is that environmental provisions in IIAs often appear in the form of soft law, which does not impose affirmative obligations on states and investors, and disputes relating to these provisions are generally not allowed to be submitted to ISA for settlement.[13]

The incorporation of environmental provisions in IIAs

The international community now faces unprecedented environmental challenges. Many states share the view that IIAs should also be made more environmentally friendly. Nowadays, an increasing number of IIAs incorporate one or more environmental provisions. Although such IIAs remain quite small in number, there is a clear trend that IIAs globally are made more accommodative to environmental concerns. For instance, though environmental provisions in China's IIAs appear inadequate in general, an empirical study reveals a clear trend that China's BITs are in the process of "greenization", in the sense that a larger number and better quality of environmental provisions are incorporated therein.[14]

Most environmental provisions in IIAs are exceptive provisions. Similar to other exceptions in IIAs, an environmental exception also serves the purpose of exempting the host states from the liability for taking IIA-inconsistent environmental measures. An environmental provision may be incorporated as one or more sub-provisions of the clause of general exceptions in IIAs. An environmental exception is often an "implied and standard" constituent of general exceptions. For instance, the clause of general exceptions of the 2004 Canadian Model BIT covers measures "to protect human, animal or plant life or health"[15] and those "for the conservation of living or non-living exhaustible natural resources".[16] The two paragraphs in combination are equivalent to an environmental exception.

An environmental provision can also be incorporated in IIAs as a carved-in exception of the substantive provisions. To reconcile the tension between the regulatory power of states and their obligation to protect foreign investments, some IIAs include an environmental exception in the expropriation and FET clauses to exclude certain regulatory measures from being held as an expropriation or violation of an FET standard.

A carved-in environmental exception in the indirect expropriation provision of IIAs is commonly seen, especially in IIAs of developed states, such as the 2012 US Model BIT[17] and the CETA Chapter Ten.[18] A typical exception of this type reads as following:

> Except in rare circumstances, such as when a measure or series of measures are so severe in the light of their purpose that they cannot be reasonably viewed as having been adopted and applied in good faith, non-discriminatory measures of a Party that are designed and applied to protect legitimate public welfare objectives, such as health, safety and the environment, do not constitute indirect expropriation.[19]

Typically, under the carved-in environmental exception, environmental measures do not constitute an act of indirect expropriation "except in rare circumstances". Almost no IIA exceptions define "rare circumstances", it is thus subject to the interpretation of arbitrators on a case-by-case basis.

A carved-in environmental exception may also exist in FET clauses, although it is less commonly seen. A typical such exception is found in the 2005 China–Madagascar BIT, reading as follows,

> Legal or *de facto* obstacles to the fair and equitable treatment mainly mean, but not limited to: non-equitable treatment of all kinds of restrictions on the means of production and management, non-equitable treatment of all kinds of restrictions on sale of products at home and abroad, as well as other measures with similar effect. But measures for reasons of security, public order, health, ethical and environmental protection and other reasons, these measures shall not be regarded as obstacles.[20]

As can be seen, this exception has the clear purpose of exempting certain environmental measures from the scope of the FET clause. The scope of this exception is broad, defined by a non-exhaustive list that covers not only security, public order, health, ethical and environmental protection reasons, but also "other reasons". However, this provision is insufficiently clear. In particular, the words "not as obstacles" do not appear explicit enough to make this exception sufficiently binding. In practice, it remains possible for arbitrators to interpret the words in a manner inconsistent with the contracting states' real intention.

In addition, an environmental provision can also take the form of a stand-alone exception, especially in IIAs without a clause of general exceptions. Such an exception is designed exclusively for the preservation of state regulatory power in taking health, safety or environmental measures. These exceptions may take the form of two models, following the security exception and general exceptions styles respectively.

A typical security exception-model environmental provision can be found in the 2007 Model BIT of Norway. Under the title of "Right to Regulate", Article 12 of this Model BIT reads that,

> Nothing in this Agreement shall be construed to prevent a Party from adopting, maintaining or enforcing any measure otherwise consistent with this Agreement that it considers appropriate to ensure that investment activity is undertaken in a manner sensitive to health, safety or environmental concerns.

This provision has several distinct features. First, the words "nothing in this Agreement" shows that environmental measures of the contracting states shall be exempted from all IIA obligations. Second, the words "adopting, maintaining or enforcing" imply that this exception applies to both existing and future measures. Third, the words "it considers appropriate" suggests that this exception is self-judging in nature, and the contracting states shall enjoy a broad margin of appreciation in taking environmental measures.

A typical example of a general exceptions-model environmental provision is Article 10(4) of the 2013 China–Tanzania BIT, which is entitled "health, safety and environmental measures", providing in relevant part that,

> Provided that such measures are not applied in an arbitrary or unjustifiable manner, or do not constitute a disguised restriction on international investment, nothing in this Agreement shall be construed to prevent a Contracting Party from adopting or maintaining environmental measures necessary to protect human, animal or plant life or health.

This exception has two distinct features. First, it does not use the typical words "it considers", which implies that it is not self-judging in nature. Second, the invocation requirements of this exception are high, including non-arbitrariness and unjustifiableness, and no disguised restriction. These requirements are almost identical to those in the chapeau of GATT Article XX.

The application of environmental provisions in ISA

In ISA practice, environmentally sensitive investment disputes frequently appear.[21] There is no reported ISA case in which an environmental exception has been applied. This is mainly because only a limited number of IIAs have an environmental exception, and the threshold requirements for the invocation of the exception are very high. It is particularly the case if the environmental exception is a self-judging one.

The IIA clauses primarily and frequently invoked in environmentally sensitive ISA cases are indirect expropriation and FET clauses.[22] In such cases, a typical issue confronting the arbitrators is to determine whether an environmental measure amounts to an act of (indirect) expropriation or a violation of FET standards under the applicable IIA. While foreign investors should not be allowed to abuse the expropriation or FET clauses to evade host states' regulation, host states should not be allowed to take regulatory measures in an arbitrary manner or to incur excessive harm to foreign investors under the camouflage of protecting public interests.

Therefore, to correctly deal with these cases, a proper distinction between expropriation or FET violation and environmental regulation should be drawn. As held by the tribunal in S.D. Myers v. Canada, such a distinction "screens out most potential cases of complaints concerning economic intervention by a state and reduces the risk that governments will be subject to claims as they go about their business of managing public affairs."[23]

ISA case law suggests that, despite the frequent occurrence of environmentally sensitive expropriation and FET claims, no consistent jurisprudence in differentiating environmental measures and an act of indirect expropriation or FET violation has been established.[24] Such a distinction can only be made on a case-by-case basis with all attending circumstances considered.[25] The lack of differentiation seems to imply that, when making expropriation and FET decisions, the environmental sensitivity of the measures is seldom considered. As discussed, the ICSID tribunal in Santa Elena v. Costa Rica clearly refused to draw a distinction between environmentally sensitive regulatory measures from "general expropriation measures".[26]

Only in a few ISA cases have the arbitrators considered the sensitivity of the environmental measures. In Methanex v. U.S.[27] for instance, the investor challenged the environmental measures taken by California of the U.S. relying on NAFTA Chapter Eleven, claiming, *inter alia*, that the measures constitute expropriation. The tribunal considered not only the general legality tests, but also the general situation of environmental protection in California, and ruled that "specific commitment" of the host state should be considered for the disputed environmental measure to constitute an act of indirect expropriation. In the light of the expropriation clause of NAFTA Chapter Eleven, the introduction of the "specific commitment" requirement implies that the tribunal has impliedly raised the legality requirements for expropriation when dealing with environmentally sensitive cases.[28]

A few recent IIAs expressly incorporate the "specific commitment" requirement in the FET clauses. For instance, CETA Chapter Ten provides that, when making an FET determination, arbitrators may take into account,

> whether a Party made a specific representation to an investor to induce a covered investment, that created a legitimate expectation, and upon which the investor relied in deciding to make or maintain the covered investment, but that the Party subsequently frustrated.[29]

Though this provision does not expressly address environmental concerns, its limiting language ("specific representation") potentially raises the threshold for FET violation and is thus helpful for states to prevent environmental measures from being held as FET violation.[30]

That arbitrators often neglect the environmental sensitivity of the regulatory measures in making expropriation and FET determinations has been criticized for ignoring public interest.[31] On this issue, although the tribunal in Methanex v. U.S. seems to have set up a good model, it would be impractical to expect other tribunals to follow, because many states do not have a comparable environmental protection situation as that in California, which makes it ungrounded to apply the "specific commitment" requirement established in Methanex v. U.S.

In light of the above discussion, one advice is to insert an environmental exception in IIAs in the form of a standalone clause, a paragraph of the clause of general exceptions or a carved-in exception in the expropriation and FET clauses. Such an exception should be carefully drafted so that, in ISA, arbitrators may be guided, as far as possible, to draw a proper line between environmental measures and acts of indirect expropriation or FET violation.

The response of IIAs to the public health crisis

It is not until quite recently that there has been an attempt to scrutinize the interplay between investors' rights and public health.[32] Indeed, the high tension between public health regulation and foreign investment protection is long-standing. Rich and powerful tobacco companies especially have often used litigation and arbitration in different dispute settlement forums, including national courts, international arbitration, the WTO or RTA tribunals, and ISA, to threaten states in an effort to block state regulatory measures that may adversely influence their profits. In particular, because most IIAs allow ISA, the costly ISA is often used to create a "regulatory chill" effect on the host states.

Tobacco control is an important part of international and national public health governance, and is unquestionably a legitimate goal for state regulation. Under some international treaties and almost all national laws, states shall bear an obligation to protect public health.[33] The tension between public health and the tobacco business has drawn wide attention since the initiation of the landmark ISA case of Philip Morris v. Australia in 2012.[34] In addition, Philip Morris also initiated an ICSID case against Uruguay.[35]

In 2012, the Australian government enacted the "plain packaging" regulations in order to protect public health, which gave rise to a dispute between the tobacco giant Philip Morris and Australia. The applicable BIT, the 1993 Australia–Hong Kong BIT, has no environmental exception. Philip Morris claimed, *inter alia*, that the Australian regulations constitute indirect expropriation and a violation of the FET provision, and requested compensation. As the tribunal held that the claims were inadmissible,[36] it is unknown how the expropriation and FET provisions of the BIT would be applied and interpreted, and how the public health concern would be addressed. Regardless of the outcome of this dispute, the initiation of the arbitration and even the threat of ISA had already created a profound "regulatory chill" effect on states. Such disputes send out a clear message that IIAs and ISA may be used, or abused, to block state efforts in pursuing legitimate public health and other public welfare goals.

Australia is not the only or the first state that has suffered from threats from powerful tobacco companies when taking public health measures. Canada, for instance, had a similar experience. In 1994, Canada planned to introduce the Tobacco Products Control Act, but R. J. Reynolds Tobacco Company threatened to initiate ISA against Canada, relying on NAFTA Chapter Eleven. Although the Canadian Supreme Court invalidated the Act in 1995, which ultimately put the plain packaging debate to rest, the threat is widely believed to have influenced the Canadian Parliament's deliberations on plain packaging and deterred the government from taking legislative action.[37]

As a landmark effort to deal with rampant tobacco litigation and ISA threats, the TPP incorporates a provision that exclusively deals with investment claims with respect to tobacco control measures, which allows the contracting states to unilaterally decide whether to allow such claims to be submitted to ISA. This provision states that:

Article 29.5
Tobacco Control Measures

A Party may elect to deny the benefits of Section B of Chapter 9 (Investment) with respect to claims challenging a tobacco control measure of the Party. Such a claim shall not be submitted to arbitration under Section B of Chapter 9 (Investment) if a Party has made such an election. If a Party has not elected to deny benefits with respect to such claims by the time of the submission of such a claim to arbitration under Section B of Chapter 9 (Investment), a Party may elect to deny benefits during the proceedings. For greater certainty, if a Party elects to deny benefits with respect to such claims, any such claim shall be dismissed.

The TPP is the first major trade agreement to "protect tobacco control measures". This provision is an exception to the ISA provisions of the TPP and is a timely and necessary response to the long-standing tension between public health and the tobacco industry. This exception has several features. First, its application scope is strictly confined to tobacco control measures, while public health measures of broader range are not covered. Second, it only exempts the contracting states of their obligation of ISA under the investment chapter, while substantive obligations under this chapter are not necessarily exempted. In other words, a foreign investor may still challenge the tobacco control measures of a contracting state in a national court. Third, different from many existing exceptions in IIAs, this exception is not automatically applicable. Tobacco control measures may still be challenged in ISA in situations where a contracting state does not phase out such a possibility or waives its rights.

Labour/human rights provisions

International investment law and human rights law have different regulatory focuses and approaches.[38] IIAs and internationalized investment contracts between states and foreign investors almost never refer to the human rights of third parties or the obligations of states under human rights law.[39] In recent years, however, an increasing number of IIAs incorporate provisions of labour rights and standards. Human-rights-sensitive investment disputes are also frequently seen in ISA practice.

One may have noted that while the term "labour rights" is often used in IIAs, the term "human rights" receives more mentions in ISA. Thus, at the outset, it is necessary to clarify these two terms. Strictly speaking, labour rights and human rights are not identical, and their relationship can be viewed from different perspectives.[40] In general, human rights are rights inherent to all human beings that are universal and inalienable,[41] while labour rights refer to entitlements that relate specifically to the role of being a worker.[42] Some labour rights are recognized in human rights conventions and can be protected as human rights. For instance, the right to leisure and rest, including reasonable limitation of working hours and periodical holidays with pay is expressly recognized as a human right in the Universal Declaration of Human Rights.[43] Similarly, the right to protection from unjustified dismissal and the right to fair and just working conditions are also recognized as human rights in the European Union Charter of Fundamental Rights.[44] Some other labour rights are granted and protected by national laws and do not necessarily amount to human rights, such as the minimum salary for workers. While recognizing the differences between human rights and labour rights, these two terms are used interchangeably in the current study for the sake of simplicity.

Incorporation of human rights provisions in IIAs

Human rights issues are usually addressed through specialized treaties. Even if a human rights provision is incorporated in an IIA, it often appears in the preambles or as a soft law rule and is aspirational and declaratory.[45] It is thus doubtful whether IIAs are sufficiently helpful in addressing human rights concerns associated with transnational investment activities.

The previous efforts to incorporate human rights provisions in IIAs seem unsuccessful in general. For instance, human rights issues were discussed during the MAI negotiations, but no meaningful results were produced.[46] The MAI draft text contains several labour rights provisions, including the preamble, a clause of "not lowering standards", and an annex that associates the MAI with the 2011 OECD Guidelines on Multinational Enterprises (OECD Guidelines). These provisions are defective, because of the lack of substantive labour rights, a material discrepancy from other international trade regimes and their more extensive and sophisticated treatment of labour rights.[47]

In recent years, to respond to the call for better human rights protection in international investment governance, some IIAs, especially those of developed states, incorporated labour rights provisions as substantive provisions, which appear more "effective" and concrete than those in the preambles. A typical human rights provision is Article 13 of the 2012 U.S. Model BIT. This Article deals exclusively with labour rights, entitled "investment and labor", stating in relevant part that,

1.1   The Parties reaffirm their respective obligations as members of the International Labor Organization ("ILO") and their commitments under the ILO Declaration on Fundamental Principles and Rights at Work and Its Follow-Up.[48]

1.2   The Parties recognize that it is inappropriate to encourage investment by weakening or reducing the protections afforded in domestic labor laws. Accordingly, each Party shall ensure that it does not waive or otherwise derogate from or offer to waive or otherwise derogate from its labor laws where the waiver or derogation would be inconsistent with the labor rights referred to in subparagraphs (a) through (e) of paragraph 3, or fail to effectively enforce its labor laws through a

> sustained or recurring course of action or inaction, as an encouragement for the establishment, acquisition, expansion, or retention of an investment in its territory.

Though this Article clearly refers to the ILO core labour standards, which are composed of: freedom of association; freedom from forced labour; freedom from child labour; and non-discrimination in employment – thus linking the IIA standard with the mainstream international standard – it also explicitly bans lowering labour rights standards as an incentive to foreign investments. Such a ban is necessary to phase out a possible "race to the bottom", given that some states may deem low labour standards and weak labour rights to be a "comparative advantage" in attracting foreign investment in the global market.[49]

Notwithstanding its merits, this Article remains weak on labour rights protection. First, though it seems to associate the BIT with the ILO core labour standards, it does not impose any affirmative obligations on the contracting states to protect labour rights. It is also unclear how such reference could be operated, given the ambiguity of the term "reaffirm". Second, the enforcement of this Article is insufficient. While this BIT excludes issues relating to labour rights from the realm of ISA, it only requires the contracting states to try to settle the issues through interstate consultation, which is by nature a "best efforts requirement".[50]

To some states, however, human rights remain a less touched-upon issue in IIA-making. China, for instance, has a long-rooted objection towards inclusion of human rights provisions in trade and investment treaties.[51] Though China has concluded a large number of IIAs, none expressly mention human rights protection in the preamble, and ILO core standards have never been referred to in China's IIAs. Only a few Chinese IIAs contain provisions that deal with regional arrangements that may involve labour rights issues[52] or the transfer of labourer benefit and compensation.[53] In a strict sense, these provisions cannot be said to be exceptions because they actually do not touch upon human rights protection.

Even in China's most recent IIAs with developed states, such as the 2012 China–Canada BIT, the 2012 China–Japan–Korea TIT, the 2013 China–Switzerland FTA and the 2015 China–Australia FTA, human rights issues are rarely mentioned. The exclusion of human rights provisions from these IIAs has been criticized. For instance, after the China–Switzerland FTA was concluded, some Swiss NGOs criticized the Swiss government, which did "not even dare to mention the word human rights in the agreement", despite this term appearing in the preamble of the FTA.[54]

Human rights issues in ISA practice

Human rights issues are not isolated from ISA.[55] Human-rights-sensitive ISA cases are frequent and numerous, and no uniform jurisprudence has been produced to date.[56] These cases touch upon various aspects of human rights. For instance, in Suez v. Argentina,[57] the right to water for the local people is involved; in Glamis Gold v. U.S.,[58] the cultural right of the local indigenous people is involved. In these cases, arbitrators need to decide, among other issues, whether human rights issues raised in ISA should be considered in settling investment disputes.

Human rights claims may be raised in ISA in different scenarios,[59] which can be roughly categorized into conflicting obligations claims and human rights violation claims. In general, arbitrators are reluctant to attaching significant weight to the provisions of international human rights treaties in ISA.[60] Consideration of human rights issues in ISA practice may give rise to various systematic concerns, such as the hierarchical order of IIAs and human rights treaties, and the scope of arbitral jurisdiction on human rights claims based on IIA violation.

Conflicting obligations claims raised by host states

A typical scenario in which human rights issues are raised in ISA is that a foreign investor claims that the host state's measure constitutes a violation of the applicable IIA, especially the expropriation and FET clauses, and the host state argues that the measure is taken for human rights protection purposes. It is also possible that, during the ISA proceedings, a non-disputing party is allowed to submit amicus curiae briefings claiming that the dispute involves profound human rights impacts. Such claims can be seen as "conflicting obligations" claims in the sense that the host state's obligations under the IIA and those under the human rights treaties are in conflict, and the host state claims that the latter obligations should prevail.

In dealing with this type of cases, the arbitrators have made inconsistent decisions. In some cases, arbitrators refused to consider the human rights arguments. Azurix v. Argentina is a good example for explaining the links and conflicts between human rights law and IIA.[61] In this case, the investor, Azurix, concluded a concession with Argentina for water and sewage services. Azurix claimed that Argentina failed to fulfil the infrastructure repair obligations, which led to Azurix's failure in providing satisfactory water services under the concession agreement and also to Argentina's refusal to pay. Azurix claimed that the refusal amounted to expropriation under the Argentina–U.S. BIT. Argentina held that there existed a conflict between the BIT and the human rights treaties that protect consumers' rights, and claimed that such conflict should be resolved in favour of human rights.[62] Though the tribunal acknowledged the public purpose of Argentina's measure, it refused to discuss Argentina's argument on the incompatibility of the obligations under human rights treaties and the BIT.[63]

In Siemens v. Argentina,[64] Argentina argued that protection of the contractual rights of Siemens in a time of economic and social crisis would lead to human rights violations of its citizens. In particular, Argentina argued that in its legal system, the constitution and international human rights treaties entered into by Argentina are the supreme law of the nation, and treaties have primacy over domestic laws. Although the tribunal recognized such a hierarchy, it refused to discuss this issue further as Argentina failed to provide convincing reasons to support its hierarchy arguments.[65]

In other cases, the arbitrators took human rights issues into account when making expropriation and FET decisions. In such cases, human rights law may play two roles. First, it may be used to highlight a host state's legal obligations to non-parties to the arbitration, and may be accepted as a margin-of-appreciation factor; second, it may play an assistive role in treaty interpretation, providing a lens for interpreting and determining the boundaries of any parallel obligations owed to foreign investors.[66]

A typical ISA case in which human rights law serves as a margin-of-appreciation factor is Biwater v. Tanzania.[67] In this case, Biwater concluded a concession agreement with Tanzania for a water and sewage project. Following Tanzania's cancellation of the agreement in 2005, Biwater initiated arbitration in ICSID, asserting expropriation and FET claims under the Tanzania–U.K. BIT. Several NGOs were allowed to submit amicus curiae briefings to the tribunal. These briefings highlighted the tension between the host state's obligation under international human rights law (protection of the residents' right to water) and that under the BIT (protection of foreign investment), claiming that,

> Human rights and sustainable development issues are factors that condition the nature and extent of the investor's responsibilities, and the balance of rights and obligations as between the investor and the host State. They conclude that foreign corporations engaged in projects intimately related to human rights and the capacity to achieve sustainable development (such as the project here), have the highest level of responsibility to meet their duties and obligations as foreign investors, before seeking the protection of international law.[68]

The tribunal took the amicus curiae arguments into consideration when interpreting the FET clause of the BIT. It rejected Biwater's FET claims, as it found that the treatment the investor could legitimately expect from the state was partly determined by the "particular investment environment" it had voluntarily entered. Such an environment was characterized by the fact that Tanzania was a developing state and that the Tanzanian state was bound by international human rights obligations to protect the right to water of its citizens.[69]

International human rights law may also play an assistive role in interpreting IIA provisions in ISA. It has been suggested that in several ISA cases, such as Tecmed v. Mexico,[70] and Mondev v. U.S.,[71] the tribunals seemed to hold that human rights jurisprudence might help to illuminate—by way of analogy—how certain IIA provisions might be construed.[72] For instance, in Tecmed v. Mexico, the Spanish company, Tecmed, invested in Mexico in a project related to land, buildings and other assets. Due to Mexico's refusal to renew the licence, Tecmed alleged that the project was lost and that Mexico had violated the provisions of the Mexico–Spain BIT, including the clauses of expropriation, FET, and full protection and security. In the ISA proceedings, when interpreting the expropriation provision of the BIT, the tribunal held that,

> In addition to the provisions of the Agreement, the Arbitral Tribunal has to resolve any dispute submitted to it by applying international law provisions (Title VI.1 of the Appendix to the Agreement), for which purpose the Arbitral Tribunal understands that disputes are to be resolved by resorting to the sources described in Article 38 of the Statute of the International Court of Justice considered, also in the case of customary international law, not as frozen in time, but in their evolution.[73]

While following such an interpretative method, the tribunal took into account a series of ECHR cases when examining whether a regulatory expropriation could be established in this case,[74] including Matos e Silva, Lda., and Others v. Portugal,[75] Mellacher and Others v. Austria,[76] and Pressos Compañía Naviera and Others v. Belgium.[77]

Human rights violation claims raised by individual investors

A less frequently seen scenario in which human rights issues may be involved in ISA is when an individual foreign investor claims that the host state's measures *per se* constitute a violation of his/her human rights under international human rights law. These type of claims are clearly an outlier in the investment treaty context and look similar to human rights claims in some respects even though asserted under an IIA.[78] In such cases, the arbitral tribunals need to decide, first, whether they have jurisdiction to deal with the human rights claims; and second, whether international human rights law should be applied in ISA.

Regarding the jurisdictional issue, the compromissory clause of the underlying IIA should be consulted, as it defines the scope of the arbitral jurisdiction. If the IIA contains a broad compromissory clause, such as one that allows "any disputes relating to an investment" to be submitted to arbitration, the arbitrators are likely to assert jurisdiction over the human rights claims in ISA. In contrast, if the compromissory clause is a restricted one, which excludes the admissibility of human rights claims, it seems that the arbitrators should not deal with such claims.

Regarding the applicable law issue, many IIAs, especially the ICSID Convention, allow arbitrators to apply "international law and national law" in ISA.[79] The term "international law" is not necessarily limited to IIAs, and can be interpreted to cover other international law rules, including international human rights treaties. For instance, in SPP v. Egypt,[80] it has been argued that an international treaty other than the applicable BIT, i.e. the UNESCO Convention for the Protection of the World Cultural and Natural Heritage, should be applied. The ICSID tribunal viewed that the Convention is relevant to the dispute and considered the arguments relating thereto.[81] Besides, when the applicable arbitration rules grant arbitrators discretionary power in deciding the applicable substantive rules, such as the UNCITRAL Arbitration Rules, it is also possible that the arbitrators would apply general international law, including international human rights law, although such cases should be exceptional.[82]

A typical case in which an investor claims that the host state's conduct constitutes a violation of IIA is Trinh Vinh Binh v. Vietnam,[83] which has not been made public. According to some commentators and NGOs, the Claimant, a Vietnamese-Dutch dual national, claimed that the way he was treated by the Vietnamese police and security authorities, especially detention for an excessive period of 18 months and suffering "torture" and "inhumane treatment" while in custody, seriously deviated from international norms of due process and human rights and should serve to violate the full protection and security and FET provisions in the Netherlands–Vietnam BIT.[84]

The root reason that human rights issues may be involved in ISA lies in the fact that both international human rights law and international investment law deal with state–private relationships. In both sets of relationships, states are in the position of obligation bearer vis-à-vis individuals. More specifically, states are required to protect not only the human rights but also the property rights of foreign investors that are admitted to their territories. Such a situation provides foreign investors an opportunity of both "forum shopping" and "treaty shopping". Thus, it is possible for the investors to choose between ISA and human rights dispute settlement mechanisms, and between international human rights law in lieu of or in addition to IIAs. Although there have been a number of human-rights-sensitive ISA cases, it is largely unclear whether and to what extent such "parallel shopping" by foreign investors should be dealt with in ISA.

Corporate social responsibility (CSR) provisions

CSR norms have gained increasing attention and acceptance in global investment governance, and are incorporated in IIAs. Though there exists no universally accepted definition of CSR, this term can be generally understood as a form of voluntary self-regulation by private enterprises, organizations, and other entities, which encompasses the economic, legal, ethical, and discretionary or philanthropic expectations that society has of organizations at a given point in time.[85] The enforcement of CSR norms engages multiple stakeholders, such as governments, MNEs, civil societies and organizations.[86]

From an international law perspective, CSR norms often exist in the form of soft law and are enforced primarily in a voluntary and self-regulatiory manner by private actors.[87] As CSR norms embrace human rights, environmental protection, anti-corruption and a wide range of other social responsibilities, they bear a close link with sustainable development. Such a link is confirmed by various CSR instruments. For instance, the EC Communication concerning CSR, entitled "Corporate Social Responsibility: A Business Contribution to Sustainable Development",[88] clearly highlights that CSR can contribute to sustainable development.

CSR norms in global investment governance

The issue of investor responsibility is traditionally and primarily addressed through two approaches: host-state approach and home-state approach. Each approach has its pros and cons.

On the one hand, foreign investors and the operation of foreign investments are subject to the national laws of the host states. As such, the effectiveness of this approach depends largely on the legislation and law enforcement of the host states. In reality, this approach is often ineffective for two main reasons. First, while developed states may enjoy a sound legal system and an effective law-enforcement mechanism, many developing states have weak regulatory and enforcement regimes. Second, investor misconduct might involve fraud, corruption or other activities designed to evade or pervert the application of domestic law.[89] In many states, it is practically difficult for foreign investors to be held accountable for their irresponsible investment activities.

On the other hand, it is also possible that foreign investors and their overseas activities be subject to the jurisdiction of their home states. For instance, in 1977, the U.S. enacted the Foreign Corrupt Practices Act (FCPA) in response to revelations of widespread bribery of foreign officials by U.S. companies in order to win business. The anti-bribery provisions of the FCPA could be applied to both U.S. and foreign nationals or entities. Besides, under the alternative jurisdiction provisions of the FCPA enacted in 1998, U.S. companies or persons are subject to the anti-bribery provisions even if they act outside the U.S. and even if no means of interstate commerce is used.[90]

The home-state approach also has its limits. First, only a few states have enacted such national laws. Second, these laws often feature restricted subject matter jurisdiction, which is often limited to corruptive acts or human rights violations. Third, such laws are also criticized for "long-arm jurisdiction", which is deemed by many states as an intrusion of their juridical sovereignty. Finally, it is doubtful whether subjecting foreign nationals or entities and extraterritorial acts to domestic jurisdiction is truly helpful in dealing with public interest protection associated with international investment at the global level.

As neither the host-state approach nor the home-state approach can satisfactorily regulate investor activities, various suggestions have been put forward. At corporate level, MNEs are called on to make "socially responsible investment", essentially meaning that investment decisions should be made on the basis of appropriate environmental, social and governance standards.[91] According to the OECD, private CSR initiatives are diverse in objectives, origin, areas covered, and implementation mechanisms. Some initiatives address a wide range of issues, including human rights and labour rights, community development, consumer rights, the use of security forces, bribery and corruption, health and safety issues, and environmental standards; while other initiatives focus on one or a few of these issues, usually in more depth.[92]

At national level, aside from host-state regulation, home-state regulation of MNEs and their overseas investment activities is gaining increasing significance in international investment governance.[93] Many states enact legislation to promote or encourage CSR abroad. While developed states such as the U.S. and the U.K. seem to have taken the lead in this regard,[94] developing states have also made remarkable progress. China is a good example. In recent years, as China has grown into a leading investment-exporting country,[95] there has been an emerging need for China to regulate its overseas investments. It is especially the case given that Chinese investments are frequently reported to have provoked environmental concerns in some African countries.[96] To better regulate the overseas investments of Chinese investors, MOFCOM adopted the "Regulations of Overseas Investment Management" in 2014.[97] According to the Regulations, Chinese enterprises are required to "abide by the local laws and regulations of the host State, respect local customs, perform social responsibility, engage in environmental and labour protection and corporate culture building, and promote the integration with the local society".[98]

At international level, some international organizations have proposed various non-binding CSR instruments as references for states in policymaking and for MNEs in investment operation. Typical examples include the 2006 ILO Tripartite Declaration of Principles Concerning Multinational Enterprises and Social Policy,[99] the OECD Guidelines,[100] the 2011 UNHRC Guiding Principles on Business and Human Rights,[101] and the Ten Principles of the UN Global Compact, derived from major international human rights and sustainable development conventions.[102] While these instruments and initiatives have different contents and focuses, they all share the same theme, i.e. to strengthen public interest protection in investment activities and governance.

Among the various CSR instruments, the OECD Guidelines are probably the most influential. Since the original adoption in 1976, they have served for forty years as the only multilaterally agreed and comprehensive code of responsible business conduct that governments have committed to promoting. The OECD Guidelines provide non-binding principles and standards for responsible business conduct in a global context consistent with applicable laws and internationally recognized standards, and they are voluntary recommendations to foster sustainable development through responsible business conduct by MNEs.[103] They establish principles covering a broad range of issues in business ethics, including information disclosure, employment and industrial relations, environment, corruption, consumer interests, science and technology, competition, and taxation.[104]

The incorporation of CSR norms in IIAs

There are two major obstacles for IIAs to incorporate CSR norms. First, because CSR norms are soft-law norms, not made by state authorities, and these norms aim at imposing obligations on foreign investors, the idea of incorporating these norms in IIAs seems to be a departure from the state-centrism of international law.[105] Second, IIAs are originally and primarily designed for the protection of foreign investments; investor responsibility is seldom addressed in IIAs.[106] In recent years, in light of the growing call for better-regulated international investments and the increasingly important role of non-state actors in global investment governance, it has been suggested that IIAs should also be made more balanced through imposing obligations on foreign investors as well. An important way to realize this goal is to incorporate CSR provisions in IIAs.[107] Besides, as IIAs are made increasingly market-oriented, it would be a high risk for global investment governance if MNEs as major global market players are not subject to IIA regulation.[108] CSR norms may be incorporated in IIAs in different forms.

Direct incorporation of CSR norms

One way to incorporate CSR norms is to directly impose CSR obligations on foreign investors and/or host states in IIAs. Investor-targeted CSR norms can help transform foreign investors from mere "benefit receiver" to "obligation bearer" in the current IIA system. This way seems ideal for a number of reasons. First, CSR norms are not foreign to many investors. In fact, MNEs of all sizes, in both developed and developing countries, have long engaged in CSR activities rooted in the values of the companies, often in the form of a corporate code of conduct.[109] Second, many national laws also incorporate various CSR norms. Third, CSR norms exist mostly in the form of soft law, developed by private or international organizations, thus they can be modified to fit the specific needs of individual states without time-consuming IIA negotiations.

Given these merits, it seems that if IIAs expressly refer to certain CSR norms, such as the OECD Guidelines, CSR norms in IIAs can be a helpful supplement to the existing CSR-related national law and international treaties. A typical example is the CSR provision contained in the 2007 Norway Model BIT, which expressly refers to the two major CSR instruments, i.e. the OECD Guidelines and the UN Global Compact, providing that:

Article 32
Corporate Social Responsibility

The Parties agree to encourage investors to conduct their investment activities in compliance with the OECD Guidelines for Multinational Enterprises and to participate in the United Nations Global Compact.

As can be seen, this CSR provision is soft law in nature. It is aspirational and serves the aim of encouraging the contracting states to adopt CSR norms in policymaking. It has some distinct features. First, although it links with major international CSR instruments, it fails to impose CSR obligations on investors directly. Second, the words "the Parties agree" and "the Parties reaffirm" show that it does not create CSR obligations, but relies on the contracting states in enforcing the CSR norms in their national jurisdictions. Third, the word "encourage" suggests that the CSR obligations are aspirational under the IIA.

Indirect incorporation of CSR obligations

CSR norms can also be indirectly incorporated in IIAs. These provisions aim at preserving regulatory power of the host states in taking CSR-related measures to better regulate transnational investment activities of foreign investors. As CSR norms encompass a wide range of public interests and have material overlaps with the elements of sustainable development, such CSR provisions are actually an equivalent to many of the existing public interest provisions in IIAs, such as environmental and human rights provisions. Given such overlap, there seems no compelling need to further discuss CSR norms in IIAs in detail.

For the purpose of this book, a panoramic overview of the CSR provisions in IIAs is sufficient. As suggested by the OECD survey, which focuses on four major types of sustainable development elements, CSR norms are rarely referred to in the language of IIAs, but the frequency of such language has progressively increased in recent years.[110] There are a number of types of treaty languages of CSR, each playing a different role in the IIA system:

i   Language in the preamble;
ii   Language on preserving policy space;
iii Language of not lowering standards;
iv   Language establishing that, in general, environmental measures taken in order to protect public welfare objectives do not constitute indirect expropriation;
v   Language showing the contracting states' commitment to cooperate on CSR matters;
vi   Language establishing a relation between CSR matters and ISDS;
vii Language on maintaining or implementing internationally recognized standards;
viii Language establishing commitments to act in the fight against corruption; and
ix   Language encouraging the respect of CSR standards.[111]

These treaty languages are not exhaustive, but are highly representative in modern IIAs. To briefly sum up, despite the growing consensus that foreign investors should engage in responsible investment activities, IIAs remain clinging to their original purpose of investment protection. The existing CSR norms in IIAs are "pseudo" in the sense that they do not truly regulate MNEs but try to achieve this goal by requiring or proposing to the contacting states to regulate their corporates through domestic law and policy. Consequently, the regulation of foreign investors and their overseas investments are left to be dealt with mainly by the national laws of the host states and their home states.

Towards a general public interest provision in IIAs?

Though public interest protection has become increasingly important in IIA-making, public interest provisions in IIAs largely remain insufficient, ineffective and fragmented. IIAs address different types of public interest concerns in separate provisions. This may be caused by a number of reasons. First, public interest is difficult to accurately define at the international level. Second, states have different or even contradictory positions with regard to the incorporation of public interest provisions in IIAs. Third, practically speaking, states may have different policy goals with regard to the protection of different types of public interest. Thus, it might be convenient to negotiate separate provisions to cater for different types of public interest. For instance, while environmental protection seems unanimously accepted by states and appears frequently in IIAs, human rights provisions are less frequently seen. Finally, states tend to incorporate public interest provisions in IIAs in the form of soft law.

It would be helpful to have a general public interest provision in IIAs. A rare example of a "general" public interest provision can be found in the recent CETA investment chapter, which reads as follows:

Article 8.9
Investment and regulatory measures

1.1 For the purpose of this Chapter, the Parties reaffirm their right to regulate within their territories to achieve legitimate policy objectives, such as the protection of public health, safety, the environment or public morals, social or consumer protection or the promotion and protection of cultural diversity.

1.2 For greater certainty, the mere fact that a Party regulates, including through a modification to its laws, in a manner which negatively affects an investment or interferes with an investor's expectations, including its expectations of profits, does not amount to a breach of an obligation under this Section.

1.3 For greater certainty, a Party's decision not to issue, renew or maintain a subsidy:

a) in the absence of any specific commitment under law or contract to issue, renew, or maintain that subsidy; or

b) in accordance with any terms or conditions attached to the issuance, renewal or maintenance of the subsidy, does not constitute a breach of the provisions of this Section.

1.4 For greater certainty, nothing in this Section shall be construed as preventing a Party from discontinuing the granting of a subsidy or requesting its reimbursement where such measure is necessary in order to comply with international obligations between the Parties or has been ordered by a competent court, administrative tribunal or other competent authority, or requiring that Party to compensate the investor therefor.

This provision has a number of features. First, it covers a very broad range of public interests, i.e. measures aiming at achieving "legitimate policy objectives", including measures for the protection of public health, safety, the environment or public morals, social or consumer protection or the promotion and protection of cultural diversity. Some of these objectives are seldom seen in other IIAs. Second, the ambiguity of the various terms used, such as "achieve", "public objectives", "cultural diversity" and "social protection", can be expansively and flexibly construed by host states and arbitrators in practice. This may potentially help preserve a broad span of state regulatory power. Third, the words "nothing in this section" suggests that this broad provision shall be applied to the whole investment chapter. Fourth, this provision also deals with the potential problem of conflict of obligations under the CETA investment chapter and other international obligations. Fifth, this provision makes clear that mere "effect" or "consequence" of the regulatory measures shall neither be the sole nor sufficient ground for determining the violation of this chapter. Finally, this provision expressly incorporates the "specific commitment" requirement, which implies that unless an investor obtains a specific commitment from the host state, the subsidy decisions made by the state shall not be deemed as a violation of the chapter. This provision may help preserve the regulatory power of the contracting states in taking measures for a wide range of public interest purposes.

Up to the present day, CETA seems to be quite outstanding in catering for public interest, compared with other IIAs. Though this provision appears somewhat similar to the clause of general exceptions contained in some IIAs, it is broader in coverage and its threshold requirements for invocation seem lower. Despite its merits, this CETA provision fails to fundamentally change the status quo of the public interest provision in IIAs. It aims more at preserving state regulatory power rather than at imposing affirmative obligations on host states and foreign investors in protecting public interests.

That said, incorporation of a general provision of public interest in IIAs may imply a trend in future IIA-making. For instance, China is negotiating a BIT with the EU. According to a resolution on the EU–China BIT negotiation, the European Parliament stresses that investment agreements concluded by the EU:

> must not be in contradiction with the fundamental values that the EU wishes to promote through its external policies and must not undermine the capacity for public intervention, in particular when pursuing public policy objectives such as social and environmental criteria, human rights, the fight against counterfeiting, security, workers' and consumers' rights, public health and safety, industrial policy and cultural diversity.[112]

In light of such a statement, it seems possible for the future China–EU BIT to also include a general provision of public interest protection.

Conclusion

Public interest protection, such as environmental and human rights protection, directly links to sustainable development. The international community shares a growing consensus that IIAs should be made more balanced in the sense that protecting foreign investments should not be achieved at the cost of marginalizing public interest protection. Despite such consensus, IIAs seldom incorporate public interest provisions due to the lack of an international consensus on the definition and scope of public interest; the concern over the suitability of IIAs in addressing public interest issues; and the different attitudes of states towards public interest protection.

In recent years, an increasing number of public interest provisions have been incorporated in IIAs. A close reading of these provisions shows that they share four major features. (i) These provisions remain scarce in IIAs globally, and most of these provisions are included in IIAs of developed states. (ii) These provisions are fragmented in IIAs as states have different attitudes towards different types of public interest, and a standalone comprehensive public interest provision is rarely seen. (iii) Many of these provisions are specialized exceptive provisions in nature, exempting states from the liability for taking regulatory measures for public interest purposes that are otherwise inconsistent with their IIA commitments. (iv) A major portion of these provisions are soft law norms, especially human rights and CSR provisions, which greatly restrains their enforceability and effectiveness in protecting public interests.

Public-interest-sensitive investment disputes are frequently seen in ISA practice. Arbitrators seldom give sufficient consideration to public interest factors, because IIAs often lack public interest provisions and the ISA rules often disallow the host states to raise counterclaims. This also shows that the current IIA system is unable to accommodate conflicting values of investment protection and public interest protection.

Overall, the lack of public interest provisions in IIAs and the weak enforceability of these provisions seem to suggest that IIAs are not sufficiently capable in addressing public interest concerns associated with transnational investment activities. The protection of public interests remains largely within national jurisdictions and international discourses established by specialized treaties other than IIAs.

Notes

1   See e.g. A. Kulick (2012); T. Komori and K. Wellens (eds.), *Public Interest Rules of International Law: Towards Effective Implementation* (Farnham: Ashgate Publishing Limited, 2009); T. Treves, F. Seatzu and S. Trevisanut (eds.), *Foreign Investment, International Law and Common Concerns* (London and New York: Routledge, 2014); G. Sacerdoti, P. Acconci, M. Valenti and A. De Luca (eds.), General Interests of Host States in International Investment Law (Cambridge: Cambridge University Press, 2014); P. J. Martinez-Fraga and C. R. Reetz, *Public Purpose in International*

Law: *Rethinking Regulatory Sovereignty in the Global Era* (Cambridge: Cambridge University Press, 2015).

2   A. Cassese, *Human Rights in a Changing World* (Cambridge: Polity Press, 1990), at 12.

3   T. Komori and K. Wellens (eds.), *Public Interest Rules of International Law: Towards Effective Implementation* (Farnham: Ashgate Publishing Limited, 2009), at 1.

4   See e.g. P. Acconci, "The Integration of Non-Investment Concerns as an Opportunity for the Modernization of International Investment Law: Is a Multilateral Approach Desirable?", in G. Sacerdoti, P. Acconci, M. Valenti and A. De Luca (eds.)(2014), at 165–189.

5   See e.g. V. Lowe, *International Law* (Oxford: Oxford University Press, 2007), at 95–96; G. Kaufmann-Kohler, "Soft Law in International Arbitration: Codification and Normativity", 1 (1) *Journal of International Dispute Settlement* 1 (2010), at 2; A. T. Guzman and T. L. Meyer, "International Common Law: The Soft Law of International Tribunals", 9 (2) *Chinese Journal of International Law* 515 (2008), at 516.

6   In M. G. Desta, "Soft Law in International Law: An Overview", in A. Bjorklund and A. Reinisch (eds.), *Soft Law and International Investment Law* (Cheltenham, Edward Elgar Publishing Ltd., 2013), at 40 and 50.

7   T. Gruchalla-Wesierski, "A Framework for Understanding 'Soft Law'", 30 *McGill Law Journal* 37 (1984), at 44.

8   H. Hillgenberg, "A Fresh Look at Soft Law", 19 (3) *European Journal of International Law* 499 (1999), at 499.

9   R. S. Karmel and C. R. Kelly, "The Hardening of Soft Law in Securities Regulation", 34 (3) *Brooklyn Journal of International Law* 883 (2009), at 950.

10   In M. Hirsch, "Source of International Investment Law", in A. Bjorklund and A. Reinisch (eds.) (2013), at 31.

11   See e.g. D. L. Swenson, "Why Do Developing Countries Sign BITs?", 12 *University of California at Davis Journal of International Law and Policy* 130 (2005), at 131; E. Neumayer, P. Nunnenkamp and M. Roy, "Are Stricter Investment Rules Contagious? Host Country Competition for Foreign Direct Investment through International Agreements", *WTO Working Paper ERSD-2014-04* (10 March 2014), available at www.wto.org/english/res_e/reser_e/ersd201404_e.pdf.

12   See J. A. VanDuzer, "Sustainable Development Provisions in International Trade Treaties: What Lessons for International Investment Agreements?", in S. Hindelang and M. Krajewski (eds.), *Shifting Paradigms in International Investment Law: More Balanced, Less Isolated, Increasingly Diversified* (Oxford: Oxford University Press, 2016), at 172–173.

13   See D. Liang and J. Liu, "Preventing Environmental Deterioration from International Trade and Investment: How China Can Learn from NFATA's Experience to Strengthen Domestic Environmental Governance and Ensure Sustainable Development", in H. Kong and W. Wroth (eds.), *NAFTA and Sustainable Development: History, Experience and Prospects for Reform* (Cambridge: Cambridge University Press, 2015), at 316.

14   See M. Chi (2015).

15   Article 10 (1) (a), the 2004 Canadian Model BIT.

16   Article 10 (1) (c), the 2004 Canadian Model BIT.

17   Annex B.4 (B), the 2012 U.S. Model BIT.

18   Annex X.11, CETA Chapter Ten.

19   Annex B.13 (1) (c), the 2004 Canadian Model BIT.
20   Article 3.2, the China–Madagascar BIT.
21   See generally N. Bernasconi-Osterwalder and L. Johnson (eds.), *International Investment Law and Sustainable Development: Key Cases from 2000 to 2010*, IISD Publication (2010), available at www.iisd.org/publications/international-invest ment-law-and-sustainable-development-key-cases-2000-2010.
22   See ibid.
23   S.D. Myers Inc. v. Government of Canada (ad hoc arbitration under the UNCITRAL Arbitration Rules), Partial Award (13 November 2000), available at www.italaw.com/cases/documents/977, at para. 282.
24   See e.g. S. Baughen, "Expropriation and Environmental Regulation: The Lessons of NAFTA Chapter Eleven", 18 (2) *J. Environmental L.* 207 (2006), at 216–227; J. R. Marlles, "Public Purpose, Private Losses: Regulatory Expropriation and Environmental Regulation in International Investment Law", 16 (2) *Journal of Transnational Law and Policy* 275, 292 (2007).
25   See e.g. L. Y. Fortier and S. L. Drymer, "Indirect Expropriation in the Law of International Investment: I Know It When I See It, or Caveat Investor", 19 (2) *ICSID Review* 293, 314 (2004) at 314.
26   See Chapter 3 (discussing indirect expropriation clause).
27   Methanex Corporation v. United States of America (*ad hoc* arbitration under the UNCITRAL Rules), available at http://italaw.com/cases/683.
28   See M. Chi (2015), at 518.
29   Article X.9.4, CETA Chapter Ten.
30   M. Chi (2015), at 519.
31   See A. Kulick (2012), at 262–263.
32   V. S. Vadi, *Public Health in International Investment Law and Arbitration* (Oxon: Routledge, 2013), at 190.
33   V. S. Vadi, "Reconciling Public Health and Investor Rights: The Case of Tobacco", in P. Dupuy, E. Petersmann and F. Francioni, *Human Rights in International Investment Law and Arbitration* (Oxford: Oxford University Press, 2009), at 454–455.
34   Philip Morris Asia Limited v. The Commonwealth of Australia (PCA Case No. 2012-12), available at www.italaw.com/cases/851.
35   Philip Morris Brands Sàrl, Philip Morris Products S.A. and Abal Hermanos S.A. v. Oriental Republic of Uruguay (ICSID Case No. ARB/10/7), available at www.italaw.com/cases/460.
36   See Philip Morris Asia Limited v. The Commonwealth of Australia (PCA Case No. 2012-12), Award on Jurisdiction and Admissibility (17 December 2015), available at www.italaw.com/sites/default/files/case-documents/ italaw7303_0.pdf, at 186.
37   M. C. Porterfield and C. R. Byrnes, "Philip Morris v. Uruguay: Will Investor–State Arbitration Send Restrictions on Tobacco Marketing Up in Smoke?", available at www.iisd.org/itn/2011/07/12/philip-morris-v-uruguay-will-investor-state-arbi tration-send-restrictions-on-tobacco-marketing-up-in-smoke/.
38   See A. Khalfan, "International Investment Law and Human Rights", in M. C. Segger et al. (eds.), (2011), at 53.
39   J. D. Taillant and J. Bonnitcha, "International Investment Law and Human Rights", in M. C. Segger et al. (eds.), (2011), at 74.
40   See generally V. Mantouvalou (2012), at 152–171.
41   UNHRC, "What Are Human Rights", available at www.ohchr.org/EN/Issues/Pages/WhatareHumanRights.aspx.

42 See V. Mantouvalou, "Are Labor Rights Human Rights?," 3 *European Labor Law Journal* 151 (2012), at 152.
43 Article 24, UDHR.
44 Articles 29 and 30, EUCFR.
45 A. Sewlikar, "Introduction of Labor Standards in Investment Arbitration", available at http://kluwerarbitrationblog.com/blog/2014/03/18/introduction-of-labour-standards-in-investment-arbitration/.
46 See M. C. Segger *et al.* (2011), at 57.
47 See generally L. Compa, "The Multilateral Agreement on Investment and International Labor Rights: A Failed Connection", 31 *Cornell International Law Journal* 683, (2007), at 685–696.
48 See Article 13.1, the 2012 U.S. Model BIT.
49 See L. Compa, "Labour Rights and Labour Standards in International Trade", 25 *Law and Policy in International Business* 165 (1993), at 165–168.
50 See Article 13.4, the 2012 U.S. Model BIT.
51 See generally D. C. K. Chow, "Why China Opposes Human Rights in the World Trade Organization", 35 (1) *University of Pennsylvania Journal of International Law* 62 (2013).
52 Article 8 (3), the China–Thailand BIT; Article 5.1(b), the China–Singapore BIT; Article 5.1(b), the China–New Zealand BIT.
53 Article 10.3 (g), the China–ASEAN FTA investment chapter.
54 Swiss Alliance of Development Organizations, "FTA between Switzerland and China: Human Rights on the Scrap Heap" (19 July 2013), available at www.alliancesud.ch/en/policy/trade/fta-between-switzerland-and-china-human-rights-on-the-scrap-heap.
55 B. Simma, Foreign Investment Arbitration: A Place for Human Rights? 60 (4) *International and Comparative Law Quarterly* 576 (2011).
56 See generally M. Hirsch, "Investment Tribunals and Human Rights: Divergent Paths", in P. M. Dupuy, F. Francioni and E. U. Petersmann (eds.), *Human Rights in International Investment Law and Arbitration* (Oxford: Oxford University Press, 2009), at 97–114.
57 Suez, Sociedad General de Aguas de Barcelona, S.A. and Vivendi Universal, S.A. v. Argentine Republic (ICSID Case No. ARB/03/19), available at www.italaw.com/cases/1057.
58 Glamis Gold Ltd. v. United States of America (*ad hoc* arbitration under UNCITRAL Arbitration Rules), available at www.italaw.com/cases/487.
59 See generally C. Reiner and C. Schreuer, "Human Rights and International Investment Arbitration", in P. M. Dupuy, F. Francioni and E. U. Petersmann (eds.), *Human Rights in International Investment Law and Arbitration* (Oxford: Oxford University Press, 2009), at 88–94.
60 See M. Hirsch (2009), at 113–114.
61 Azurix Corp. v. The Argentine Republic (ICSID Case No. ARB/01/12), available at www.italaw.com/cases/118. For a discussion of the case, see J. Chaisse and M. Polo, "Globalization of Water Privatization — Ramifications of Investor–State Disputes in the 'Blue Gold' Economy", 38 (1) *Boston College International and Comparative Law Review* 1 (2015), at 16–23, 49–50 and 55–61.
62 Azurix Corp. v. The Argentine Republic (ICSID Case No. ARB/01/12), Award (14 July 2006), available at www.italaw.com/sites/default/files/case-documents/ita0061.pdf, at para. 254.

63 See generally T. Meshel, "Human Rights in Investor–State Arbitration: The Human Right to Water and Beyond", 6 *Journal of International Dispute Settlement* 277 (2015).

64 Siemens A.G. v. The Argentine Republic (ICSID Case No. ARB/02/8), available at www.italaw.com/cases/1026.

65 See Siemens A.G. v. The Argentine Republic (ICSID Case No. ARB/02/8), Award (6 Feb. 2007), available at www.italaw.com/sites/default/files/case-documents/ita0790.pdf, at para. 79.

66 Azurix Corp. v. The Argentine Republic (ICSID Case No. ARB/01/12), Award (14 July 2006), at para. 261. For a discussion of this issue, refer to L. Peterson, *Human Rights and Bilateral Investment Treaties: Mapping the Role of Human Rights Law in Investor–State Arbitration* (Montreal: Rights & Democracy, 2009), available at http://publications.gc.ca/collections/collection_2012/dd-rd/E84-36-2009-eng.pdf, at 11.

67 Biwater Gauff (Tanzania) Ltd. v. United Republic of Tanzania (ICSID Case No. ARB/05/22), available at www.italaw.com/cases/157.

68 Biwater Gauff (Tanzania) Ltd. v. United Republic of Tanzania (ICSID Case No. ARB/05/22), Award (24 July 2008), available at www.italaw.com/sites/default/files/case-documents/ita0095.pdf.

69 J. D. Taillant and J. Bonnitcha, "International Investment Law and Human Rights", in M. C. Segger et al. (2011), at 75.

70 Técnicas Medioambientales Tecmed, S.A. v. The United Mexican States (ICSID Case No. ARB (AF)/00/2), available at www.italaw.com/cases/1087.

71 Mondev International Ltd. v. United States of America (ICSID Case No. ARB(AF)/99/2), available at www.italaw.com/cases/715.

72 L. Peterson, *Human Rights and Bilateral Investment Treaties: Mapping the Role of Human Rights Law in Investor–State Arbitration* (Montreal: Rights & Democracy, 2009), available at http://publications.gc.ca/collections/collection_2012/dd-rd/E84-36-2009-eng.pdf, at 23.

73 Técnicas Medioambientales Tecmed, S.A. v. The United Mexican States (ICSID Case No. ARB (AF)/00/2), Award (29 May 2003), available at www.italaw.com/sites/default/files/case-documents/ita0854.pdf, at para. 116.

74 Técnicas Medioambientales Tecmed, S.A. v. The United Mexican States (ICSID Case No. ARB (AF)/00/2), Award (29 May 2003), at paras. 121–122.

75 ECHR, Case of Matos e Silva, Lda., and Others v. Portugal (Application No. 15777/89), Judgment (Merits and Just Satisfaction) (16 September 1996), available at http://hudoc.echr.coe.int/eng?i=001-58063.

76 ECHR, Case of Mellacher and Others v. Austria (Application No. 10522/83; 11011/84; 11070/84), Judgment (19 December 1989), available at http://hudoc.echr.coe.int/eng?i=001-57616.

77 ECHR, Case of Pressos Compañía Naviera and Others v. Belgium (Application No. 17849/91), Judgment (Merits) (20 November 1995), available at http://hudoc.echr.coe.int/eng?i=001-58056.

78 See L. Peterson (2009), at 18–19.

79 See e.g. Article 42, ICSID Convention.

80 Southern Pacific Properties (Middle East) Limited v. Arab Republic of Egypt (ICSID Case No. ARB/84/3), available at www.italaw.com/cases/3300.

81 Southern Pacific Properties (Middle East) Limited v. Arab Republic of Egypt (ICSID Case No. ARB/84/3), Award on the Merits (9 March 1993), available at

www.italaw.com/sites/default/files/case-documents/italaw6314_0.pdf, at para. 150–154; for a brief discussion of this issue, refer to L. Peterson (2009), at 22.

82 See C. Reiner and C. Schreuer (2009), "Human Rights and International Investment Arbitration", in P. M. Dupuy, F. Francioni and E. U. Petersmann (eds.), *Human Rights in International Investment Law and Arbitration* (Oxford: Oxford University Press, 2009), at 84–85.

83 Trinh Vinh Binh v. Vietnam (*ad hoc* arbitration under the UNCITRAL Arbitration Rules), available at www.italaw.com/cases/155.

84 L. Peterson (2009), at 24–25.

85 UNEP, "Corporate Social Responsibility and Regional Trade and Investment Agreements" (2011), available at http://unep.ch/etb/publications/CSR%20publication/UNEP_Corporate%20Social%20Responsibility.pdf, at 13.

86 See K. Gordon, J. Pohl and M. Bouchard, "Investment Treaty Law, Sustainable Development and Responsible Business Conduct: A Fact Finding Survey", *OECD Working Papers on International Investment* 2014/01, available at www.oecd.org/investment/investment-policy/WP-2014_01.pdf, at 8.

87 See generally I. Bantekas, "Corporate Social Responsibility in International Law", 22 *Boston University International Law Journal* 309 (2004).

88 European Commission, "Communication from the Commission" (Doc. No. COM(2002) 347), available at http://trade.ec.europa.eu/doclib/docs/2006/february/tradoc_127374.pdf.

89 See A. Newcombe, "Investor Misconduct", in A. de Mestral and C. Lévesque (eds.), *Improving International Investment Agreements* (London and New York: Routledge, 2013), at 196.

90 See Stacey L. McGraw and Stacey E. Rufe, The Foreign Corrupt Practices Act: An Overview of the Law and Coverage-Related Issues (21 March 2014), available at http://apps.americanbar.org/litigation/committees/insurance/articles/janfeb2014-foreign-corrupt-practices-act.html#_edn6; The Criminal Division of the U.S. Department of Justice and the Enforcement Division of the U.S. Securities and Exchange Commission, "A Resource Guide to the FCPA U.S. Foreign Corrupt Practices Act" (14 November 2012), available at www.justice.gov/sites/default/files/criminal-fraud/legacy/2015/01/16/guide.pdf, at 11–12.

91 H. Fung, S. Law and J. Yau, *Socially Responsible Investment in a Global Environment* (Cheltenham: Edward Elgar Publishing, 2010), at 4.

92 See OECD, *Employment and Industrial Relations — 2008 Annual Report on the OECD Guidelines for Multinational Enterprise*, available at www.oecd.org/corporate/mne/employmentandindustrialrelations-2008annualreportontheoecdguidelinesformultinationalenterprises.htm, at 237–238.

93 See generally, J. A. Zerk, *Multinationals and Corporate Social Responsibility: Limitations and Opportunities in International Law* (Cambridge: Cambridge University Press, 2006), at 145–197.

94 See ibid., at 151.

95 MOFCOM, "Spokesperson's Remarks on Outward Investment and Economic Cooperation of the Ministry of Commerce Comments on China's Outward Investment and Economic Cooperation in 2015", available at http://english.mofcom.gov.cn/article/newsrelease/policyreleasing/201602/20160201251488.shtml.

96 See D. H. Shinn, "The Environmental Impact of China's Investment in Africa", 49 (1) *Cornell International Law Journal* 25 (2016), at 25.

97   MOFCOM, "Regulations of Overseas Investment Management", adopted by 27th Ministerial Affairs Meeting of the Ministry of Commerce of the People's Republic of China on 19 August 2014, effective as of 6 October 2014, available at www.mof com.gov.cn/article/b/c/201409/20140900723361.shtml (original in Chinese).

98   Ibid., at Article 20.

99   ILO, *Tripartite Declaration of Principles concerning Multinational Enterprises and Social Policy* (adopted by the Governing Body of the International Labour Office at its 204th Session, Geneva, November 1977, as amended at its 279th Session, November 2000, and 295th Session, March 2006), available at www.ilo.org/ wcmsp5/groups/public/—-ed_emp/—-emp_ent/—-multi/documents/publication/ wcms_094386.pdf.

100   OECD, *Guidelines for Multinational Enterprises (2011 edition)*, available at www.oecd.org/daf/inv/mne/48004323.pdf.

101   UNHRC, *Guiding Principles on Business and Human Rights* (2011), Doc. No. HR/PUB/11/04, available at www.ohchr.org/Documents/Publications/Guiding PrinciplesBusinessHR_EN.pdf, at 1.

102   UNGC, *The Ten Principles of the United Nations Global Compact*, available at www.unglobalcompact.org/what-is-gc/mission/principles.

103   OECD, available at http://mneguidelines.oecd.org/guidelines/.

104   OECD, "The OECD Guidelines for Multinational Enterprises", OECD Policy Brief (June 2001), available at www.oecd.org/investment/mne/1903291.pdf, at 2.

105   M. Karavias, *Corporate Obligations under International Law* (Oxford: Oxford University Press, 2013), at 6.

106   See M. V. Stichele and S. van Bennekom, "Investment Agreements and Corporate Social Responsibility (CSR): Contradictions, Incentives and Policy Option", *SOMO Discussion Paper 1* (November 2015), available at www.somo.nl/ wp-content/uploads/2005/12/Investment-agreements-and-Corporate-Social-Responsibility.pdf, at 1

107   See e.g., N. L. Bridgeman and D. B. Hunter, "Narrowing the Accountability Gap: Toward a New Foreign Investor Accountability Mechanism", 20 (2) *Georgetown International Environmental Law Review* 187 (2008).

108   See P. Muchlinski, "Regulating Multinational Enterprises", in M. Bungenberg, C. Herrmann, M. Krajewski and J. P. Terhecht (eds.), *European Yearbook of International Economic Law 2016* (Basel: Springer International Publishing AG, 2016), at 403–419.

109   OECD, *Employment and Industrial Relations — 2008 Annual Report on the OECD Guidelines for Multinational Enterprise*, available at www.oecd.org/corporate/ mne/employmentandindustrialrelations-2008annualreportontheoecdguidelines formultinationalenterprises.htm, at 237–238.

110   The OECD Survey, at 10.

111   The OECD Survey, at 16–17.

112   See European Parliament, "European Parliament resolution of 9 October 2013 on the EU–China negotiations for a bilateral investment agreement (2013/2674 (RSP))", available at http://eur-lex.europa.eu/legal-content/EN/TXT/PDF/?uri= CELEX:52013IP0411&from=EN, at para. 23.

6 Procedural provisions

Traditionally, IIAs do not contain comprehensive and detailed procedural provisions. Procedural issues are often left to be decided in accordance with the applicable arbitration laws and arbitration rules or in pursuance of arbitrators' discretionary decisions.

There are different approaches to negotiating procedural rules in IIAs. Generally, "European style" IIAs contain a few concise procedural provisions, mainly providing for the contracting states' consent to ISA. Differently, "American style" IIAs often incorporate a comprehensive body of procedural rules as a section or chapter, dealing with a wide range of issues relating to the dispute settlement proceedings, such as pre-arbitration proceedings (negotiation and consultation), submission of a dispute to ISA, the composition of an arbitral tribunal, the conduct of arbitral proceedings and the enforcement of arbitral awards. As IIA-making is increasingly Americanized nowadays, there is a trend towards the procedural provisions in IIAs are becoming more comprehensive.[1]

It is sometimes difficult to draw a clear line between procedural provisions and substantive provisions in IIAs. While some provisions play a typical procedural function, such as a compromissory clause and an arbitral tribunal composition clause, others may not be easily categorized. Even substantive provisions may have a profound impact on dispute settlement. For instance, the definitions of investor and investment may dictate the jurisdiction *ratione personae* and jurisdiction *ratione materiae*; a denial of benefits clause may decide whether an investor is qualified to be protected by the IIA; an umbrella clause may "transform" a contract-based claim to a treaty-based one; and an MFN clause may, arguably, be applied to import more favourable procedural rules from other IIAs.

Some procedural provisions in IIAs may bear close connection with sustainable development. As mentioned, sustainable development is closely related to the principle of good governance and the principle of public participation and access to information and justice. It is clear that these principles are inherently linked with IIA provisions relating to transparency, third-party (amicus curiae) participation and the arbitral appeal system, to name the typical ones. Therefore, the design and function of these provisions may not only

DOI: 10.4324/9781315642840-9

influence the dispute settlement proceedings, but may also profoundly influence the realization of sustainable development goals. Typical procedural provisions will be discussed in this chapter.

Restrictive compromissory clauses

A typical feature of modern IIAs is that foreign investors are granted direct recourse to arbitration against host states. Such direct recourse to ISA serves two main purposes. On one hand, as foreign investors do not necessarily need to exhaust local remedies in the host states, the settlement of investment disputes are "privatized" and "internationalized". On the other hand, as ISA may exempt the home states from exercising diplomatic protection over their investors (diplomatic protection can only be exercised if the host states refuse to enforce arbitral awards), investment dispute settlement is "depoliticized".[2] Mainly for such reasons, ISA has become a preferred alternative in settling investment disputes.

Over the past decades, with the rapid increase of the number of IIAs, there has been an explosion of ISA cases,[3] especially those under the ICSID Convention and the ICSID Additional Facility Rules.[4] In treaty-based ISA, the arbitral jurisdiction is based on and limited to the compromissory provisions of the applicable IIAs.[5] Thus the compromissory clause of IIAs may play a critical role in preserving state regulatory power by granting, limiting or prohibiting foreign investors from submitting sustainable development-related issues to ISA. Roughly speaking, there are two opposing modes of compromissory clauses.

First, the restrictive compromissory clause. Such a clause means that IIAs expressly limit the types of disputes that can be submitted to ISA and/or exclude certain disputes from being admissible to ISA. For instance, according to Article 24 (1) of the 2012 U.S. Model BIT, an investor may submit "an investment dispute" against the respondent state under Articles 3 through 10. These Articles only relate to investment protection and treatment, but do not include sustainable development, such as the provisions of "investment and labor" (Article 13), "investment and environment" (Article 12) and "transparency" (Article 11).

It is clear that, despite the fact that the 2012 U.S. Model BIT has incorporated a number of important sustainable development provisions, alleged violation of these provisions is not a legal ground for foreign investors to have recourse to ISA. Such disputes should be submitted to the national courts of the host states. In this sense, the restrictive compromissory clause helps the contracting states in preserving regulatory power in taking measures for sustainable development purposes.

Second, the open compromissory clause. Such a clause means that IIAs employ general and broad terms with regard to the admissibility of disputes to ISA. Typical clauses can be found in many recent Chinese IIAs. For instance, Article 15 (2) of the China–Japan–Korea TIT provides that "any investment dispute" shall be submitted to ISA if it cannot be settled through prior negotiation and consultation, without further restrictions. Article 15 (1) of the TIT sets forth a broad definition of the key term "investment dispute", providing that,

> For the purposes of this Article, an investment dispute is a dispute between a Contracting Party and an investor of another Contracting Party that has incurred loss or damage by reason of, or arising out of, an alleged breach of any obligation of the former Contracting Party under this Agreement with respect to the investor or its investments in the territory of the former Contracting Party.

Judging by the plain language, though an investment dispute under this TIT should meet several requirements to be admissible to ISA, this TIT does not impose any restriction on the character of the dispute. These requirements, if not read with other applicable provisions of the TIT, would allow foreign investors to submit any kinds of disputes to ISA, including sustainable development-related disputes, as far as the disputes are "with respect to the investor or its investment". This would subject state regulatory measures for sustainable development purposes to the scrutiny of international arbitrators in accordance with international law (the TIT and even beyond). Such an open compromissory clause potentially limits the contracting states' regulatory power.

Though compromissory clauses *per se* do not serve sustainable development goals directly, they may play a helpful or an impeding role in helping preserve state regulatory power by limiting, to varying extents, the access of foreign investors to ISA. It is thus advisable that states negotiate a compromissory clause with certain restrictions, which may assist the states in achieving sustainable development goals in an indirect manner.

Transparency provisions in IIAs

Arbitration is traditionally viewed as a confidential dispute settlement mechanism between private parties. Because ISA is originally modelled after commercial arbitration, confidentiality is naturally "inherited". The lack of differentiation of ISA from commercial arbitration has formed a part of the debate over the legitimacy of ISA. Many arbitrators are private commercial lawyers who tend to treat states and investors "equally", without considering the uniqueness of states as a public governing authority.[6] In comparison, public-law lawyers appear more willing to handle investment disputes against the background of general international law.[7] The "clash" of these different conceptual paradigms could make a difference to the outcome of the dispute.[8] Today, as the public-law nature of ISA has been progressively recognized, confidentiality of ISA has been subject to increasing criticism, as it appears inconsistent with good governance and the rule-of-law standard. It seems natural that ISA should be made more transparent. Accordingly, various transparency provisions have been incorporated in IIAs nowadays.

Tension between confidentiality and transparency of ISA

Confidentiality has long been deemed an important feature of commercial arbitration.[9] It is particularly the case when comparing arbitration with litigation. Generally, confidentiality of arbitration refers to the obligations of the disputing parties, the arbitrators, and the arbitral institutions not to disclose information or documents concerning the arbitration proceedings to third parties and to the public – including but not limited to the submission of the dispute to arbitration, the documents produced in the proceedings, the decisions, awards and the reasoning of the arbitrators. Confidentiality of arbitration relies on the national law and the applicable arbitration rules, and especially, party autonomy plays a central role in defining the confidentiality obligations in arbitration.[10] Though there are no international uniform rules and arbitral practice on the exact scope and contents of the confidentiality obligation, many institutional rules and national laws cater extensively for confidentiality of arbitration.

As the ISA system borrows its main elements from the system of commercial arbitration,[11] the two arbitration systems are inherently linked with each other. Proponents of confidentiality of ISA typically draw on parallels with experiences in commercial arbitration,[12] arguing that ISA should be confidential and open only to participation by the disputing parties, unless those parties agree otherwise, as confidentiality and party autonomy are the two hallmarks of traditional arbitration.[13]

Despite the similarity and the link between the systems of ISA and commercial arbitration, the public-law nature of ISA has been gradually revealed and widely recognized. Such nature gives rise to the concern over the confidentiality of ISA, and the tension between confidentiality and transparency in ISA has become high.[14] Enhanced transparency of ISA is helpful in addressing the legitimacy crisis of the current international investment law.[15] As B. Stern has insightfully argued,

> This system [the ISA system], which was traditionally based on private legitimacy arising from the consent of the parties, seems to now be in search of public legitimacy, which it is thought can be obtained from a certain degree of openness to civil society.[16]

There are a number of reasons for enhancing the transparency of ISA. First, ISA has distinct public policy implications. It typically "targets" state regulatory measures that involve public interests; if the state "loses the case", the compensation would be paid out of state revenue. The enforcement of ISA awards may also involve diplomatic and political factors.[17] Second, inconsistency of ISA awards has been frequently criticized as a key reason of the legitimacy crisis of the ISA system, while enhanced transparency could be helpful in establishing more consistent ISA jurisprudence. Third, enhanced transparency can also help cure the democratic deficit in the current ISA system, in which the legality of a state's exercise of public power is scrutinized under the standards crafted by arbitrators who are appointed by the disputing parties and have no genuine democratic legitimacy.[18] Finally, the call from civil societies for greater public involvement in ISA has also played a promotional role in enhancing the transparency of the ISA system.[19]

Consequently, while confidentiality remains a distinct feature almost intact in commercial arbitration,[20] ISA has become increasingly transparent. It has been observed that "probably the most striking difference between ISA and international commercial arbitration lies in their level of confidentiality or transparency".[21] The broadening transparency gap between the two arbitration systems seems to suggest that ISA should be conducted in a "public law approach". This approach emphasizes the public nature of investment disputes, implying that ISA proceedings need to be presumptively public and open to participation by interested parties, such as NGOs as *amici*, irrespective of the wishes of the disputing or treaty parties.[22]

In ISA practice, there appeared a trend in the arbitration community to separate ISA from commercial arbitration.[23] In several high-profile NAFTA Chapter Eleven cases, such as Methanex v. U.S. and UPS v. Canada,[24] the tribunals distinguished ISA from commercial arbitration in support of more transparency in ISA. For instance, the tribunal in Methanex v. U.S. held that,

> In this respect, the current dispute is to be distinguished from a typical commercial arbitration on the basis that a state was the Respondent, the issues had to be decided in accordance with a treaty and the principles of public international law and a decision on the dispute could have a significant effect extending beyond the two Disputing Parties.[25]

A similar trend can also be found in ICSID arbitration. For example, in Biwater v. Tanzania,[26] the tribunal found that, when confronting two competing interests between "the need for transparency in treaty proceedings" and "the need to protect the procedural integrity of the arbitration", ISA and commercial arbitration should be differentiated, holding that,

> Considerations of confidentiality and privacy have not played the same role in the field of investment arbitration, as they have in international commercial arbitration. Without doubt, there is now a marked tendency towards transparency in treaty arbitration.[27]

The international community shares a growing consensus of improving global investment governance. This would imply that the ISA system be reformed more transparent. In the non-binding G20 Guiding Principles for Global Investment Policymaking adopted during the G20 Meeting of trade ministers in July 2016, the world's economic leaders united to call for more transparency in investment policymaking and dispute settlement.[28] As international investment law is likely to continue to face demands for increased transparency, openness, predictability, and fair balance between investors' rights and public interests,[29] the transparency of ISA is likely to be further improved.

The different dimensions of transparency under IIAs

An increasing number of IIAs incorporate transparency provisions in various types. In the context of IIAs, the notion of transparency in ISA is very broad.[30] Transparency obligations are principally imposed on the contracting states, but they may also profoundly affect private investors and other stakeholders in ISA (such as a non-disputing party). These obligations may either be contained in separate provisions or integrated in one provision of the IIAs. Besides, IIAs may also provide various ways for the contracting states to fulfil transparency obligations, such as consultation and exchange of information, making information publicly available, answering requests for information and notification of information.[31]

Transparency provisions in IIAs are designed in different dimensions and with varying levels of "intrusiveness" to the contracting states, the disputing parties and the arbitrators of ISA. Roughly speaking, the transparency obligations under modern IIAs have three dimensions, i.e. informational transparency, adjudicative transparency, and participatory transparency. Accordingly, they also represent varying levels of "intrusiveness".

Before discussing the dimensions of the transparency obligations in IIAs, a few points should be noted at the outset. First, though transparency obligations are typically imposed on the contracting states of IIAs, they may have profound impacts that go beyond the states. For instance, participatory transparency obligations may impact non-disputing parties (amicus curiae) and even arbitrators. Second, transparency obligations on states are not absolute. Many IIAs contain exceptive provisions to exempt states' transparency obligations in certain circumstances.[32] For instance, some IIAs exempt the contracting states from making public various types of "confidential information".[33] Third, transparency obligations are not always isolated from each other. For instance, when a non-disputing party lodges a request to participate in the ISA as amicus curiae, such a request encompasses transparency obligations in both adjudicative dimensions (access to key arbitral documents or attending the hearings) and participatory dimensions (submission of amicus curiae briefs).

Informational transparency obligations in IIAs

Informational transparency obligations are imposed on IIA contracting states. The states are required to publish or make available to foreign investors or the general public their relevant laws, regulations, rules and policies (or the making of these instruments) that may influence the legal rights and obligations of investors and the business environment of the states. IIA provisions concerning informational transparency often denote the lowest level of transparency obligation. They reflect the traditional concerns of foreign investors regarding the transparency of host-state activity, statements, policies, regulations, and decision-making.[34]

In the globalization era, informational transparency is indispensable for global governance. For instance, the principle of transparency is viewed as a basic principle of WTO law, which is relatively clearly defined as the publication of national laws, regulations, judicial decisions and administrative rulings of general application related to trade.[35] Additionally, the reports of WTO panels and the AB are also routinely made public on the official website of the WTO.[36] Further, under some WTO agreements, member governments are also required to notify other members of any new or changed rules which may affect trade and to set up "enquiry points" to respond to requests on new or existing measures.[37]

Informational transparency also constitutes a basic requirement of the rule of law. According to a report of the Secretary-General of the UN, rule of law,

> refers to the principle of governance to which all persons, institutions and entities, public and private, including the state itself, are accountable to laws that are publicly promulgated, equally enforced and independently adjudicated, and which are consistent with international human rights norms and standards.[38]

This definition, especially the words "laws that are publicly promulgated" reveals that informational transparency is a core element of the rule of law.

Transparency provisions are common in IIAs. The contracting states may agree on the scope of "information" to be made public. For instance, according to Article 21 of the ASEAN Comprehensive Investment Agreement, entitled "Transparency", the information that should be made public includes: (1) investment-related agreements; (2) new law or any changes to existing laws, regulations or administrative guidelines; and (3) relevant laws, regulations and administrative guidelines of general application.[39] In comparison, the regulations that should be made public under the Canada–China BIT seem broader in coverage:

> laws, regulations and policies pertaining to the conditions of admission of investments, including procedures for application and registration, criteria used for assessment and approval, timelines for processing an application and rendering a decision, and review or appeal procedures of a decision.[40]

Besides, some IIAs also lay down certain formal requirements for the publication of "investment-related regulations". For instance, the 2012 U.S. Model BIT, in its provision of "Transparency", requires regulations of general application adopted at the central level be published in "a single official journal of national circulation" and shall "include in the publication an explanation of the purpose and rationale for the regulations".[41] Some other IIAs also require the contracting states to establish "enquiry points" for the purpose of furnishing the regulations that are subject to the transparency requirement to the public.[42]

Adjudicative transparency obligations in IIAs

Adjudicative transparency essentially requires the publication of ISA-related documents or public access to the arbitral proceedings and hearings in particular. The term "ISA-related documents" in its strict sense is not a legal term in international investment law. It may be used with varying scopes and contents. Broadly understood, ISA-related documents include, but are not limited to, the pleadings and submissions of the disputing parties, the procedural decisions and awards of the arbitrators, the submissions of non-disputing parties, expert witness statements and the minutes or records of the arbitral hearings.

Whether and to what extent ISA-related documents should be made public depends on a variety of factors, such as the applicable IIAs, arbitration laws and procedural rules, the discretion of the arbitrators, and the agreement of the disputing parties. In reality, while some ISA-related documents are easily accessible by the public, others may be quite difficult to obtain.[43]

Many IIAs contain provisions of adjudicative transparency. This is partly a response to the current legitimacy crisis of ISA. The exact scope of ISA-related documents varies among IIAs. The 2012 U.S. Model BIT contains a provision entitled "Transparency of Arbitral Proceedings", according to which a wide range of ISA-related documents shall be promptly transmitted to the non-disputing contracting party and made available to the public subject to a few exceptions:

a)   the notice of intent;
b)   the notice of arbitration;
c)   pleadings, memorials, and briefs submitted to the tribunal by a disputing party and any written submissions submitted pursuant to Article 28(2) [Non-Disputing Party submissions] and (3) [*Amicus* Submissions] and Article 33 [Consolidation];
d)   minutes or transcripts of hearings of the tribunal, where available; and
e)   orders, awards, and decisions of the tribunal.[44]

With regard to public access to hearings, this provision requires arbitrators to "conduct hearings open to the public" and "determine, in consultation with the disputing parties, the appropriate logistical arrangements".[45]

According to the CETA investment chapter, ISA-related documents that should be made public are governed by the UNCITRAL Transparency Rules.[46] In addition, the CETA also requires many other types of ISA-related documents to be made public, including the request for consultations, the notice requesting a determination of the respondent, the notice of determination of the respondent, the agreement to mediate, the notice of intent to challenge a member of the tribunal, the decision on challenges to a member of the tribunal, the request for consolidation and Exhibits, subject to Article 3 (1) and (2) of the UNCITRAL Transparency Rules.[47] With regard to access to hearings, the CETA contains a very similar provision to the 2012 U.S. Model BIT, under which hearings shall be open to the public unless the tribunal determines otherwise.[48]

Compared with the above IIAs, IIAs of many other states appear conservative by limiting the types of ISA-related documents, and by restricting or even denying public access to arbitral hearings. For instance, according to the Canada–China BIT, the Article of "Public Access to Hearing and Documents" only expressly requires the publication of ISA awards, subject to the redaction of confidential information.[49] With regard to other types of ISA-related documents, publication will only be made on an *ad hoc* basis when a disputing party considers it necessary.[50] Besides, with regard to public access to hearings, this BIT sets up clear and strict requirements,

> Where, after consulting with a disputing investor, a disputing Contracting Party determines that it is in the public interest to do so and notifies the Tribunal of that determination, hearings held under this Part shall be open to the public. To the extent necessary to ensure the protection of confidential information, including business confidential information, the Tribunal may hold portions of hearings in camera.[51]

As can be seen, under the Canada–China BIT, an arbitral tribunal has no authority to decide whether hearings should be made public; only the disputing state can determine this issue, subject to a lenient requirement of "consulting with the disputing investor". Although this provision is silent as to the situation where a third party applies to the arbitral tribunal to attend the hearings, it can be presumed that such permission can only be given with the consent of the disputing state. Overall, this provision features a low level of adjudicative transparency.

Participatory transparency provisions in IIAs

Participatory transparency primarily concerns non-disputing party participation in ISA proceedings. Such participation is ordinarily justified on the basis that this "friend of the court" is in a position to provide the court or tribunal with its special perspective or expertise in relation to the dispute.[52] In legal literature, the term "non-disputing party" is often used interchangeably with "the public", "third party" or "amicus curiae" ("friend of the court"), though their differences are recognized. While in many ISA cases, non-disputing parties often appear to be NGOs and civil society groups in the capacity of amicus curiae, intergovernmental organizations and even sovereign states may also be non-dispute parties in some cases.[53]

In practice, the requests of non-disputing parties to participate in ISA typically include three specific requests: (i) access to arbitral documents, (ii) permission to attend the hearings, and (iii) permission to make legal arguments, often in the form of amicus curiae briefs. These requests encompass several dimensions of transparency. Access to arbitral documents and hearings is covered by adjudicative transparency; submission of amicus curiae briefs is covered by participatory transparency. Among these requests, amicus curiae participation in

ISA is a highly contentious issue in international investment law.[54] This will be further discussed in the next section.

Observations of transparency provisions in IIAs

Several observations can be drawn from the study of the transparency provisions in IIAs. First, an increasing number of IIAs incorporate transparency provisions of various types. This is partly a response to help tacklethe legitimacy crisis of the current IIA and ISA systems.

Second, existing transparency provisions in IIAs are of different levels, depending on the intrusiveness of the transparency obligations. In general, informational transparency provisions are widely accepted in IIAs. Adjudicative transparency provisions are also often seen in IIAs, but their application usually requires the consent of the contracting states and/or the disputing parties. In comparison, participatory transparency provisions are only accepted in principle in a limited number of IIAs, and their application not only requires the disputing parties' consent, but also the assessment of arbitrators on a case-by-case basis.

Third, unlike many other IIA provisions that are mainly developed through IIAs, transparency provisions are developed not only through the discourse of IIA-making, but are dependent on the development of many other international legal instruments, including multilateral treaties and institutional arbitral rules. To put it differently, transparency provisions are included in IIAs not only as a result of the bilateral bargain between the contracting states but, more importantly, they are a timely reaction of the contracting states to the growing international trend of rule of law and good governance.

The globalization of transparency provisions

In addition to IIAs, states' transparency obligations may also be grounded on other legal instruments, which codify the recent development of transparency provisions in international investment law. In this regard, a few international legal instruments deserve highlighting, such as the 2006 amendments to the ICSID Arbitration Rules,[55] the UNCITRAL Rules on Transparency Rules in Treaty-based Investor–State Arbitration (UNCITRAL Transparency Rules),[56] and the Mauritius Transparency Convention.[57]

The 2006 amendments to the ICSID Arbitration Rules

The ICSID has long been aware of the concerns over the non-transparent manner of ICSID arbitration shown by NGOs, scholars and others. The ICSID Secretariat officially kicked off research for improvement of ICSID arbitration in 2004. In a report released in October 2004, entitled "Possible Improvement of the Framework for ICSID Arbitration", the ICSID identified a number of outstanding issues where improvements may be needed, including, *inter alia*, publication of awards and access of third parties to ICSID arbitration.[58]

As a result, the ICSID amended its arbitration rules in 2006, which incorporates several procedural innovations. As suggested by some commentators, the amendments made improvements in three major aspects regarding the transparency of ICSID arbitration, including the opening of hearing, the publication of arbitral awards and the admission of *amicus* briefings.[59]

Regarding the opening of hearings, the amendments authorize ICSID tribunals to allow third parties to attend or observe oral hearings if none of the disputing parties to the proceedings objects, and after consultation with the ICSID Secretary-General. They further require the tribunals to preside over open proceedings to "establish procedures for the protection of proprietary or privileged information".[60] In contrast, the old ICSID Arbitration Rules only allowed the tribunal to open hearings to third parties if the disputing parties agree.

Regarding the publication of awards, though the amendments do not authorize the ICSID to publish the awards without the consent of the parties, they provide that the ICSID "shall promptly" publish "excerpts of the legal reasoning" of the tribunal, without being subject to the consent of the disputing parties.[61] In contrast, the old ICSID Arbitration Rules only gave the ICSID discretion to publish "excerpts of the legal rules" of awards in the absence of disputing parties' consent.

Regarding the admission of *amicus* briefings, the amendments add an entirely new subsection entitled "submissions of non-disputing parties". Under the subsection, ICSID arbitral tribunals are expressly authorized to accept submissions from non-disputing "persons or entities" at their discretion, while the disputants, i.e. investors and the host states, are not able to either jointly or individually veto the tribunal's decision to accept *amicus* submissions.[62] The issue of amicus curiae participation in ISA will be further elaborated in the next section.

In general, the amendments represent an intelligible and well-intentioned response to perceived concerns with the ICSID arbitral process, but transparency improvements made by the amendments seem moderate and conservative.[63] First, although the procedural direction of ICSID tribunals is enhanced, the exercise of the discretion remains dependent on the consent of the disputing parties to a large extent. Second, the amendments only stress publication of awards but not all types of ISA-related documents. For such reasons, the amendments have been criticized for failing to meet the basic principle of transparency as "only the prompt, complete and accessible publication of all awards, interim and final, meets the basic principles of transparency".[64]

It is hard to assess whether the amendments are satisfactorily helpful in improving the transparency of ICSID arbitration. Yet, as J. Wong and J. Yackee have observed, by granting arbitrators more discretion and an obligation to making ICSID arbitration more transparent, the amendments represent a partial move away from the traditional version of international commercial arbitration and a corresponding shift towards something closer to a domestic litigation model.[65]

The UNCITRAL Transparency Rules

Existing arbitration rules in general provide for a limited level of transparency.[66] Though the UNCITRAL Arbitration Rules are frequently applied in international arbitration, including ISA, the existence and information of the arbitration were often not made public, even where important public policies were involved or illegal or corrupt business practices were uncovered.[67]

To respond to the call for more transparency in ISA, the UNCITRAL Transparency Rules were drafted and adopted, taking effect on 1 April 2014. The Rules shall be applied to ISA cases initiated under the UNCITRAL Arbitration Rules pursuant to an IIA concluded on or after 1 April 2014, unless the contracting states have agreed otherwise.[68] Thus, the Rules actually adopt a "default application" mode, which increases the chances for the Rules to be applied. With regard to ISA cases initiated before 1 April 2014, the Rules may also apply if the disputing parties so agree or if the contracting states to an IIA so agree after 1 April 2014.[69]

It is noteworthy that the Rules provide that transparency decisions should be made by the arbitral tribunals at their discretion. In general, there is no need for the tribunals to obtain consent from the disputing parties on an *ad hoc* basis. In particular, when making such decisions, the tribunals shall take into consideration the public interest in the transparency of treaty-based ISA.[70] In order to incorporate the UNCITRAL Transparency Rules, the UNCITRAL Arbitration Rules have also been revised in 2013.[71]

Without exploring the provisions of the UNCITRAL Transparency Rules in detail, one may find that the Rules cover a wide range of arbitral issues, including publication of information, publication of documents, submissions by third parties, submissions by non-disputing contracting states, and opening of hearings. Compared with other major rules, the UNCITRAL Transparency Rules "go a step further than the ICSID and the PCA Rules" in providing broader public access to key documents prepared during the course of proceedings.[72]

The Mauritius Transparency Convention

The Mauritius Transparency Convention is designed to provide a mechanism for the application of the UNCITRAL Transparency Rules to arbitrations arising under IIAs concluded before 1 April 2014.[73] In the preamble, the Convention clearly recognizes the need for provisions on transparency in the settlement of treaty-based ISA cases to take account of the public interest involved in ISA. Once the Convention enters into force, it will operate to constitute consent by the contracting states for the UNCITRAL Transparency Rules to be applied in proceedings, whether or not conducted under the UNICTRAL Arbitration Rules, brought under pre-April 2014 investment treaties to which they are party.[74]

Non-disputing party (amicus curiae) participation in ISA

Since the 1990s, non-disputing parties (herein used interchangeably with amicus curiae) have become more prominent before international jurisdictions, such as the WTO, ITLOS, ICJ, ECHR and some special international criminal tribunals (such as ICTY and ICTR), and this trend is likely to continue with the increased influence of non-state actors at the international level.[75] Amicus curiae participation in international adjudication has both pros and cons. On one hand, it helps protect public interests, enhance ISA transparency, improve the quality of the award and engage public scrutiny of the adjudication; on the other hand, it may also delay the process, increase costs, disregard the consent of the disputing parties and interfere with their strategies.[76]

In international investment law, amicus curiae participation in ISA is becoming a fixture in cases involving important public policy considerations.[77] Given that no uniform rules governing the admission of amicus curiae participation have been established in the international sphere,[78] arbitrators are authorized by many IIAs and arbitration rules to determine whether and how *amici* should be allowed on an *ad hoc* basis. NGOs and civil society groups are among the first and the major *amici* to be granted "third-party intervention rights" in ISA cases.[79] Intergovernmental organizations and state governments can also be *amici*. For instance, Achmea v. Slovak[80] is deemed a "significant milestone" in ISA history with regard to amicus curiae participation, not only because the *amicus* submissions were made by an intergovernmental organization (the EC) and a sovereign state (the Netherlands), but because, importantly, the *amicus* submissions were made at the invitation of the tribunal.[81]

In practice, amicus curiae participation in ISA typically requires accessing key arbitral documents, attending the oral hearings and submitting *amicus* briefings. The first two requirements fall under adjudicatory transparency. This section will focus on the issue of amicus curiae participation in ISA by drawing lessons from ISA practices.

NAFTA Chapter Eleven arbitration experiences

To some extent, arbitral tribunals under NAFTA Chapter Eleven can be seen as major supporters and rule-shapers with regard to amicus curiae participation in ISA. NAFTA tribunals have shown themselves to be responsive to concerns about transparency,[82] and their practices regarding transparency and amicus curiae participation in ISA, as well as their acceptance by the Free Trade Commission of NAFTA (FTC), are encouraging.[83]

Methanex v. U.S. is the first case to recognize the "privilege" of third-party participation in ISA proceedings as amicus curiae.[84] In this case, NAFTA Chapter Eleven and the UNCITRAL Arbitration Rules were applied. Several NGOs asked the tribunal for permission to submit written *amicus* briefs, to be granted access to the records of the arbitration, to make oral submissions in support of the written briefs, and to have observer status at the oral hearings.

The U.S. and Canada (non-party contracting state) supported amicus curiae participation, but Methanex and Mexico (non-party contracting state) opposed, raising concerns over the jurisdiction, confidentiality and fairness of the arbitral proceedings.

Neither NAFTA Chapter Eleven nor the UNCITRAL Arbitration Rules contains explicit rules on amicus curiae participation. The tribunal nonetheless decided to allow submission of *amicus* briefs, despite the objection of one of the disputing parties. According to the tribunal, Article 15 (1) of the UNCITRAL Arbitration Rules grants the tribunal discretion to conduct the arbitration "in a manner it considers appropriate, provided the parties are treated with equality and that at any stage of the proceedings each party is given a full opportunity of presenting his case". The tribunal found that "allowing a third person to make an *amicus* submission could fall within its procedural powers over the conduct of the arbitration, within the general scope of Article 15 (1) of the UNCITRAL Arbitration Rules".[85] In particular, the tribunal cited public interest as the main justification for exercising its discretion in allowing amicus curiae participation, holding that,

> There is undoubtedly public interest in this arbitration. The substantive issues extend far beyond those raised by the usual transnational arbitration between commercial parties. This is not merely because one of the Disputing Parties is a State: there are of course disputes involving States which are of no greater general public importance than a dispute between private persons. The public interest in this arbitration arises from its subject matter, as powerfully suggested in the Petitions. There is also a broader argument, as suggested by the Respondent and Canada: the Chapter 11 arbitral process could benefit from being perceived as more open or transparent or conversely be harmed if seen as unduly secretive. In this regard, the tribunal's willingness to receive amicus submissions might support the process in general and this arbitration in particular, whereas a blanket refusal could do positive harm.[86]

Another milestone NAFTA case is UPS v. Canada.[87] In this case, UPS, a U.S. investor, alleged, *inter alia*, that Canada Post engaged in unfair competition acts and that Canada failed to accord to it national treatment under NAFTA Article 1102 and MST in accordance with international law under NAFTA Article 1105. The Canadian Union of Postal Workers and the Council of Canadians request to be granted standing as parties to the arbitral proceedings; and in case of denial, the right to intervene as *amici curiae*. Canada and the U.S. supported the view that the arbitral tribunal is authorized to accept written *amici* submissions from third parties, while Mexico disagreed. Similar to Methanex v. U.S., the tribunal in UPS v. Canada allowed *amici* submissions based on two grounds: first, it has broad procedural discretion in conducting the arbitration according to Article 15(1) of the UNCITRAL Arbitration Rules;[88] second, the subject matter of this case involves important public interests.[89]

With regard to amicus curiae participation, the factual backgrounds and the decisions in Methanex v. U.S. and UPS v. Canada are quite similar. First, though both tribunals allowed amicus curiae participation, neither has made clear the assessment criteria. Second, in the absence of a provision of amicus curiae participation in NAFTA Chapter Eleven, the tribunals made their decisions through exercising their procedural discretion under Article 15 (1) of the UNCITRAL Arbitration Rules. Third, the tribunals held that consideration of public interest is an important rationale underlying their decisions.

The development of the rules regarding amicus curiae participation in NAFTA Chapter Eleven arbitration is largely driven by NAFTA jurisprudence. The decisions in Methanex v. U.S. and UPS v. Canada helped shape these rules. These decisions were quickly ratified by the three NAFTA states, who, acting as the FTC, issued a binding interpretation of NAFTA.[90] This interpretation not only makes clear that "no provision of the NAFTA limits a tribunal's discretion to accept written submissions from a person or entity that is not a disputing party", but also lays down the application requirements as well as the assessment criteria for determination of non-disputing party participation.[91] Especially when deciding amicus curiae participation in ISA, the tribunal will consider the following factors, among other things,

a) the non-disputing party submission would assist the Tribunal in the determination of a factual or legal issue related to the arbitration by bringing a perspective, particular knowledge or insight that is different from that of the disputing parties;
b) the non-disputing party submission would address matters within the scope of the dispute;
c) the non-disputing party has a significant interest in the arbitration; and
d) there is a public interest in the subject matter of the arbitration.[92]

These criteria, though not exhaustive, help clarify the standard of NAFTA tribunals in assessing the issue of amicus curiae participation. It should be noted that although this issue is in nature a procedural one, the decision of this issue nevertheless necessitates consideration of non-procedural factors. As seen in the NAFTA cases, public interest in the subject matter of the arbitration plays an indispensable role when making amicus curiae participation decisions.

ICSID arbitration experiences

Compared with NAFTA Chapter Eleven arbitration, the development of the rules of amicus curiae participation in ICSID arbitration is a different story. The ICSID amicus curiae participation rules were developed chiefly through the institutional efforts of the ICSID, rather than by jurisprudence developed by ICSID tribunals.

ICSID tribunals were originally not willing to grant permission to amicus curiae participation in arbitration absent the disputing parties' consent.[93] In an early ICSID cases, Aguas del Tunari v. Bolivia,[94] the two disputing parties concluded a concession agreement for exclusive provision of water and sewerage services as part of the respondent state's efforts of privatization of its water service industry in its third largest city. In 2001, the Claimant submitted a claim to the ICSID, alleging that Bolivia's various acts and omissions have led to the rescission of the concession agreement and constituted a breach of the provisions of the Bolivia–Netherland BIT.

During the arbitration proceeding, two NGOs submitted a "Petition to the Tribunal", requesting, *inter alia*, "standing to participate as parties" in the proceedings; and in the alternative, "the right to participate in such proceedings as *amici curiae*" at all stages of the arbitration. Especially, they requested the tribunals' permission to make submissions concerning the procedures by which this arbitration will be conducted, the arbitrability of the matters and the merits of the claims. They also sought the tribunal's permission to attend all hearings, make oral presentations during hearings and have immediate access to all submissions made to the tribunal.[95] To justify their request, the NGOs cited public interest as the ground, arguing that "the resolution of this claim will directly affect both the specific interests of Petitioners" and that "the award is likely to affect issues of broad public concern".[96]

The tribunal, after "extended and serious consideration", rejected these requests for three reasons. First, there is no authority and power entrusted in the tribunal to make the decision, while the interplay between the applicable BIT and the ICSID Convention and the consensual nature of arbitration should be considered to decide this issue. Second, the disputing parties did not consent to amicus curiae participation. Third, there is no need for witness or non-party submission at the jurisdictional stage. Especially, the tribunal unanimously held that,

> In particular, it is manifestly clear to the Tribunal that it does not, absent the agreement of the Parties, have the power to join a non-party to the proceedings; to provide access to hearings to non-Parties and, *a fortiori*, to the public generally; or to make the documents of the proceedings public.[97]

This decision has been criticized for ignoring reasonable exceptions of the public.[98] It is particularly surprising considering that this decision was made after the decisions of Methanex v. U.S. and UPS v. Canada became widely known. To some extent, such criticism has prompted the ICSID to reflect and reform its arbitration rules. In the 2004 ICSID Report, the ICSID Secretariat recognizes the transparency gap between NAFTA Chapter Eleven arbitration and ICSID arbitration and acknowledges the need to revise the ICSID Arbitration Rules, stating that,

> In two recent investor-to-State arbitrations governed by the Arbitration Rules of the United Nations Commission on International Trade Law (UNCITRAL), a form of arbitration that is also often mentioned in

investment treaties, the tribunals confirmed that they had broad authority to accept and consider submissions from third parties. Arbitrations under the ICSID and Additional Facility Arbitration Rules have not yielded similar precedents. There may well be cases where the process could be strengthened by submissions of third parties, not only civil society organizations but also for instance business groups or, in investment treaty arbitrations, the other States parties to the treaties concerned. It might therefore be useful to make clear that the tribunals have the authority to accept and consider submissions from third parties.[99]

Two years later, in Suez v. Argentina,[100] another ICSID tribunal made a different amicus curiae participation decision. This case concerned a concession agreement between the investor and Argentina regarding water and sewage services. During the arbitral proceeding, several NGOs requested to attend the oral hearing, submit *amici* briefs and be granted unlimited access to the arbitral documents.

The tribunal first recognized that neither the ICSID Convention nor the ICSID Arbitration Rules specifically authorize or specifically prohibit the submission of *amici* briefs. However, unlike in Aguas del Tunari v. Bolivia, the tribunal found that it had discretion in deciding the issue of amicus curiae participation by referring to Article 44 of the ICSID Convention. This Article provides that "If any question of procedure arises which is not covered by this Section or the Arbitration Rules or any rules agreed by the parties, the Tribunal shall decide the question". In interpreting this Article, the tribunal found Article 15 (1) of the UNCITRAL Rules as interpreted by the tribunal in Methanex v. U.S. is "substantially similar to" Article 44 of the ICSID Convention. Finally, the tribunal unanimously ruled that "Article 44 of the ICSID Convention grants it the power to admit amicus curiae submissions from suitable non-parties in appropriate cases".[101]

The tribunal further discussed the conditions for the admission of *amici* submissions by reviewing the amicus curiae practices in other jurisdictions. It identified three conditions. First, the appropriateness of the subject matter of the case. Second, the suitability of a given non-party to act as amicus curiae in that case. Third, the procedure by which the *amicus* submission is made and considered.[102] These tests, according to the tribunal at a later stage of the proceedings, are in accord with Rule 37 (2) of the 2006 amendment to the ICSID Arbitration Rules.[103] The tribunal especially stressed the public interest involved in the subject matter of this case when making the amicus curiae decision, holding that,

> In examining the issues at stake in the present case, the Tribunal finds that the present case potentially involves matters of public interest … The factor that gives this case particular public interest is that the investment dispute centres around the water distribution and sewage systems of a large metropolitan area, the city of Buenos Aires and surrounding municipalities. Those

systems provide basic public services to millions of people and as a result may raise a variety of complex public and international law questions, including human rights considerations. Any decision rendered in this case, whether in favour of the Claimants or the Respondent, has the potential to affect the operation of those systems and thereby the public they serve.[104]

Partly as a result of these efforts, the 2006 amendment to the ICSID Arbitration Rules added a completely new subsection (Rule 37.2), dealing exclusively with amicus curiae participation in ICSID arbitration. This subsection provides that:

Rule 37
Visits and Inquiries;
Submissions of Non-disputing Parties

After consulting both parties, the Tribunal may allow a person or entity that is not a party to the dispute (in this Rule called the "non-disputing party") to file a written submission with the Tribunal regarding a matter within the scope of the dispute. In determining whether to allow such a filing, the Tribunal shall consider, among other things, the extent to which:

a)   the non-disputing party submission would assist the Tribunal in the determination of a factual or legal issue related to the proceeding by bringing a perspective, particular knowledge or insight that is different from that of the disputing parties;
b)   the non-disputing party submission would address a matter within the scope of the dispute;
c)   the non-disputing party has a significant interest in the proceeding.

The Tribunal shall ensure that the non-disputing party submission does not disrupt the proceeding or unduly burden or unfairly prejudice either party, and that both parties are given an opportunity to present their observations on the non-disputing party submission.

The amendments represent an improvement with respect to amicus curiae participation in ICSID arbitration. Under Rule 37 (2), an ICSID tribunal shall have full discretion in making amicus curiae participation decisions, subject only to an obligation to first consult with the disputing parties.[105]

Since the adoption of the amendments, there have been a number of ICSID cases in which amicus curiae participation requests were submitted to and partially granted by the tribunals, such as Biwater v. Tanzania, Piero Foresti v. South Africa,[106] Bernard von Pezold v. Zimbabwe[107] and Border Timbers v. Zimbabwe.[108]

The first ICSID case to apply the revised Rule 37(2) is Biwater v. Tanzania. In this landmark case, in 2006, several NGOs submitted a joint request to the tribunal and demanded a status as *amici*, access to key arbitration documents and permission to attend oral hearings, relying on the decision in Methanex v. U.S.[109] The tribunal followed the tests established in the revised Rule 37 (2) and found that all three tests were satisfied, and granted the petition partially.[110] Although the tribunal also mentioned public interest by referring to the jurisprudence established in Methanex v. U.S. and Suez v. Argentina,[111] it is unclear how much weight the tribunal put on public interest consideration in making the amicus curiae participation decision.

Despite its merits, Rule 37(2) could be the "Achilles' heel" of ICSID arbitration. First, unlike the FTC interpretation of the NAFTA, this rule lists three considerations, which do not include public interest as a test when making amicus curiae participation decisions. What is included, however, is "interest of the non-disputing party". True, this Rule does not automatically exclude public interest consideration since, on the one hand, given the non-exhaustive nature of the list, an ICSID tribunal may still take public interest into account; on the other hand, ISA jurisprudence does not draw a clear line between "public interest" and "the interest of the non-disputing party". However, the silence of revised Rule 37(2) seems to suggest that the ICSID Arbitration Rules do not make public interest a compulsory factor when making amicus curiae participation decisions. Thus, whether public interest should be considered and what weight to be given thereto would rest on the tribunal's discretion.

Second, the rule of amicus curiae participation does not operate in isolation. Rather, the proper operation of this rule interacts with other transparency obligations. Thus, without the overall lift of the transparency obligations, even amicus curiae participation in ISA is generously allowed by ICSID arbitrators its positive effects may still be limited. On this point, it has been suggested that,

> The theory of *amicus* submissions rests at least partially on the notion that amici will provide tribunals with relevant arguments that the parties will not, or cannot, provide themselves. Without prior access to party submissions, amici will have, at most, a merely speculative sense of the factual and legal arguments that the parties have made or intend to make, and will probably tend to offer tribunals arguments largely redundant to, or even irrelevant to, those contained in party submissions.[112]

In a sense, it seems that public interest is stressed less in ICSID arbitration than in NAFTA arbitration in making amicus curiae participation decisions. An explanation of such a difference lies in the different decision-making mechanism under the NAFTA and ICSID regimes. Considering the sharp difference of the number of contracting states of the NAFTA and the ICSID Convention, rule-making in the ICSID regime is more difficult than in the NAFTA regime.[113]

The establishment of an ISDS appeal mechanism

Compared with litigation, arbitration is known as a single-instance dispute settlement alternative, for the sake of efficiency. In other words, "the goal of correctness yields to the goal of finality".[114] However, there is a growing call that the pursuit of efficiency should not be pursued at the cost of fair and just adjudication, which necessitates an appeal mechanism in ISDS. In international adjudication, an appeal mechanism is especially necessary since it is a warranted means to harmonize an increasingly fragmented international jurisprudence and law, aiming at achieving a higher level of consistency.[115]

There are several reasons to justify the creation of an appeal mechanism in the existing ISDS system. First, states and investors have increasing concerns over the inconsistency and incoherence of ISA jurisprudence. An appeal mechanism can be helpful in addressing such concerns. Second, unlike commercial arbitration, ISA involves sovereign states' exercise of public authorities that may have profound and harmful effects on aliens and their properties. Thus, the legal, diplomatic and social consequences of ISA are more profound than those of commercial arbitration. Third, even if a second-instance proceeding is allowed for ISA under some treaties, national laws and institutional arbitration rules, such proceeding cannot address the inconsistency concern because it is strictly confined to the prescribed procedural aspects. For instance, though the ICSID Convention provides for an annulment mechanism,[116] this mechanism is fundamentally different from an appeal mechanism because "annulment is only concerned with the legitimacy of the process of decision. It is not concerned with its substantive correctness".[117] Likewise, though judicial review of foreign arbitral awards by national courts is allowed under the New York Convention, such review is strictly confined to several prescribed procedural aspects of arbitration and public policy.[118]

In the international sphere, the discussion of an appeal mechanism in ISDS is highlighted in the 2004 ICSID Report, which explores, *inter alia*, the necessity and possibility of establishing an appeal mechanism in the ICSID arbitration system.[119] According to the Report, by as early as mid-2005, as many as twenty states may have signed IIAs with provisions on an appeal mechanism for ISA awards.[120] However, in a follow-up report, the ICSID, after carefully analysing the pros and cons of an appeal mechanism, suggested that, though an appeal mechanism is conducive to the consistency and coherence of ICSID case law, "it would be premature to attempt to establish such an ICSID mechanism at this stage".[121]

This view is shared by some commentators as well. For instance, B. Legum has observed that the current environment of international investment law is "ill-suited to appeals" and that the need for an appeal mechanism in ISDS has not been established.[122] Especially, he mentioned that even if an appeal mechanism is established, it is not likely to be able to address the consistency concern of ISA, arguing that,

> But the different decisions stemmed from a contrasting appreciation of the facts of the case, not from a fundamentally different understanding of the applicable law. Under the model of appellate review adopted by the few international appellate bodies in existence today, this difference in

appreciation of the facts would be corrected on appeal only if no reasonable arbitrator could have possibly so understood the facts of the case.[123]

In the national plane, many states have positively responded to an appeal mechanism in ISDS. The EU seems to be a pioneer of trying to establish an appeal mechanism in ISDS. In the CETA investment chapter, an appeal mechanism is made possible according to its Article entitled "Appellate Tribunal".[124] The appellate mechanism has several features. First, it can be initiated "unilaterally" by any disputing party, and no agreement between the disputing parties is required.[125] Second, the Appellate Tribunal may review both procedural and substantive aspects of an ISA award, such as the application and interpretation of applicable law, and the appreciation of facts and domestic law. It also has the competence of upholding, modifying or reversing an ISA award.[126] Such competence distinguishes this mechanism from the ICSID annulment mechanism and the judicial review under the New York Convention.

In the U.S., the discussion of an appeal mechanism for ISDS moved into the mainstream since 2002, when the U.S. Congress enacted the Bipartisan Trade Promotion Authority Act, which identified for U.S. FTAs a negotiating objective of "providing for an appellate body or similar mechanism to provide coherence to the interpretations of investment provisions in trade agreements".[127] Thus in a number of IIAs, the U.S. and its partner states have expressed the possibility of establishing an appeal mechanism for review of ISA awards, such as the investment chapter of the Singapore–U.S. FTA[128] and the 2012 U.S. Model BIT.[129]

Other states have also shown an interest in an appeal mechanism in ISDS. For instance, the investment chapter of the 2015 Australia–China FTA provides that the contracting states shall conduct negotiations with regard to the establishment of an appellate mechanism to review ISA awards rendered under this chapter, and such review shall not only cover procedural issues, but also "questions of law".[130]

Admittedly, an appeal mechanism could be helpful in ensuring the consistency and coherence of ISA jurisprudence. However, such a function should not be overstated. As these appeal mechanisms are established under specific IIAs, and IIAs remain fragmented globally, it is difficult for the IIA-specific appeal mechanisms to address the consistency concern of ISA jurisprudence satisfactorily at the global level. In this sense, an international investment court could be of help. Though the EU has put forward a long-term perspective of establishing such a court system,[131] it remains to be seen whether the international community, especially major economic powers, would truly support this proposal.

Interstate consultation mechanism provisions

States are the contracting parties of IIAs. Cooperation between states is important for the enforcement of IIA obligations. Most IIAs provides for an interstate consultation mechanism. This can play a facilitative role in helping the contracting states achieve sustainable development goals without breaking their IIA commitments. Interstate consultation may occur for both cooperation and dispute settlement purposes and may take different forms.

Interstate consultation for cooperation purpose

Interstate consultation may occur for cooperation purposes. Some recent IIAs provide for a requirement of interstate consultation, mainly for facilitating cooperation between the contracting states.

The 2012 China–Canada BIT is an example. Article 18 of this BIT, entitled "Consultation", makes it possible for the contracting states to consult for various purposes.[132] Especially, this Article calls for interstate consultation for addressing environmental issues.[133] According to the drafters of this BIT, the main purpose of this Article is to affirm that the contracting states should not encourage investment by sacrificing the environment. Thus in a case where one of the contracting states offers such encouragement, the other party is entitled to request consultations to address such concerns.[134] In this sense, this Article helps establish a workable mechanism for the contracting states to discuss and settle environmental issues, which is helpful to the contracting states in preserving regulatory power in making environmental policies.[135]

Similarly, the 2012 U.S. Model BIT contains an interstate consultation provision with regard to labour rights issues, providing that a contracting state may request consultations with the other Party regarding any matter arising under this Article, and the other contracting state shall respond to this request within thirty days and shall thereafter "consult and endeavor to reach a mutually satisfactory resolution".[136] Similarly, such an interstate consultation mechanism is created for the contracting states in better to understand and coordinate their labour rights policies.

Interstate consultation for dispute settlement purposes

Interstate consultation is commonly used in confrontational occasions, as a form of state intervention in the settlement of interstate or investor–state disputes. There are some typical occasions where interstate consultation is necessitated for dispute settlement purposes.

First, states are under an obligation to settle disputes in a peaceful manner and in good faith under general international law.[137] It is almost universal that IIAs contain provisions for settling disputes relating to the interpretation and application of the IIAs between the contracting states through consultation, other diplomatic means and arbitration.[138] Such provision often requires the disputing states to try to settle the dispute through friendly consultation before resorting to other recourses. For instance, Article 37(1) of the 2012 U.S. Model BIT provides in relevant part that,

Subject to paragraph 5, any dispute between the Parties concerning the interpretation or application of this Treaty, that is not resolved through consultations or other diplomatic channels, shall be submitted on the request of either Party to arbitration for a binding decision or award by a tribunal in accordance with applicable rules of international law.

Second, interstate consultation may be an implied prerequisite for the initiation or continuation of ISA of certain types of investment disputes, such as those relating to tax or financial (prudential) measures. Under such provisions, if an investor intends to claim that a tax or financial measure of a contracting state constitutes an act of expropriation, the investor must refer this dispute to the competent authorities of both contracting states. The two authorities have exclusive competence in deciding whether the measure constitutes expropriation within a certain period of time before the investor can submit the dispute to ISA.[139]

Last but not the least, interstate consultation may also be an implied requirement during ISA proceedings. Some IIAs provide an opportunity for jointly interpreting IIA for the contracting states during the course of ISA, thus restricting the arbitrators' treaty-interpretation power. For instance, according to the NAFTA, the FTC, composed of representatives of the contracting states or their designees, has the power to, *inter alia*, "resolve disputes that may arise regarding its interpretation or application."[140] The FTC's interpretation of the NAFTA is binding on Chapter Eleven arbitral tribunals.[141] Such a joint interpretation mechanism by a non-judicial or political body is unique and has profoundly influenced the IIA-making of NAFTA contracting states with many third states.[142] In a number of NAFTA Chapter Eleven cases, such as Pope & Talbot v. Canada,[143] Mondev v. U.S.,[144] ADF v. U.S.,[145] Waste Management v. Mexico,[146] Methanex v. U.S. and UPS v. Canada, the FTC issued joint interpretations of a pertinent NAFTA provision while the arbitral proceedings were pending.

In the first scenario, interstate consultation is an express requirement of the IIA. In the second and third instances, interstate consultation is not an express requirement. However, for the purpose of issuing joint interpretations or achieving mutual decisions, consultation seems inevitable and indispensable. In this sense, interstate consultation can be deemed an implied requirement.

Conclusion

Procedural provisions of IIAs often aim at shaping a dispute settlement mechanism tailored specifically for investment disputes. The existing ISA system has its origins in international commercial arbitration and shares the various characteristics thereof. Yet, as ISA involves sovereign states, it acquires a strong public nature. Such a nature has been widely recognized in practice, giving rise to high tension between the two arbitration systems.

The incompatibility of the two arbitration systems is a contributing factor to the legitimacy crisis of ISA and of international investment law at large. To help confront this crisis, various procedural innovations have been made in IIAs and major arbitration rules. Among these innovations, rules of ISA transparency, amicus curiae participation in ISA, and the appeal mechanism of the ISDS system seem outstanding. These innovations may directly serve sustainable development goals. Greater procedural transparency (including amicus curiae participation) in ISA represents a core element of good governance and the rule of law, and an opportunity to appeal is an important step in delivering justice. Good governance and access to justice are important constituent principles of sustainable development. In this sense, the procedural innovations of IIAs and arbitration rules help make IIAs more compatible with sustainable development.

Besides, other procedural provisions in IIAs may also contribute to sustainable development in an indirect manner. Proper compromissory clauses may restrict foreign investors to submit sustainable development disputes to ISA, such as those relating to environment, labour rights and transparency. Interstate consultation clauses enable states to consult certain sustainable development issues or to intervene in ISA proceedings when necessary. They may play a role of restricting or defining the scope of the adjudicative power of arbitrators.

It should be noted that the application of the procedural provisions in IIAs rely heavily on the discretion of arbitrators. Thus in ISA cases involving sustainable development elements, arbitrators are expected to play a critical role not only in ensuring the smooth progress of the arbitration proceedings, but they can also play an important role in ensuring that sustainable development elements are not marginalized in the course of dispute settlement.

Notes

1   See generally M. Chi, "From Europeanization toward Americanization: The Shift of China's Dichotomic Investment Treaty-Making Strategy", 23 (2) *Canadian Foreign Policy Journal* 158 (2017).

2   UNCTAD, "Investor–State Disputes: Prevention and Alternatives to Arbitration", *UNCTAD Series on International Investment Policies for Development* (2010), available at http://unctad.org/en/docs/diaeia200911_en.pdf, at 3.

3   B. Simma, "Foreign Investment Arbitration: A Place for Human Rights?", 60 (4) *International and Comparative Law Quarterly* 573 (2011), at 574–575.

4   ICSID, "The ICSID Caseload – Statistics" (Issue 2016-2), available at https://icsid.worldbank.org/apps/icsidweb/resources/pages/icsid-caseload-statistics.aspx, at 7.

5   See C. Reiner and C. Schreuer, "Human Rights and International Investment Arbitration", in P. M. Dupuy, F. Francioni and E. U. Petersmann (eds.), *Human Rights in International Investment Law and Arbitration* (Oxford: Oxford University Press, 2009), at 83.

6   See e.g. T. W. Wälde, "Procedural Challenges in Investment Arbitration under the Shadow of the Dual Role of the State–Asymmetries and Tribunals' Duty to Ensure, Pro-actively, the Equality of Arms", 26 *Arbitration International* 3, (2010), at 4–5.

7   See e.g. S. W. Schill, "W(h)ither Fragmentation? On the Literature and Sociology of International Investment Law", 22 *European Journal of International Law* 875 (2011), at 888.

8   See A. Roberts, "Clash of Paradigms: Actors and Analogies Shaping the Invest-ment Treaty Regime", 107 (1) *American Journal of International Law* 45 (2013).

9   See H. Bagner, "Confidentiality – A Fundamental Principle in International Commercial Arbitration?", 18 (2) *Journal of International Arbitration* 243 (2001), at 244–245.

10   See F. De Ly, M. Friedman and L. R. di Brozolo, "Confidentiality in International Commercial Arbitration", 28 (3) *Arbitration International* 355 (2012), at 355–396.

11   M. Gehring and M. Scherer, "Public Interest in Investment Arbitration", in D. Euler, M. Gehring and M. Scherer (eds.), *Transparency in International Investment Arbitration: A Guide to the UNCITRAL Rules of Transparency in Treaty-Based Investor–State Arbitration* (Cambridge: Cambridge University Press, 2015), at 8.

12   G. B. Born and E. G. Shenkman, "Confidentiality and Transparency in Commercial and Investor–State International Arbitration", in C. A. Rogers and R. P. Alford (eds.), *The Future of Investment Arbitration* (Oxford: Oxford University Press, 2009), at 6.

13   A. Roberts (2013), at 48; T. Ishikawa, "Third Party Participation in Investment Treaty Arbitration", 59 *International and Comparative Law Quarterly* 373, (2010), at 375; J. E. Viñuales, "Amicus Intervention in Investor–State Arbitration", 61 *Dispute Resolution Law Journal* 72 (2006), at 75; Y. Fortier, "The Occasionally Unwarranted Assumption of Confidentiality", 15 *Arbitration International* 131 (1999), at 131.

14   See C. G. Buys, "The Tension between Confidentiality and Transparency in Inter-national Arbitration", 14 (1) *American Review of International Arbitration* 121 (2003).

15   See e.g. S. D. Franck (2005).

16   See B. Stern, "Civil Society's Voice in the Settlement of International Economic Disputes", 22 (2) *ICSID Review* 280 (2007), at 347.

17   See generally A. Asteriti and C. Tams, "Transparency and Representation of the Public Interest in Investment Treaty Arbitration", in S. W. Schill (ed.), *International Investment Law and Comparative Public Law* (Oxford: Oxford University Press, 2011), at 792.

18   See e.g. G. van Harten, *Investment Treaty Arbitration and Public Law* (Oxford: Oxford University Press, 2007), at 5; S. W. Schill, "Enhancing International Investment Law's Legitimacy: Conceptual and Methodological Foundations of a New Public Law Approach", 52 (1) *Virginia Journal of International Law* 57 (2011), at 67.

19   See e.g. E. Levine, "Amicus Curiae in International Investment Arbitration: The Implications of an Increase in Third-Party Participation", 29 *Berkeley Journal of International Law* 200 (2011); B. Choudhury, "Recapturing Public Power: Is Investment Arbitration's Engagement of the Public Interest Contributing to the Democratic Deficit?", 41 *Vanderbilt Journal of Transnational Law* 775 (2008); A. Newcombe and A. Lemaire, "Should Amici Curiae Participate in Investment Treaty Arbitrations?", *Vindobona Journal of International Law and Arbitration* 22 (2001).

20   J. J. Coe Jr., "Transparency in the Resolution of Investor–State Disputes – Adoption, Adaptation, and NAFTA Leadership", (54) *Kansas Law Review* 1339 (2006), at 1342.

21   K. Böckstigel, "Commercial and Investment Arbitration: How Different Are They Today?", 28 (4) *Arbitration International* 577 (2012), at 587.

22   A. Roberts (2013), at 48; R. P. Buckley and P. Blyschak, "Guarding the Open Door: Non-Party Participation Before the International Centre for Settlement of Investment Disputes", 22 *Banking and Finance Law Review* 353 (2007), at 355.

23   R. Teitelbaum, "A Look at the Public Interest in Investment Arbitration: Is It Unique? What Should We Do about It?", 5 (1) *Berkeley Journal of International Law Publicist* 55 (2010), at 56.

24   United Parcel Service of America Inc. v. Government of Canada (under UNCITRAL Arbitration Rules), *Decision of the Tribunal on Petitions for Intervention and Participation as Amici Curiae* (17 October 2001), available at www.italaw.com/sites/default/files/case-documents/ita0883.pdf, at para. 70.

25   See Methanex Corporation v. U.S., *Decision of the Tribunal on Petitions from Third Persons to Intervene as "Amici Curiae"* (15 January 2001), available at www.italaw.com/sites/default/files/case-documents/ita0517_0.pdf, at para. 17.

26   Biwater Gauff (Tanzania) Ltd. v. United Republic of Tanzania (ICSID Case No. ARB/05/22), available at www.italaw.com/cases/157.

27   Biwater Gauff (Tanzania) Ltd. v. United Republic of Tanzania, Procedural Order No. 3 (29 September 2006), available at www.italaw.com/sites/default/files/case-documents/ita0089.pdf, at para. 114.

28   See G20 Trade Ministers Meeting Statement, 9–10 July 2016, Shanghai, available at www.oecd.org/daf/inv/investment-policy/G20-Trade-Ministers-Statement-July-2016.pdf, at paras. II, III AND IV.

29   S. W. Schill, "Enhancing International Investment Law's Legitimacy: Conceptual and Methodological Foundations of a New Public Law Approach", 52 (1) *Virginia Journal of International Law* 57 (2011), at 69.

30   K. F. Gómez, "Rethinking the Role of Amicus Curiae in International Investment Arbitration: How to Draw the Line Favorably for the Public Interest", 35 (2) *Fordham International Law Journal* 513 (2012), at 528.

31   See UNCTAD, "Transparency", *UNCTAD Series on Issues in International Investment Agreements* (2004), available at http://unctad.org/en/Docs/iteiit20034_en.pdf, at 13–47.

32   Ibid., at 50–54.

33   Article 21.2, ASEAN Comprehensive Investment Agreement.

34   UNCTAD, "Transparency in IIAs", *UNCTAD Series on Issues in International Investment Agreements II* (2012), available at http://unctad.org/en/PublicationsLibrary/unctaddiaeia2011d6_en.pdf, at 15.

35   See Article X, GATT 1947; Article III, GATS and Article 63, the TRIPs Agreement.

36   The reports of the panels and the AB are available at www.wto.org/english/tratop_e/dispu_e/dispu_e.htm.

37   Annex B, the SPS Agreement.

38   UN, "Report of the Secretary-General on the Rule of Law and Transitional Justice in Conflict and Post-Conflict Societies" (3 August 2004) (S/2004/616), available at www.un.org/en/ga/search/view_doc.asp?symbol=S/2004/616, at para 6.

39   Article 21.1 (a), (b) and (c), ASEAN Comprehensive Investment Agreement.

40   Article 17.2, Canada–China BIT.

41   Article 11.4, 2012 U.S. Model BIT.

42   Article 21.1 (d), ASEAN Comprehensive Investment Agreement.

43   See generally J. Maupin, "Transparency in International Investment Law: The Good, the Bad and the Murky", in A. Bianchi and A. Peters (eds.), *Transparency in International Law* (Cambridge: Cambridge University Press, 2013), at 142–170.

44   Article 29.1, 2012 U.S. Model BIT.
45   Article 29.2, 2012 U.S. Model BIT.
46   Article 8.36.1, CETA.
47   Articles 8.36.2, and 8.36.3, CETA.
48   Article 8.36.5, CETA.
49   Article 28 (1), Canada–China BIT.
50   Article 28 (3) and (4), Canada–China BIT.
51   Article 28 (2), Canada–China BIT.
52   L. Bartholomeusz, "The Amicus Curiae before International Courts and Tribunals", 5 *Non-State Actors and International Law* 209 (2005), at 211.
53   See E. Levine (2011), at 212–214.
54   See generally L. Bastin, "The Amicus Curiae in Investor–State Arbitration", 1 (3) *Cambridge Journal of International and Comparative Law* 208 (2012), at 208–214; L. Bartholomeusz (2005), at 212–272.
55   Available at https://icsid.worldbank.org/apps/ICSIDWEB/icsiddocs/Pages/ICSID-Convention-Arbitration-rules.aspx.
56   Available at www.uncitral.org/uncitral/en/uncitral_texts/arbitration/2014Transparency.html.
57   Available at www.uncitral.org/uncitral/en/uncitral_texts/arbitration/2014Transparency_Convention_status.html.
58   ICSID Secretariat, "Possible Improvement of the Framework for ICSID Arbitration", ICSID Secretariat Discussion Paper (22 October 2004), available at https://icsid.worldbank.org/apps/ICSIDWEB/resources/Documents/Possible%20Improvements%20of%20the%20Framework%20of%20ICSID%20Arbitration.pdf.
59   See J. Wong and J. Yackee, "The 2006 Procedural and Transparency-Related Amendments to the ICSID Arbitration Rules", in K. Sauvant (ed.), *Yearbook on International Investment Law and Policy 2009–2010* (Oxford: Oxford University Press, 2010), at 257–261; G. Born, S. P. Finizio, D. W. Ogden, R. D. Kent, J. V. H. Pierce and D. W. Bowker, "Investment Treaty Arbitration: ICSID Amends Investor–State Arbitration Rules", available at www.wilmerhale.com/pages/publicationsandnewsdetail.aspx?NewsPubId=90393.
60   ICSID Arbitration Rule 32.
61   ICSID Arbitration Rules 48.
62   ICSID Arbitration Rules 37 (2).
63   See J. Wong and J. Yackee (2010), at 258.
64   H. Mann, A. Cosbey, L. Peterson and K. von Moltke, "Comments on ICSID Discussion Paper, 'Possible Improvements of the Framework for ICSID Arbitration'" (2004 ICSID Report), www.iisd.org/pdf/2004/investment_icsid_response.pdf, at 8.
65   See J. Wong and J. Yackee (2010), at 272–273.
66   See OECD, "Transparency and Third Party Participation in Investor–State Dispute Settlement Procedures", OECD Working Papers on International Investment (2005/01), available at http://dx.doi.org/10.1787/524613550768, at 2.
67   L. Johnson and N. Bernasconi-Osterwalde, "New UNCITRAL Arbitration Rules on Transparency: Application, Content and Next Steps", available at http://ccsi.columbia.edu/files/2014/04/UNCITRAL_Rules_on_Transparency_commentary_FINAL.pdf, at 4.
68   Article 1.1, the UNCITRAL Transparency Rules.
69   Article 1.2, the UNCITRAL Transparency Rules.
70   Article 1.4 (a), the UNCITRAL Transparency Rules.

71   Article 1.4, the 2013 UNCITRAL Arbitration Rules.
72   See D. Wilkie, "UNCITRAL Unveils New Transparency Rules – Blazing a Trail Towards Transparency in Investor–State Arbitration?", available at http://kluwer arbitrationblog.com/2013/07/25/uncitral-unveils-new-transparency-rules-blazing-a-trail-towards-transparency-in-investor-state-arbitration/.
73   Article 1.1. the Mauritius Convention on Transparency.
74   E. Shirlow, 'A Step toward Greater Transparency: The UN Transparency Convention', available at http://kluwerarbitrationblog.com/2015/03/30/a-step-toward-greater-transparency-the-un-transparency-convention/.
75   L. Bartholomeusz (2005), at 285.
76   K. F. Gómez, "Rethinking the Role of Amicus Curiae in International Investment Arbitration: How to Draw the Line Favorably for the Public Interest", 35 (2) *Fordham International Law Journal* 513 (2012), at 543–553.
77   J. A. VanDuzer, "Enhancing the Procedural Legitimacy of Investor–State Arbitration through Transparency and Amicus Curiae Participation", 52 *McGill Law Journal* 681 (2007), at 723.
78   See e.g. UNCTAD, "Transparency", *Series on Issues in International Investment Agreements II* (2012), available at http://unctad.org/en/pages/Publication Webflyer. aspx?publicationid=425; OECD (2005/01) H. Mann, 'Reconceptualizing International Investment Law: Its Role in Sustainable Development", 17 *Lewis and Clark Law Review* 521 (2013); L. Bastin, "The *Amicus Curiae* in Investor–State Arbitration", 1 (3) *Cambridge Journal of International and Comparative Law* 208 (2012), at 208; E. Levine (2011); A. Sabater, "Towards Transparency in Arbitration (A Cautious Approach)", 5 *Berkeley Journal of International Law* 47 (2010); B. Choudhury, "Recapturing Public Power: Is Investment Arbitration's Engagement of the Public Interest Contributing to the Democratic Deficit?", 41 *Vanderbilt Journal of Transnational Law* 775 (2008); A. Newcombe and A. Lemaire (2001).
79   E. Levine (2011), at 209.
80   Achmea B.V. v. The Slovak Republic, UNCITRAL (PCA Case No. 2008-13), available at www.italaw.com/cases/417 (last accessed 20 November 2016).
81   M. Dimsey, "Submission by a Third Person", in D. Euler, M. Gehring and M. Scherer (eds.), *Transparency in International Investment Arbitration: A Guide to the UNCITRAL Rules of Transparency in Treaty-Based Investor–State Arbitration* (Cambridge: Cambridge University Press, 2015), at 153–154.
82   J. A. VanDuzer (2007), at 685.
83   See C. Forcese, "Does the Sky Fall?: NAFTA Chapter 11 Dispute Settlement and Democratic Accountability" 14 *MSU-DCL Journal of International Law* 315 (2006).
84   E. Levine (2011), at 209.
85   Methanex Corporation v. U.S. (*ad hoc* arbitration under UNCITRAL Arbitration Rules), *Decision of the Tribunal on Petitions from Third Persons to Intervene as "Amici Curiae"* (15 January 2001), available at www.italaw.com/sites/default/files/case-documents/ita0517_0.pdf, para. 31.
86   Ibid., at para. 49.
87   United Parcel Service of America Inc. v. Government of Canada (under UNCITRAL Arbitration Rules), available at www.italaw.com/cases/1138.
88   United Parcel Service of America Inc. v. Government of Canada (under UNCITRAL Arbitration Rules), *Decision of the Tribunal on Petitions for Intervention and Participation as Amici Curiae* (17 October 2001), available at www.italaw.com/sites/default/files/case-documents/ita0883.pdf, at para. 63.

89   Ibid., at para. 70.

90   J. Wong and J. Yackee (2010), at 252–253.

91   FTC, "Statement of the Free Trade Commission on Non-Disputing Party Participation", available at www.state.gov/documents/organization/38791.pdf, at paras. A.1, B.2 and B.6.

92   *Id.*, at para. B.6.

93   See E. Levine (2011), at 208.

94   Aguas del Tunari, S.A. v. Republic of Bolivia (ICSID Case No. ARB/02/3), available at www.italaw.com/cases/57.

95   Aguas del Tunari, S.A. v. Republic of Bolivia, *Petition of la Coordinadora para la Defensa del Agua y Vida, la Federacion Departmental Cochabambina de Organizaciones Regantes, Semapa Sur, Friends of the Earth-Netherlands, Oscar Oliver, Moar Fernandez, Father Luis Sanchez, and Congressman Jorge Alvarado to the Arbitral Tribunal*, available at www.italaw.com/sites/default/files/case-documents/ ita0018.pdf, at 19.

96   Ibid., at 2.

97   Aguas del Tunari, S.A. v. Republic of Bolivia, *Letter from the ICSID Tribunal to the NGOs regarding Petition to Participate as Amicus Curiae* (29 January 2003), available at www.italaw.com/sites/default/files/case-documents/ita0019_0.pdf, at 1–2.

98   See L. Mistelis, "Confidentiality and Third-Party Participation: UPS v. Canada and Methanex Corp. v. USA", in T. Weiler (ed.), *International Investment Law and Arbitration: Leading Cases from the ICSID, NAFTA, Bilateral Treaties and Customary International Law* (London: Cameron May, 2005), at 169.

99   ICSID Secretariat, 2004 ICSID Report., at 9.

100 Suez, Sociedad General de Aguas de Barcelona, S.A. and Vivendi Universal, S.A. v. Argentine Republic (ICSID Case No. ARB/03/19), available at www.italaw.com/cases/1057.

101 Suez v. Argentina, *Order in Response to a Petition for Transparency and Participation as Amicus Curiae* (19 May 2005), available at www.italaw.com/sites/default/files/ case-documents/ita0815.pdf, at paras. 8–16.

102 Ibid., at para. 17.

103 Suez v. Argentina, *Order in Response to a Petition by Five Non-Governmental Organizations for Permission to Make an Amicus Curiae Submission* (12 February 2007), available at www.italaw.com/sites/default/files/case-documents/ita0823.pdf, at para. 15.

104 Suez v. Argentina, Order of 19 May 2005, at para. 19.

105 See J. Wong and J. Yackee (2010), at 262–263.

106 Piero Foresti, Laura de Carli and Others v. The Republic of South Africa (ICSID Case No. ARB(AF)/07/01), available at www.italaw.com/cases/446 (last accessed 20 November 2016).

107 Bernhard von Pezold and Others v. Republic of Zimbabwe (ICSID Case No. ARB/10/15), available at www.italaw.com/cases/1472 (last accessed 20 November 2016).

108 Border Timbers Limited, Border Timbers International (Private) Limited & Hangani Development Co. (Private) Limited v. Republic of Zimbabwe (ICSID Case No. ARB/10/25), available at www.italaw.com/cases/1470.

109 Biwater Gauff (Tanzania) Ltd. v. United Republic of Tanzania (ICSID Case No. ARB/05/22), *Petition for Amicus Curiae Status* (27 November 2006), available at www.italaw.com/sites/default/files/case-documents/ita0090.pdf, at 1, 10–14.

110 Biwater Gauff (Tanzania) Ltd. v. United Republic of Tanzania (ICSID Case No. ARB/05/22), Procedural Order No. 5 (2 February 2007), available at www.italaw. com/sites/default/files/case-documents/ita0091_0.pdf, at para. 50.

111 Ibid., at paras. 51–52.

112 J. Wong and J. Yackee (2010), at 269.

113 Ibid., at 233.

114 C. Schreuer, "From ICSID Annulment to Appeal: Half Way Down the Slippery Slope", 10 *The Law and Practice of International Courts and Tribunals* 211 (2011), at 211.

115 N. Gal-Or, "The Concept of Appeal in International Dispute Settlement", 19 (1) *European Journal of International Law* 43 (2008), at 45.

116 Article 52(1), the ICSID Convention.

117 See C. Schreuer, "From ICSID Annulment to Appeal: Half Way Down the Slippery Slope", 10 *The Law and Practice of International Courts and Tribunals* 211 (2011), at 212.

118 See Article V, the New York Convention.

119 ICSID Secretariat, 2004 ICSID Report, at 14–16 and Annex (Possible Features of an ICSID Appeals Facility).

120 Ibid., at 14.

121 Ibid., at 4.

122 B. Legum, "Options to Establish an Appellate Mechanism for Investment Disputes", in K. Sauvant (ed.), *Appeals Mechanism in International Investment Disputes* (Oxford: Oxford University Press, 2008), 234–238.

123 Ibid., at 237.

124 Article 8.28, CETA.

125 Article 8.28.9 (a), CETA.

126 Article 8.28 (2), CETA.

127 B. Legum (2008), at 231–232.

128 Article 15.19 (10), Singapore–U.S. FTA.

129 Article 28 (1), 2012 U.S. Model BIT.

130 Article 9.23, 2015 Australia–China FTA.

131 Refer to Chapter II.

132 Article 18.1, the Canada–China BIT.

133 Article 18.3, the Canada–China BIT.

134 Ministry of Foreign Affairs, Trade and Development of Canada, *Final Environmental Assessment of the Canada–China Foreign Investment Protection Agreement (FIPA)*, available at www.international.gc.ca/trade-agreements-accords-commerciaux/agr-acc/china-chine/finalEA-china-chine-EEfinale.aspx?lang=en.

135 Manjiao Chi (2015), at 524.

136 Article 13.4, the 2012 U.S. Model BIT.

137 See e.g. Article 33, the United Nations Charter.

138 See J. W. Salacus, *The Law of Investment Treaties* (2nd edn.) (Oxford: Oxford University Press, 2015), at 399; UNCTAD, *Dispute Settlement: State-State, UNCTAD Series on Issues of International Investment Agreements* (2003), Doc. No. UNCTAD/ITE/IIT/2003/1, at 16.

139 See e.g. Article 21.2, the 2012 U.S. Model BIT; Article 21.5, the China–Japan–Korea TIT.

140 Article 2001.2, the NAFTA.

141 Article 1131.2, the NAFTA.

142   See G. Kaufmann-Kohler, "Interpretive Powers of the Free Trade Commission and the Rule of Law", in F. Bachand (ed.), *Fifteen Years of NAFTA Chapter 11 Arbitration* (New York: Juris Publishing, 2011), at 176–178.

143   Pope and Talbot Inc. v. The Government of Canada (*ad hoc* arbitration under UNCITRAL Arbitration Rules), available at www.italaw.com/cases/863).

144   Mondev International Ltd. v. United States of America (ICSID Case No. ARB(AF)/99/2), available at www.italaw.com/cases/documents/716.

145   ADF Group Inc. v. United States of America (ICSID Case No. ARB (AF)/00/1), available at www.italaw.com/cases/43.

146   Waste Management, Inc. v. United Mexican States (ICSID Case No. ARB(AF)/00/3), available at www.italaw.com/cases/1158.

Part III

Transforming IIAs to be more compatible with sustainable development

7 'Reconceptualizing' IIAs from the governance perspective

The world is in the era of globalization. A typical aspect of globalization is the emergence of technically specialized cooperation networks with a global scope, and spheres of life and expert cooperation that transgress national boundaries and are difficult to regulate through traditional international law.[1]

Globalization necessitates a paradigm shift of global investment governance. Currently, the global investment governance regime relies primarily on IIAs and ISDS, mostly at bilateral level. This regime seems inadequately compatible with the goal of global governance. A typical concern is that the current IIA and the ISDS systems are unable to satisfactorily respond to the sustainable development concerns associated with transnational investment activities. Abundant studies suggest that the root reason lies in the fact that the IIAs and ISDS systems improperly restrain states from taking necessary regulatory measures for sustainable development purposes, such as environmental and human rights protection.

States have diverse responses to such a situation. The EU has proposed to reform the current ISDS system during the course of the negotiation of the TTIP.[2] Some Latin American countries such as Bolivia, Ecuador and Venezuela, have denounced the ICSID Convention and decided to terminate their BITs.[3] Other countries, such as South Africa, conducted a constitutional review of the BIT programme and found that the current BIT system inappropriately subjects vital national interests to unpredictable international arbitration that may constitute direct challenges to legitimate, constitutional and democratic policy-making.[4]

A skeletal review of global governance

Traditionally, states are the basic units that structure international political life and the ultimate sources of legal and coercive authority within their territories. States are formally autonomous from external interference and accorded exclusive recognition of their status as such within the international community.[5] Accordingly, the space in which a state can exercise its regulatory authority is equated to its territory.

Deepening globalization has weakened such "territory-based" regulatory authority and gives rise to an urgent call for global governance. While global

DOI: 10.4324/9781315642840-11

governance has generated a great deal of discussion in recent decades, it remains as a new, vague, complex and flexible concept. Global governance can be understood from different perspectives.[6] A typical description of this concept has been given in a report entitled "Our Global Neighbourhood" issued by the Commission on Global Governance in 1995, providing the following,

> Governance is the sum of the many ways individuals and institutions, public and private, manage their common affairs. It is a continuing process through which conflicting or diverse interests may be accommodated and cooperative action may be taken. It includes formal institutions and regimes empowered to enforce compliance, as well as informal arrangements that people and institutions either have agreed to or perceive to be in their interest.

At the global level, governance has been viewed primarily as intergovernmental relationships, but it must now be understood as also involving non-governmental organizations (NGOs), citizens' movements, multinational corporations, and the global capital market. Interacting with these are global mass media of dramatically enlarged influence.[7]

Global governance has a number of distinct features. First, it implies that states no longer monopolize the law-making power, and soft-law instruments and private standards emerge as rules regulating global affairs. Second, it implies an increasing reliance on non-confrontational and cooperative law-enforcement mechanisms. Finally and fundamentally, the role of various non-state and sub-state actors in the law-making and law-enforcement processes becomes increasingly prominent.[8]

Especially, the rise of non-state actors on the stage of international affairs is probably the most striking aspect of global governance. Notwithstanding the central role states play in international affairs, states are no longer deemed as "the natural, default organizational structure of human community".[9] State authorities increasingly delegate more and more regulatory discretion to various forms of public and private, formal and informal institutions. Willingly or unwillingly, sovereigns surrender their monopoly on regulatory power, which formerly defined the notion of sovereignty, to actors whose reach defies political boundaries.[10]

Prompted partly by the shift of regulatory power from states to non-state actors, the way in which such power is exercised has also been changed. While legally binding national and international law (hard law) remain the primary normative basis for global governance, non-formal norms (e.g. soft law and private contracts) also play an important role, though soft law has been widely criticized and even dismissed as a factor in international affairs.[11] Through formal norms (international or domestic), informal standards and private contracts, global bodies, including states and non-state actors, shape the rights, interests and expectations of diverse stakeholders across political boundaries.[12] For such reasons it has been suggested that global governance actually means "governance without government".[13]

Unsurprisingly, global governance now addresses almost all areas of public and private life. It seems self-evident that the intensity, speed and volume of global interactions reflect increasing interdependence, which has nudged us toward examining international relations through the lens of global governance.[14]

To non-Westerners, global governance appears to be a "Western term", as it presumes the validity of a number of norms of "good governance" rooted in Western experiences, such as the market economy, human rights, democracy, accountability and rule of law.[15] The concept of "good governance" is described by the United Nations Economic and Social Commission for Asia and the Pacific (UNESCAP) as the following:

> Good governance has eight major characteristics. It is participatory, consensus oriented, accountable, transparent, responsive, effective and efficient, equitable and inclusive and follows the rule of law. It assures that corruption is minimized, the views of minorities are taken into account and that the voices of the most vulnerable in society are heard in decision-making. It is also responsive to the present and future needs of society.[16]

Despite its attractiveness, global governance also raises challenges. A typical challenge is that "global governance is the globalization of local governance", given that the international system is founded on the principle of national sovereignty, that the Westphalian order remains the basis of the international architecture, and that global governance can only result from the action of sovereign states.[17] Such a challenge implies that state sovereignty needs to be reconceptualized and reconstructed in the context of global governance.

The incompatibility of IIAs with global governance

In the era of globalization, investment activities become transnationalized and swiftly complicated. Globalized investment activities call for not only broader market access but also an effective global governance regime. International investment law, with IIAs as the cornerstone, appears insufficiently capable of supporting such a regime. This is mainly caused by the fragmentation of international law, state-centrism of international investment law and the inherent structural imbalance of existing IIAs.

The fragmentation of international investment law

International law is fragmented. It is often considered that international law is composed of different branches or regimes that are separate from each other, such as international investment law, international environmental law and international human rights law.[18] As insightfully pointed out by M. Koskenniemi, as international law is increasingly diversified and expansive, its various branches tend to develop their own rules and rule systems on the basis of multilateral treaties, acts of international organizations, specialized treaties and customary patterns that are tailored to the needs and interests of each branch but rarely take account of the outside world.[19]

International investment law as a specialized branch of international law is shaped and developed with the joint contribution of host states, investors and home states during the course of conducting and regulating international investment transactions.[20] Normatively, it is composed of national, contractual and international legal frameworks. The national legal framework consists of the legislation, regulations, administrative acts and judicial decisions of the governmental authorities over the investment or the investor. The contractual framework consists of various types of investment contracts governing numerous important matters relating to the organization, structure, operation and functioning of the investment and the respective rights and obligations of investors. The international legal framework for investment consists of various branches of international law and international legal institutions.[21]

The fragmentation of international law could seriously restrict the compatibility of IIAs with global governance. First, IIAs as an important norm supplier of investment governance, are separated from other branches of international law. Such separation makes it difficult for IIAs to address broader concerns associated with transnational investment activities. IIAs as *lex specialis* should be confined to determinations only of whether investor rights have been violated, while non-investment considerations, such as human rights norms or multilateral environmental commitments, cannot weigh in on that equation.[22]

Even IIAs norms *per se* are extremely fragmented. This is in sharp contrast with some other specialized bodies of international law. For example, in international trade law, WTO law provides a set of "universal trade rules" for almost all major trading countries. In comparison, few uniform rules have been established in IIAs, despite the recent normative convergence of some IIA rules. Rather, the diversity and amount of IIAs is astonishingly great. There are nearly 3000 BITs and over 300 other types of IIAs globally, and the number of IIAs is still on the rise.[23] As IIAs are mostly negotiated on a bilateral and regional basis, states are subject to different obligations and standards thereunder. This gives rise to the "spaghetti bowl phenomenon" in international investment law.[24] Furthermore, the "radiating effect" or "multilateralization effect" of MFN clauses may further complicate the existing IIA web, and create deeper uncertainty when determining states' IIA obligations.[25]

The state-centrism of international investment law

The sovereign state system, born and developed in modern Europe, was firmly established on a global scale and the independent, sovereign, nation state was a common, global institution which was adopted and taken for granted by humanity as a whole.[26] International society in the twentieth century was structured as state-centric and such a character is likely to persist.[27]

That the international society is state-centric may partly explain the state-centrism of international law, since international law is traditionally defined as the law created by and governing relations between states, which is reflected in a highly statist doctrine of sources that recognizes states, and only states, as the creators of international law.[28] The state-centric international law has several features. First, non-state actors are not deemed as "participants" in international affairs; second, many soft-law rules are excluded from the realm of international law as they are not necessarily made by states; third, international law focuses primarily on interstate relationships, and the protection of the individual rights and the common interest of the international community appears insufficient.

As can be seen, the notions of state-centrism of international law and global governance seem to conflict. While the former stresses the central role of states in international society, the latter implies surrender of the states' sovereign power. The recent developments and debates surrounding international humanitarian intervention,[29] combating terrorism,[30] and suppression of piracy[31] clearly demonstrate the compatibility gap between the state-centric international law and global governance. In light of such a gap, it has been suggested that international law should not confine itself to regulating official or public action, but must regulate action in the private sphere as well, and that international law should do more to engage non-state actors in its processes of norm-making and enforcement.[32]

To some extent, contemporary international law appears less state-centric. A distinct characteristic of contemporary international law is the wide range of participants in international affairs, which include not only states and international organizations, but also non-state actors, such as NGOs, public and private companies, and individuals.[33] The application of international law has also been expanded to areas considered to be of internal concern to the state, despite the fact that it is intended to regulate the external affairs of states with each other.[34]

International investment law as a specialized branch of international law is also state-centric. The making of international investment law is limited to states. IIAs are concluded as a result of interstate negotiations, often on a bilateral basis. Even today, states remain reluctant to include soft-law norms in IIAs in an enforceable way. Although IIAs aim primarily at protecting foreign investors and investments, private investors have no formal role to play in IIA-making. At the enforcement stage, IIAs generally grant private investors direct access to ISA. Investors may challenge the national investment governance regime of the host states. Yet such challenges are often seen by states as "attacks" on the regulatory power inherent to sovereigns.

Besides, almost all prominent proposals for reforming the existing IIA and ISA systems remain state-centred to a large extent, while a governance perspective is rarely adopted. As discussed earlier, these proposals focus primarily on "protecting state regulatory power". In contrast, they seldom deal with typical "global governance issues", such as the role of non-state actors, regulation of MNEs, major players in transnational investment activities, application of soft law norms and democracy in the IIA-making process.

The structural imbalance of IIAs

IIAs play an insufficient role as a major norm supplier for an effective global-investment governance regime. Such insufficiency is mainly caused by the structural imbalance of modern IIAs.

First and foremost, the existing IIAs fail to draw a proper balance between the rights of foreign investors and those of the host states. As R. Dolzer has pointed out, empirically speaking, IIAs contain only rights for foreign investors and very limited rights, if any, for host states.[35] As mentioned, IIAs aim primarily at protecting foreign investors and investments, though they are negotiated by states. For such reasons, IIAs are often silent on the issue of preservation and exercise of the regulatory power of host states and the engagement of other non-state actors.

Second, the existing IIAs fail to draw a proper balance between the rights and obligations of investors, which can be typically shown by the fact that they seldom incorporate provisions that directly impose obligations on foreign investors. Substantively, IIAs codify a number of international law standards for the treatment and protection of foreign investments, while investors' conduct is largely left to be regulated through national laws and non-binding soft law relating to CSR. Procedurally, IIAs grant foreign investors direct access to ISA unilaterally, but seldom grant states the same procedural rights to initiate arbitration or to raise counter-claims against investors. IIAs also fail to provide full ISA access for non-disputing party stakeholders, especially the victims of or groups affected by transnational investment activities.

Last but not the least, the existing IIAs fail to draw a balance between the protection of investments and that of public (non-investment) interest. IIAs are mainly designed to regulate the relationships between international investors, host states and home states,[36] but such a design marginalizes the protection of public interest that may be adversely affected by transnational investment activities. Though, as discussed, there is a tendency for IIAs to be made increasingly accommodating towards public interest protection, public interest provisions, such as those relating to the protection of the environment, labor rights, public safety and national security, remain insufficient in IIAs. This makes IIAs incapable of satisfactorily addressing public interest concerns associated with transnational investment activities. Recent years have witnessed a number of ISA disputes and other undesirable situations involving irresponsible investors or investments that resulted in public interest damages.[37]

The structural imbalance of IIAs is a reflection of the inappropriate division of IIA rights and obligations among the various stakeholders of transnational investment activities, including but not limited to states (host state, home state and other states), investors (foreign and national investors), impacted individuals and groups (such as NGOs, indigenous peoples) and the public. True, given the diversity of stakeholders and the complicated relationships forged therewith, it would be difficult to draw a proper balance. Besides, it is also unclear as to what constitutes proper balance. That said, there is no denying that the structural imbalance of IIAs heavily restricts IIAs from playing a more constructive role in global investment governance.

ISA and global investment governance

Though ISA has its origin in commercial arbitration, the involvement of a state transforms ISA from a mere dispute settlement mechanism to one in which the public nature of the state needs to be recognized. Reviewing and deciding on the legality of state acts by private arbitrators in accordance with rules and standards of international law could be provocative to many states. One commentator has observed that the failure of some arbitrators to recognize the public nature of ISA and to allow states a sufficient margin to determine and implement various policy goals, has contributed to the legitimacy crisis in which the IIA system currently finds itself.[38] The incompatibility between the private nature of arbitration and the public nature of state involvement restricts ISA in supporting an effective global investment governance regime.

The "regulatory chill" effect of ISA

ISA or even a mere threat of ISA can play a deterring function in a state's public policy decision-making, a phenomenon often described as "regulatory chill".[39] Despite the lack of a uniform definition, "regulatory chill" can be divided into three categories, according to some commentators. First, "anticipatory chill", where state policymakers take into account potential disputes with foreign investors before they begin drafting regulatory or legislative changes for the public interest. Second, "specific response chill", meaning the freezing of a specific regulatory measure once policymakers have become aware of the risk of an investment dispute. Third, "precedential chill", which occurs when a state changes a regulation in response to a settled or resolved investment dispute because it fears future arbitrations based on the same regulation.[40]

There are several reasons to explain the "regulatory chill" effect of ISA on states. First, ISA essentially subjects a state's regulatory measures to the scrutiny of private arbitrators according to international law. Second, ISA is both costly and time-demanding. The legal fees as well as the possible compensation can be a heavy burden on many states.[41] The financial cost of ISA can grow unbearably high for many states, especially developing states.[42] Third, given the increasing procedural transparency of ISA, states may be reluctant to get involved in ISA as respondents, because this is likely to be deemed to be a sign of the deterioration of the legal environment of the state.

There are ample examples to show the "regulatory chill" effects of ISA. For instance, Canada has decided to cease the promulgation of the planned regulatory measures for public purposes in order to avoid being sued in ISA.[43] In 2001, the Canadian government proposed to prohibit the display of "light" and "mild" descriptors on tobacco packaging in Canada. Phillip Morris, a tobacco giant, submitted a report to the Canadian government, claiming that the proposed regulations would violate Canada's obligations under the NAFTA, the WTO Agreement on Technical Barriers to Trade (TBT) and the Agreement on Trade Related Aspects of Intellectual Property (TRIPS). The report especially pointed out that the ban would constitute, among others, an expropriation and a violation of fair and equitable treatment under NAFTA Chapter Eleven, because it would interfere with Phillip Morris' trademark rights.[44] The Canadian government finally did not move ahead with the plans. It has been advised that Phillip Morris's arbitration threats may have been a possible factor in the outcome.[45]

Today, the "regulatory chill" effect of ISA is more pronounced as states shoulder broader and heavier duties to deliver public goods, and as MNEs are growing more powerful. Such effects potentially degrade the ability of states to take regulatory measures for public purposes. Developing countries may suffer more profoundly because they are subject to more claims, and awards against them appear financially more important.[46]

The inability of ISA to protect non-investment interests

Although a foreign investor and its host state are both involved in the same investment transaction, they do not necessarily share the same objectives. The clashes of contrasting objectives are most evident in investment disputes that touch upon non-commercial issues.[47] ISA cases involving non-investment issues, such as human rights or environment issues, are becoming increasingly common.[48] In such cases arbitrators need to decide, first, whether the non-investment interests should be considered; and if so, whether non-investment interests should be favoured over investment protection.

ISA case law suggests that arbitrators sometimes refuse to consider non-investment interests, and even if such interests are considered, they are often marginalized to give way to the protection of investments.[49] In Biloune v. Ghana, Mr. Biloune, a Syrian national investor, sought compensation for the alleged violation of his human rights as a result of Ghana's detention and deportation of him when claiming for compensation for an alleged expropriation. The tribunal found that it had no jurisdiction to hear the human rights issue because the applicable BIT required the dispute to be "in respect of foreign investment".[50]

In Azurix v. Argentina, as mentioned, the respondent state raised the inconsistency between the BIT provisions and international human rights law to defend its BIT-inconsistent measures. It further argued that such conflict should be resolved in favour of human rights. The tribunal found that it failed to understand the incompatibility in the specifics of the case because this issue had not been fully argued.[51]

Marginalization of non-investment interest in ISA can be deemed a typical consequence of the "tension of discourse" between international investment law and other branches of international law. On one hand, IIAs do not contain sufficient and enforceable public interest provisions to deal with ISA disputes that involve non-investment interest. On the other hand, though non-investment interests may be addressed through other specialized international law discourses, such as IETs or human rights treaties, these discourses do not provide a platform to settle investment disputes effectively.

It is true, though, that the primary aim of IIAs is to protect foreign investors and investments. ISA is the enforcement mechanism designed to reach this aim. However, recognizing this aim does not necessarily lead to the conclusion that non-investment interests should be marginalized in ISA. The international community is increasingly aware of the need for IIAs to not only cater to the need for investment protection, but should also be made accommodating in protecting the public interest as necessary, such as the protection of the environment, labour rights, public health and national security.

As already mentioned, IIA-making efforts have been made towards this end. Some IIAs incorporate an increasing number of public interest provisions; some clearly refer to external public interest standards; some incorporate exception languages in FET and indirect expropriation clauses; some adopt the GATT-style clause of general exceptions and security exceptions. Though these provisions are different, they serve the same purpose of preserving state regulatory power, thus giving the states broader space for taking measures for public interest purposes.

However, such IIA-making efforts cannot be automatically translated to better protection of non-investment interest. ISA practice so far seems to suggest that these provisions have not functioned to their full potential or that they are insufficiently helpful. For instance, despite the fact that an increasing number of IIAs incorporate general exceptions, there is no reported ISA case in which such exceptions have been successfully invoked. Likewise, while some IIAs recognize the need to protect labour rights, they clearly preclude the provision of labour rights from the ambit of ISA.[52]

Conclusion

International investment law is a specialized branch of international law. IIAs are the core component of international investment law. In the era of globalization, transnational investment activities become increasingly complex and expansive. Such activities may give rise to profound public interest and sustainable development concerns. Such a reality calls for an effective global-investment governance regime that is favourable to the promotion of sustainable development. However, the fragmentation, state-centrism and structural imbalance of international investment law paralyse IIAs in supplying adequate normative and systematic support to the establishment of such a regime.

ISA provides a mechanism of enforcement of IIAs that is available to private investors. Such a mechanism subjects state regulatory measures to the external scrutiny of international arbitrators. While ISA may help protect foreign investors and investments, it could also have a "regulatory chill" effect on states. ISA case law also suggests that non-investment interest associated with transnational investment activities is unlikely to be protected in ISA.

The incompatibility of IIAs and ISA with global governance calls for reconceptualization and reform of the existing IIA and ISA systems. Through the lens of governance, IIAs should not only be deemed as treaties that record states' commitments for investment protection, but must be also viewed as a special arrangement of right and obligation divisions among the main stakeholders of transnational investment activities. Likewise, ISA should not only be deemed a mere dispute settlement mechanism, but must be also viewed as a privatized administrative tool that can be used in reviewing, correcting and reshaping states' regulatory behaviour. Such a reconceptualization could be helpful for the design of a more effective regime for global investment governance.

Notes

1   M. Koskenniemi, "Fragmentation of International Law: Difficulties Arising from the Diversification and Expansion of International Law" (Report of the Study Group of the International Law Commission), A/CN.4/L.682 (13 April 2006), at 244.

2   The European Commission, "Why the New EU Proposal for an Investment Court System in TTIP Is Beneficial to Both States and Investors", available at http://europa.eu/rapid/press-release_MEMO-15-6060_en.htm.

3   C. Schreuer, "Denunciation of the ICSID Convention and Consent to Arbitration", in M. Waibel, A. Kaushal, K. L. Chung and C. Balchin (eds.), *The Backlash against Investment Arbitration: Perceptions and Reality* (The Hague: Kluwer Law International, 2010), at 353–368; UNCTAD, "Denunciation of the ICSID Convention and BITs: Impact on Investor–State Claims", *IIA Issue Note*, No. 2, December 2010, available at http://unctad.org/en/Docs/webdiaeia20106_en.pdf.

4   See X. Carim, "Lessons from South Africa's BITs Review", *Columbia FDI Perspectives*, No. 109 (25 November 2013), available at http://ccsi.columbia.edu/files/2013/10/No_109_-_Carim_-_FINAL.pdf.

5   L. Kazemi, *Monopoly Broken? Investment Governance beyond the Sovereign State* (Thesis for Doctor of Philosophy) (UMI Number: 3420848, 2010), at 1.

6   See generally S. Reich, "What Is Globalization: Four Possible Answers", *Kellogg Institute Working Paper #261* (December 1998), available at www3.nd.edu/~kellogg/publications/workingpapers/WPS/261.pdf.

7   Commission on Global Governance, "Our Global Neighborhood", available at www.gdrc.org/u-gov/global-neighbourhood/index.htm, at Chapter I.

8   See generally E. Benvenisti, "The Law of Global Governance", 368 *Recueil des cours* 47 (2013).

9   L. Anderson, "Antiquated before They Can Ossify: States that Fail before They Form", 58 (1) *Journal of International Affairs* 1 (2004), at 1.

10   E. Benvenisti (2013), at 66.

11   See K. W. Abbott and D. Snidal, "Hard and Soft Law in International Governance", 54 (3) *International Organization* 421 (2000), at 421–423.

12   E. Benvenisti (2013), at 66.

13   See e.g. J. N. Rosenau and E. O. Czempiel (eds.), *Governance without Government* (Cambridge: Cambridge University Press, 1992); B. G. Peters and J. Pierre, "Governance without Government: Rethinking Public Administration", 8 (2) *Journal of Public Administration Research and Theory* 223 (1998).

14   T. G. Weiss, D. C. Seyle and K. Coolidge, "The Rise of Non–State Actors in Global

Governance: Opportunities and Limitations", *One Earth Foundation Future Discussion Paper*, available at http://acuns.org/wp-content/uploads/2013/11/gg-weiss.pdf, at 4.

15 See H. Wang and J. N. Rosenau, "China and Global Governance", 33 (3) *Asian Perspective* 5 (2009), at 6.

16 See UNESCAP, "What Is Good Governance?", available at www.unescap.org/sites/default/files/good-governance.pdf.

17 P. Lamy, "Global Governance: From Theory to Practice", 15 (3) *Journal of International Economic Law* 721 (2012) at 721.

18 S. Schlemmer-Schulte, "Fragmentation of International Law: The Case of International Finance & Investment Law versus Human Rights Law", 25 *Global Business and Development Law Journal* 409 (2012), at 410.

19 See generally M. Koskenniemi (2006).

20 J. W. Salacuse, *The Three Laws of International Investment: National, Contractual and International Frameworks for Foreign Capital* (Oxford: Oxford University Press, 2013), at 35.

21 Ibid., at 35–42.

22 D. Schneiderman, "Legitimacy and Reflexivity in International Investment Arbitration: A New Self-Restraint", 2(2) *Journal of International Dispute Settlement* 471 (2011), at 471–476.

23 UNCTAD, International Investment Agreement Navigator, available at http://investmentpolicyhub.unctad.org/IIA.

24 See generally, J. Chaisse and S. Hamanaka, "The Investment Version of the Asian Noodle Bowl: The Proliferation of International Investment Agreements", *ADB Working Paper Series on Regional Economic Integration*, No. 128 (April 2014), available at www.cuhk.edu.hk/law/proj/BITSel/download/Hamanaka_Shintaro.pdf.

25 See S. W. Schill, *The Multilateralization of International Investment Law* (Cambridge: Cambridge University Press, 2009).

26 See O. Yasuaki, "A Transcivilizational Perspective on International Law", 342 *Recueil des cours* 77 (2009), at 106–107.

27 O. Yasuaki (2009), at 102.

28 See A. Roberts and S. Sivakumaran, "Lawmaking by Non-State Actors: Engaging Armed Groups in the Creation of International Humanitarian Law", 37 *Yale Journal of International Law* 108 (2012), at 111.

29 J. Holzgrefe, "The Humanitarian Intervention Debate", in J. Holzgrefe and R. Keohane (eds.), *Humanitarian Intervention: Ethical, Legal and Political Dilemmas* (Cambridge: Cambridge University Press, 2003), at 18.

30 See M. Asada, "Security Council Resolution 1540 and International Legislation", T. Komori and K. Wellens (eds.), *Public Interest Rules in International Law: Towards Effective Implementation* (London and New York: Routledge, 2016), at 141–142.

31 S. Marks, "State-Centrism, International Law, and the Anxieties of Influence", 19 *Leiden Journal of International Law* 339, (2006), at 341.

32 See e.g. M. Shaw, *International Law* (5th edn.) (Cambridge: Cambridge University Press, 2003), at 176–177.

33 Z. Dabone, "International Law: Armed Groups in a State-Centric System", 93 *International Review of the Red Cross* 395 (2011), at 396.

34 See Y. Tanaka, "Protection of Community Interests in International Law: The Case of Law of the Sea", in A. von Bogdandy and R. Wolfrum (eds.), 15 *Max Planck Yearbook of United Nations Law* (2011), at 329–375.

35   R. Dolzer, "The Impact of International Investment Treaties on Domestic Administrative Law", 37 *NYU Journal of International Law and Policy* 953 (2005), at 954.

36   J. W. Salacuse (2013), at 35.

37   See generally H. G. Fung, S. A. Law and J. Yau, *Socially Responsible Investment in Global Environment* (Cheltenham and Northampton, Edward Elgar, 2010); B. J. Richardson, *Socially Responsible Investment Law: Regulating the Unseen Polluters* (New York: Oxford University Press, 2008).

38   A. Roberts, "The Next Battleground: Standards of Review in Investment Treaty Arbitration", 16 *International Council for Commercial Arbitration Congress Series* 170 (2011), at 173.

39   See e.g. K. Tienhaara, "Regulatory Chill and the Threat of Arbitration: A View from Political Science", in C. Brown and K. Miles (eds.), *Evolution in Investment Treaty Law and Arbitration* (Cambridge: Cambridge University Press, 2011), at 606–628.

40   See generally C. Tietje and F. Baetens, "The Impact of Investor–State-Dispute Settlement (ISDS) in the Transatlantic Trade and Investment Partnership" (Study prepared for the Minister for Foreign Trade and Development Cooperation, Ministry of Foreign Affairs, The Netherlands), Reference: MINBUZA-2014.78850, at 41.

41   C. M. Gomezperalta, "How States Can Cope with the Growing Threat of Arbitration", available at www.robertwrayppllc.com/how-states-can-cope-with-the-growing-threat-of-arbitration/.

42   See UNCTAD Policy Framework (2012), at 79.

43   K. P. Gallagher and E. Shrestha, "Investment Treaty Arbitration and Developing Countries: A Re-Appraisal", *Global Development and Environment Institute Working Paper No. 11-01* (2011), available at https://ase.tufts.edu/gdae/Pubs/wp/11-01Treaty ArbitrationReappraisal.pdf, at 6.

44   See Philip Morris International Inc., "Submission by Philip Morris International Inc. in Response to the National Centre for Standards and Certification Information Foreign Trade Notification No. G/TBTIN/CAN/22", available at www.essentialaction.org/tobacco/pmresponsetonoi.pdf, at 6–9.

45   K. P. Gallagher and E. Shrestha (2011), at 6.

46   Ibid., at 7–10.

47   B. Choudhury, "Democratic Implications Arising from the Intersection of Investment Arbitration and Human Rights", 46 (4) *Alberta Law Review* 983 (2009), at 989.

48   See e.g. N. Bernasconi-Osterwalder and L. Johnson (eds.), *International Investment Law and Sustainable Development: Key Cases from 2000 to 2010*, available at www.iisd.org/publications/international-investment-law-and-sustainable-development-key-cases-2000-2010.

49   B. Choudhury (2009), at 989.

50   See generally C. Reiner and C. Schreuer (2009), at 99–100.

51   Ibid., at 102–103.

52   For instance, Article 13 of the 2012 U.S. Model BIT provides for "Investment and Labor", however Article 24.1(a) (i) (A) of this BIT impliedly excludes disputes arising out of Article 13 from being submitted to ISA.

8 Filling the compatibility gap between IIAs and sustainable development

Sustainable development and investment protection are often deemed to be conflicting goals of IIAs. Such conflict should prompt careful assessment in IIA-making. As suggested by B. Simma, when states commit themselves to the obligations of foreign investment protection through IIAs, they should determine the optimal degree of police powers and regulatory authority to be retained during the life of the investments, according to their obligations towards public interest protection.[1]

As discussed earlier, international investment law is not sufficiently compatible with sustainable development. Such incompatibility becomes more pronounced as investment disputes involving various sustainable development elements appear more frequently. To help address this situation, states in recent years have come to realize the need for more inclusive and balanced IIAs. It has been suggested that international investment law should abandon the traditional preoccupation with safeguarding investors' rights and focus more on sustainable development instead.[2]

As discussed already, the existing proposals for IIA reform primarily take a normative perspective, focusing on designing IIA provisions that can either preserve state regulatory power or limit foreign investors' access to ISA. Readily recognizing the merits of these proposals, this chapter tries to suggest ways of making IIAs more compatible with sustainable development from the governance perspective. The suggestions in this chapter do not aim at replacing existing proposals but should be seen as supplements to them.

The compatibility gap between IIAs and sustainable development

States are subject to various restrictions when negotiating IIAs that are compatible with sustainable development. Realizing such restrictions and inadequacy is helpful to properly understand how and why states can or cannot make IIAs more compatible with sustainable development.

IIAs as supplier of sustainable development norms

IIAs are the primary source of norms for the regime of global investment

DOI: 10.4324/9781315642840-12

governance. IIAs' norms not only stand for a series of commitments by the host states to foreign investors, but also form the primary source of law to be applied in settling investment disputes. Without a sufficient norm supply from IIAs, an effective global investment governance regime can hardly be imagined.

As the major norm supplier of the global investment governance regime, IIAs face a serious shortage of sustainable development norms. As discussed, except in the forewords, few IIAs clearly mention sustainable development.[3] In general, sustainable development provisions in IIAs remain insufficient. Most such provisions are "balancing provisions", aiming at preserving state regulatory powers, rather than imposing sustainable development obligations on the host states or foreign investors. The public interest provisions in IIAs often appear in the form of soft-law rules, and only have limited enforceability and effectiveness. Besides, it is only recently that some IIAs began to incorporate certain good governance provisions, such as clauses of transparency and third-party participation. Despite the merits of these procedural innovations, IIAs in general fail to take into account all stakeholders of international investment activities, and fail to properly balance the procedural rights of host states and foreign investors.

Overall, the sustainable development provisions in IIAs fail to adequately reflect the concept of sustainable development in its full dimensions, especially the social dimension. Thus, despite the increase of sustainable development provisions in IIAs, the shortage of norm-supply in IIAs remains outstanding.

The defective substantive-procedural balance of IIAs

Because ISA is a major and powerful way of enforcing the substantive commitments of IIAs, it is necessary that IIAs strike a sensible balance between the substantive and procedural rules. Such a balance is especially important for making IIAs compatible with sustainable development, as many IIAs try to preserve state regulatory power through excluding certain types of disputes from the realm of ISA.

To illustrate this issue, a brief comparison of the 2012 U.S. Model BIT and the China–Japan–Korea TIT is helpful. The 2012 U.S. Model BIT contains several clauses dealing with environment,[4] labour rights,[5] and essential state security.[6] According to the compromissory clause of this BIT,[7] disputes relating to environmental and labour rights clauses are inadmissible for ISA. Such disputes have to be settled by national courts or interstate consultation.

On the other hand, the China–Japan–Korea TIT is one of the most sustainable development-compatible IIAs China has concluded. This TIT also includes several sustainable development provisions, including a clause of environmental measures,[8] and an environmental exception of indirect expropriation.[9] However, the compromissory clause of this TIT does not set forth a threshold on the admissibility of disputes for ISA.[10] In light of such a broad compromissory clause, the inclusion of the sustainable development provisions in this TIT may not be truly helpful in preserving state regulatory power, since it is possible for foreign investors to submit sustainable development-related disputes to ISA as far as the disputes are "related to an investment".

True, there is no fixed pattern to strike a substantive-procedural balance in IIAs. Yet one thing is clear: if the contracting states truly intend to preserve state regulatory power for taking sustainable development measures, it is advisable that they ban foreign investors from submitting such disputes to ISA. Striking a proper substantive-procedural balance in IIA is in essence an issue of harmonization. States need to harmonize the sustainable development provisions and the compromissory provision. Such a balance is particularly important in IIA-making, given the uncertain role of ISA in promoting sustainable development.

The weak normativity of sustainable development in international investment law

Despite states' continued treatification efforts, sustainable development remains a "weak" norm in international law. It is "weak" in two senses. First, the exact contents of sustainable development remain unclear. As mentioned earlier, sustainable development is frequently perceived as a balancing paradigm between environmental needs and economic growth, but not a legal norm that entails ascertainable obligations and rights. In ISA practice, arbitral tribunals appear reluctant to consider sustainable development concerns. Such reluctance is often "justified" by the "tension of discourse" (international investment law is not the proper discourse in addressing sustainable development concerns) and treaty interpretation (e.g. the primary objective and purpose of IIAs is protecting foreign investors and investments).

Second, sustainable development is a "weak" norm because it has not been widely accepted as a legal norm in the international law system. The incorporation of sustainable development typically occurs in IETs. Although some elements of sustainable development have entered into the normative framework of international environmental law, especially IETs, such as the principle of common but differentiated responsibility,[11] it has not acquired sufficient normativity in other areas of international law, including international investment law.

Though a growing number of IIAs incorporate various public interest, environmental and human rights provisions nowadays, this does not substantially raise the level of the IIAs' compatibility with sustainable development. First, these provisions only represent some elements of sustainable development, while many other elements are left out. Second, these provisions in general fail to generate concrete and enforceable sustainable development obligations on states and foreign investors.

The weak normativity of sustainable development in international investment law is detrimental to the development of a global investment governance regime truly accommodative to sustainable development. Indeed, if the normativity of sustainable development stays unimproved, even if an IIA incorporates a sustainable development clause, the real effectiveness of this clause would remain uncertain.

Increasing the supply of sustainable development norms

While acknowledging that IIAs should primarily aim at protecting foreign investments and investors, it is advisable that they also be made more compatible with sustainable development. As mentioned, the current insufficiency of IIAs in achieving sustainable development goals lies in the insufficient supply of norms, defective substantive-procedural balance and weak normativity of sustainable development in IIAs. Thus, the first step to enhance the compatibility of IIAs with sustainable development is to enhance the supply of sustainable development norms to IIAs. This can be achieved in several ways.

First, more "balancing provisions" should be incorporated in IIAs. The existing IIAs are often viewed as "unbalanced" in the sense that they are insufficiently helpful in preserving state regulatory power. Thus, the majority of the existing proposals of IIA reform focus on designing provisions that can better preserve state regulatory power, i.e. "balancing provisions". For instance, it has been suggested that the U.S. experience of NAFTA Chapter Eleven arbitration has had a direct influence on its attitudes in more recent FTA and BIT negotiations, and led to modifications to its model BIT.[12]

Most of the proposed "balancing provisions" deal with allocation of the rights and obligations between the host states and foreign investors. They mainly relate to substantive provisions, such as FET, indirect expropriation, public interest protection and exception clauses. As discussed earlier, many recent IIAs, especially those concluded by developed countries, incorporate such "balancing provisions".[13] Though incorporation of "balancing provisions" in IIAs may help preserve state regulatory power, the practical effects of these provisions remain unclear. On one hand, it remains to be seen how arbitrators interpret these provisions in ISA practice; on the other hand, it is also uncertain whether and to what extent these provisions would discourage foreign investors.

Second, better "good governance" provisions should be incorporated in IIAs. In addition to incorporating "balancing provisions", IIAs can also be made more compatible with sustainable development by including provisions that can help the contracting states achieve good governance of foreign investments. As discussed, good governance comprises, among other things, the notions of transparency, participation, accountability and the rule of law. Aside from the FET clause, which is by nature a classic expression of the rule of law, some recent IIAs incorporate provisions relating to the various elements of good governance, such as procedural transparency and third-party participation provisions.

Third, reference to external standards should also be increased in IIAs. Provisions compatible with sustainable development may also be incorporated into IIAs by reference to relevant external standards, such as the OECD Guidelines. This method has several advantages. First, it is flexible and feasible. As IIAs are becoming complicated, the IIA-making process has quickly become a burdensome task to many states, especially those with limited treaty-making capacity. Incorporation by reference enables states to reach an agreement without going through the hardship of treaty negotiation. Second, many sustainable development norms have already been drafted by NGOs and international organizations in the form of soft-law rules. These rules provide sufficient external standards for states to consider in IIA-making.

Fourth, most the sustainable development provisions in IIAs are soft-law norms. While it is widely acknowledged that soft law plays an increasingly important role in global governance,[14] the extent to which these provisions can help promote sustainable development depends largely on how the contracting states and investors enforce them on a voluntary basis. In light of this, IIAs can be made more compatible with sustainable development through hardening these soft-law rules, i.e. transforming soft law to hard law, which would strongly improve the implementation of these norms.[15]

Soft-law norms may be hardened once normative positions and rationalistic preferences have moved sufficiently to make a binding commitment politically acceptable. Hardening of soft law is possible through the strategic and persistent use of the soft-law rules.[16] This rule-making method has been widely used in some legal fields, such as security regulation. For instance, international anti-bribery norms evolved from national hard law, to soft law, to international treaty law in the form of the 1997 Convention on Combating Bribery of Foreign Officials in International Business Transactions ("Anti-Bribery Convention") over the past three decades. Such transformation is achieved through strategic use of soft-law instruments, and diplomatic and public pressure can cement the commitment to becoming a hard-law instrument. Initially, these norms were introduced and applied in the U.S. in response to evidence of widespread illegal payments to government officials by large U.S. companies, which was followed by multilateral efforts to combat corruption. Then, the OECD, at the behest of the U. S., used soft-law instruments to move its members towards a firm commitment against bribery. After accepting several soft-law instruments, OECD members found it easier to accept (or more difficult to resist) a hard-law instrument in international business transactions. Such efforts ultimately resulted in the conclusion of the Anti-Bribery Convention.[17]

This transformation path may also make sense in making sustainable development rules in IIAs. Many sustainable development norms, such as CSR norms, have already acquired hard-law status in many national legal systems, and have been incorporated in many IIAs in the form of soft law. With persistent state practice, it is possible that at least some of these norms can be hardened IIAs.

Finally, it should be mentioned that, although this book proposes increasing sustainable development norm-supply to IIAs, it does not argue that IIAs should be expanded indefinitely to be able to address every concern associated with transnational investment activities. Rather, whether and how to incorporate sustainable development norms in IIAs depends primarily on the contracting state's position. Such a position is not formed in the abstract and can be changed over time depending on the actual situation of the state. A state needs to take into account a wide range of factors in IIA-making, including political willingness, economic situation, civil society demands, bargaining power, external pressure and development strategy, just to list a few. Understandably, a state with strong political willingness towards environmental protection and a developed economy is more likely to support sustainable investment in investment policy-making. Likewise, it is unsurprising if a state decides in favour of economic development over environmental protection in IIA-making during a certain development period or with specific partners. In this sense, consensus-building among the states should be a core aspect in making future IIAs more compatible with sustainable development.

Harmonizing sustainable development provisions in IIAs

Given that IIAs are typically negotiated on a bilateral basis, and that states may have different or even conflicting policy goals, it is almost impossible for IIAs to incorporate sufficient and uniform sustainable development provisions. Such a situation may be further complicated by the inconsistent interpretation of IIA provisions in ISA. Thus, to make IIAs more compatible with sustainable development, it is necessary to harmonize the sustainable development provisions in IIAs. Such harmonization may take place at two levels, i.e. inter-IIA harmonization and intra-branch harmonization.

Inter-IIA harmonization towards greater normative convergence of sustainable development provisions

Inter-IIA harmonization of sustainable development provisions requires that greater normative convergence of these provisions in different IIAs should be achieved. As discussed earlier, IIAs are drastically different in their sustainable development provisions. Some IIAs contain multiple sustainable development provisions, while others contain fewer or even none. Also, the quality of these provisions varies among IIAs. While some provisions are merely declaratory and can hardly be enforced, some are confined to a limited scope, and others can be broadly applied to exempt the contracting states from their IIA obligations. Consequently, some IIAs appear more accommodative to sustainable development than others. Such normative diversity can be amplified through the application of MFN clauses as is commonly seen in many IIAs.

It is advisable that states make efforts to harmonize sustainable development provisions to achieve greater convergence at the global level. As it seems unlikely that a multilateral investment treaty can be concluded in the near future, such a harmonization process could start at the bilateral and regional level. Although it seems difficult to propose a roadmap and to predict the result of this process, the issuance of a model IIA that features greater compatibility with sustainable development seems a sensible method. On this issue, as mentioned in Chapter 2, several proposals for reforming the current IIA system have been made. These proposals, especially the IISD Model IIA, provide helpful guidance and reference for the making of a model IIA that is more compatible with sustainable development goals. Such a model IIA may also serve as the blueprint for the negotiation of a multilateral IIA in the longer term.

In addition, at the bilateral and regional level, it is also desirable that leading trading states, such as the U.S., the EU and China, build a consensus that promoting sustainable development should be a priority in IIA-making. As a matter of fact, some IIAs recently concluded by these countries, such as the CETA and the TPP, appear more compatible with sustainable development than most of the existing IIAs.[18] Though the China–EU BIT and China–U.S. BIT remain in the negotiation, the parties have made it clear that these BITs should be made more compatible with sustainable development goals.[19] The consensus built among these states during the negotiation of these landmark IIAs is likely to lead global IIA-making in the future.

Intra-branch harmonization of conflicting norms through proper treaty interpretation

Intra-branch harmonization of international investment law and other branches of international law or general international law essentially requires reconciling the normative conflict between IIA norms and other international law norms, such as human rights treaty norms. Such harmonization could be realized via proper application of the various treaty interpretation tools enshrined in the VCLT in ISA practice. To a large extent, the harmonization is also helpful in addressing the "tension of discourse" in global investment governance.

The concept of sustainable development is a multifaceted one that captures economic development, social development and environmental protection. Not every aspect of sustainable development is sufficiently addressed in international law. Also, international law rules that address these aspects are scattered in various different branches, as a result of the fragmentation of international law. The rules of the different branches are not always compatible and are sometimes conflicting. Such conflicts typically exist between special law and general law and between successive norms, which could ultimately cause deviating institutional practices and, possibly, the loss of an overall perspective on the law.[20]

The normative conflict of the rules of different specialized branches of international law brings about profound challenges to states because their regulatory measures for sustainable development purposes may conflict with their IIA obligations. For instance, in Azurix v. Argentina, Argentina claimed that it faced conflicting obligations under the BIT and international human rights law. Though it is difficult to establish a hierarchical order of the conflicting norms within the international law system, such conflict can be reconciled if arbitrators can fully perceive the sustainable development sensitivity of the dispute and appropriately interpret IIA provisions under the VCLT treaty interpretation framework.

As intra-branch harmonization relies heavily on arbitrators, it is necessary to discuss at the outset the role of the arbitrators in promoting sustainable development through ISA. Arbitrators not only control the arbitral proceedings, but they also make case law that governs investor–state relations.[21] In ISA, it is almost implied that arbitrators have broad discretion in treaty interpretation. Through applying the different treaty interpretation tools allowed by the VCLT, arbitrators may come to different conclusions. Yet, as a matter of fact, arbitrators are sometimes criticized on the grounds of interpreting IIA provisions expansively, neglecting public interests and the regulatory power of states, and producing inconsistent jurisprudence.[22]

That said, it is also important to note that arbitrators may play a constructive role in addressing the "tension of discourse" through treaty interpretation when settling investment disputes that are sensitive to sustainable development. Existing studies suggest that arbitrators may use two treaty interpretation tools to achieve intra-branch harmonization of IIAs and other international law, i.e. the application of the principle of system integration, and the evolutionary interpretation of IIA to reflect the changed treaty object and purpose.

First, the principle of system integration should be applied in treaty interpretation. Treaty interpretation not only serves the clinical purpose of ascertaining the intent of the contracting states, but may also play the role of "system integration".[23] According to Article 31(3)(c) of the VCLT, when interpreting treaty provisions "any relevant rules of international law applicable in the relations between the parties" should be considered. This VCLT provision is often deemed as an expression of the principle of system integration, aiming at seeking coherence and uniformity in treaty interpretation.[24]

According to this principle, treaty interpretation is not conducted in the abstract; rather, it is premised on the presumption that, despite international law-making being fragmented and decentralized, any new rule has been made with the awareness of other existing rules.[25] When interpreting treaty provisions, reference should be made to the "normative environment" of the treaty, which includes all sources of international law. Essentially, this principle requires that when several treaty norms bear on a single issue, they should, to the greatest extent possible, be interpreted so as to give rise to a single set of compatible obligations.[26]

As investment disputes involving sustainable development are on the rise, arbitrators often face the situation in which states' IIA obligations and the obligations under other international law norms are inconsistent or conflicting. Such a situation necessitates the application of the principle of system integration in ISA.

The need for system integration has received increasing attention in ISA. IIAs form a part of the international legal system, and the rules of interpretation are themselves one of the means by which the system as a whole gives form and meaning to individual rules.[27] IIAs are "informed by, and in conversation with, general international law", and through treaty interpretation, IIAs are open to outside influence, which could lead to "system integration" of international investment law with other branches of international law.[28] In this sense, the use of the principle of system integration in ISA may be a useful reconciling tool in striking a balance between states' sustainable development obligations and their IIA obligations.

Second, the evolutionary interpretation of IIAs may help arbitrators defend sustainable development goals as well. As stated in Article 31(1) of the VCLT, a treaty shall be interpreted "in the light of its object and purpose". It has been established in ISA that investment protection is the object and purpose of IIAs. As such, IIA provisions should be interpreted to reflect such object and purpose, which often results in the "pro-investment bias" in ISA.

Such an interpretation method is criticized. Treaty object and purpose is not static. Ascertaining the object and purpose of IIAs involves an evolutionary interpretation of IIA terms.[29] The underlying, long-term purpose of investment policies and IIAs today is best captured by the more complex concept of sustainable development, for several reasons. First, a positive relativity between the inflow of FDI and the economic development of state cannot be affirmatively established. Second, development should be seen as a broader process involving economic, social, political and legal considerations, and mere economic growth without social equity and environmental justice could hardly be regarded as making a meaningful contribution to development. Third, sustainable development is a widely accepted policy objective of the global community, and plays an important role in investment policymaking.[30] Now that sustainable development promotion, which consists of the simultaneous pursuit of economic prosperity, environmental quality and social equity, is established as the object and purpose of IIAs, it is possible and necessary for arbitrators to interpret IIA provisions in favour of sustainable development.

Today, total exclusion of sustainable development considerations in interpreting IIAs by arbitrators is subject to increasing criticism for neglecting the public interest.[31] In addition, since public interest regulations and conduct of a state are promulgated and taken by elected officials in order to protect the welfare of the state's citizens and nationals, "interference with these regulations by unelected and unappointed arbitrators is not consistent with basic principles of democracy".[32]

However, it remains largely unclear how effectively arbitrators can use the various treaty interpretive tools in an innovative and persuasive way to reconcile the normative conflicts between international investment law and other branches of international law, such as human rights law and environmental law. ISA case law seems to suggest a passive picture. The pro-investment bias in interpreting IIA provisions remains to a large extent, which mainly results from the selective use of interpretive tools, overreliance on prior arbitral and judicial decisions, and the liberal understating of treaty object and purpose.[33] Furthermore, even if IIAs can be interpreted in a way more compatible with sustainable development goals, it still remains uncertain whether, and to what extent, the coherence and uniformity of the interpretive practices can be maintained in light of the proliferation of IIAs and the *ad hoc* nature of ISA.[34]

Remedying the democratic deficit of IIA-making

Traditionally, treaty-making was not in any way connected with the word democracy, which is often used in the context of politics.[35] Recently, however, the democratic deficit in treaty-making has generated growing concern. As treaties can have a wide range of implications for a state's legal and administrative systems, economy, and individual citizens, there is concern that treaties entered into by the executive, without significant parliamentary or public involvement, are undemocratic.[36] For instance, the WTO negotiations have been criticized for lack of legitimacy because of the lack of input from historically marginalized groups, including the poor, women, and indigenous peoples.[37]

Under the notion of democratic treaty-making, treaty-making no longer revolves around the underlying traditional issue of the use of the external affairs power by a state and the role of the executive versus parliament. Rather, enhanced transparency in treaty-making and wider stakeholder engagement, particularly the involvement of non-state stakeholders, should be present in treaty-making as well.[38]

This book submits that an important but often neglected factor to explain why IIAs are insufficient in addressing sustainable development concerns associated with transnational investment activities is the democratic deficit in IIA-making. In particular, IIA-making lacks sufficient involvement of non-state stakeholders. Such a democratic deficit should be remedied by improving the transparency of IIA-making process and enhancing the engagement of non-state stakeholders in IIA-making.

Improving the transparency of the IIA-making process

Transparency promises a more accountable, more democratic and more legitimate system of global governance. Somewhat ironically, secrecy in treaty negotiations and confidentiality in dispute settlement are two hallmarks of investment law so far.[39] Indeed, as mentioned, while milestone progress has been made on the transparency of ISA, highlighted by the adoption of the UNCITRAL Transparency Rules and the Mauritius Transparency Convention, transparency in IIA-making remains at a low level and is less discussed. "Secret" IIA-making, which remains as the mainstream practice in many states, is viewed as a major contributing factor to the democratic deficit of IIAs and may create profound challenges for democratic governance and accountability.[40]

In recent years, many states have realized the need for a more transparent treaty-making process. In this connection, Australia seems to be a good example. Since 1996, the Australian government has introduced reforms to treaty-making practice, aiming primarily at curing the democratic deficit in its treaty-making.[41] A key measure of the reform is to enhance the transparency of treaty-making through introducing a "significantly higher level of consultation in treaty-making before treaties are signed and to communicate more information to stakeholders and the public about how treaties will affect them".[42]

In its recent report, the Australian Parliament (the Foreign Affairs, Defence and Trade Committee) observed that "while the committee accepts that absolute transparency in treaty-making is an unrealistic expectation, absolute secrecy in the current globalized environment of treaty-making is equally unrealistic and therefore in need of changing".[43] It also held that "the benefits of increased transparency during free trade negotiations outweigh a perceived risk to the national interest from public disclosure".[44] The Australian government has also noted that this reform "provides greater transparency in the treaty-making process and ensures that interested groups and individuals are in a position to contribute freely to Australia's negotiating position".[45]

Similarly, in the EU, while the current debate concerning the democratic deficit in EU's trade and investment treaty-making largely focuses on the relationship between the EU and its member states, surrounding the EU's treaty-making competence after the Lisbon Treaty,[46] this debate also contains an EU–public dimension. As a response to the persistent criticism of the secrecy of IIA negotiations, transparency has forcefully entered the negotiations on CETA and TTIP. The EU initiated a large-scale online public consultation that prompted heated public discussion over the ISDS mechanism enshrined in the draft TTIP agreement.[47]

The EU's online consultation during the treaty-making process has profound democratic implications. As observed by S. W. Schill, it changes the way the public and EU government communicate with each other and opens up new paths for democratic input into the EU's treaty-making process. More importantly, the consultation parts with the usual assumption that the interests of the public are represented and mediated through the member states. It is suggested that the direct corridor of communication between the EU and the public through the consultation can give a voice to interests not well-represented through the EU member states and can allow for new trans-border interest coalitions.[48]

The issue of transparency in treaty-making, in essence, is more political than legal. Yet, in light of the growing recognition of the principle of transparency in international and national governance and the profound impact of IIAs on public interest, it would not be surprising if states were to prefer a more transparent IIA-making process in the future.

Enhancing the engagement of non-state stakeholders

As pointed out by J. Alvarez, the power of treaty-making is traditionally withheld by states, because matters of interstate diplomacy were regarded as confidential matters reserved for states.[49] According to the constitutions of many states, state treaty-making power rests primarily or exclusively on the executive body.[50] Non-state actors, such as individuals and NGOs, are often institutionally excluded from the treaty-making process under both international and national laws.

The twentieth century has witnessed growing friendliness in treaty-making towards non-state actors, both international organizations at first and NGOs at a later stage.[51] Today, non-state actors, NGOs in particular, are playing an increasingly important role in international relations and in norm-creating, including treaty-making.[52] In fact, the involvement of non-state actors in treaty-making in various different capacities, as a way of realizing participatory democracy, is gaining momentum.[53]

Public participation can be particularly necessary in the making of treaties involving public interest considerations. For instance, during the making of the Framework Convention on Tobacco Control, the WHO held public hearings, received over 500 submissions and allowed verbal testimonies from representatives of 144 organizations and institutions before the hearings panel.[54] On the other hand, exclusion of public participation is criticized for endangering the legitimacy of treaty-making. For example, during the Copenhagen climate change negotiations in 2009, many environmental NGOs were disappointed because their efforts to play a participatory role had been frustrated, and it has been suggested that the exclusion of NGOs from the making of MEAs could violate international law, as the 1992 Rio Declaration and the UNCSD's Agenda 21 provide that "NGOs play a vital role in the shaping and implementation of participatory democracy".[55]

At national level, many states have taken steps to cure the democratic deficit in treaty-making as well. For instance, the Law Commission of New Zealand realizes the importance of sufficient representation of indigenous peoples in treaty-making, and has proposed various recommendations to reform its treaty-making process, including wider public participation.[56]

Though some states routinely conduct a feasibility study before officially starting treaty negotiations, and solicit public opinions or seek advice from experts, NGOs and industrial unions during the treaty-making process,[57] institutionalized public participation remains insufficient and is often deemed an unwelcome practice. Many states oppose greater participation of NGOs in the treaty-making process since they believe NGOs are simply special interest groups who will warp the process.[58] For instance, concerns have been voiced over lack of consultation with the Máori people, an indigenous group, in the treaty-making of New Zealand.[59] It has also been found that there is a lack of effective mechanisms for consultation and consent between the state and indigenous peoples in Paraguay in the state's policymaking and treaty-making.[60]

Public participation carries great significance in enhancing the democracy and legitimacy of IIA-making. The bargain underlying IIA-making can be understood as the following: foreign investments are expected to play a helpful role in host states' economic development, and in return host states commit to protect foreign investors and investments through IIAs.[61] In this bargain, the voice of the individuals and groups, who are prone to be adversely impacted by transnational investment activities and the host state's investment governance measures, is not sufficiently heard. The silence could make these individuals and groups vulnerable to detriment caused by foreign-investment activities.

Because IIAs are silent on the rights of local stakeholders and the obligations of foreign investors, arbitrators may also find it difficult to satisfactorily protect the local stakeholders or even to take their request into consideration. Consequently, local stakeholders, such as indigenous groups, can only try to address these concerns through the local remedies available in the host states. This is not an ideal alternative, considering that the local remedies are often insufficient and lack effectiveness in some states, and that the indigenous groups may lack adequate capability. Such a situation necessitates broader public participation in IIA-making.

What is suggested here is not that IIA-making should be made fully accessible to the public. Rather, it is hereby proposed that participatory democracy in IIA-making should be enhanced through engaging local stakeholders, NGOs and MNEs to this process in appropriate ways. The rationale behind this proposal is quite simple. Non-state stakeholders are frequently the victims of sustainable development harms brought by transnational investment activities, and they have a direct and special interest in making IIAs compatible with sustainable development. Thus, they should have the right to know how and to what extent their rights and interest would be influenced by transnational investment activities, what consequences they would bear, and how to mitigate or remedy the potential detriments.

While it is one thing to comprehend the need for non-state actor participation to cure the democratic deficit of IIA-making, it is quite another for states and international organizations to make the necessary institutional arrangement to implement this plan. Indeed, engaging non-state actors in IIA-making may bring about a number of difficulties to states. What are the appropriate ways to engage non-state actors effectively in IIA-making? How to ensure that non-state actor participation will not adversely influence the IIA-making process? How to reconcile the different viewpoints of states and non-state actors? None of these questions can be satisfactorily or easily answered. Obviously, non-state actor participation in IIA-making requires a profound institution-building and policy-making paradigm shift at national and international level.

The EU is a front-runner in democratizing trade and investment treaty-making, especially after the Lisbon Treaty. Citizens' participation in the EU's treaty-making process is "guaranteed" by the Treaty on European Union (TEU), according to which every citizen shall have the right to participate in the democratic life of the EU.[62] The Lisbon Treaty, for the first time, establishes the right to directly participate in or influence the EU decision-making process, in particular by means of the "citizens' initiative".[63] The treaty-making practice of the EU suggests a few ways of engagement for non-state actors. First, enhancing the transparency of the treaty-making process, such as the timely publishing of the relevant background documents or treaty drafts to the public. Second, conducting public surveys to solicit non-state actors' opinions on specific treaty issues that are likely to affect the public interest. Third, holding public hearings on key treaty issues, so that the treaty-making body and the public or their representatives can have an opportunity to openly discuss and debate the issues.[64]

In other parts of the world, especially in developing states, there is a different picture of the democratization of IIA-making. Here, the work of the Office of the United Nations High Commissioner for Human Rights (OHCHR) on the assessment of the impacts of international investments on indigenous peoples deserves special attention. In 2001, the OHCHR decided to appoint a Special Rapporteur on the rights of indigenous peoples. The Special Rapporteur has observed that international trade and investment treaties can cause profound detriment to the rights of indigenous peoples, finding that,

> Closely related to the development agenda are the global and regional multilateral, plurilateral and bilateral investment and trade treaties and agreements entered into by states in which indigenous peoples are found. Many of those treaties and agreements have direct implications for how lands, territories, resources and traditional knowledge systems of indigenous peoples are regarded and used … Some agreements which allow for the liberalization and deregulation of existing laws and policies, and have the effect of undermining existing human rights, social and environmental standards, can have detrimental effects on indigenous peoples.[65]

In her recent report, the Special Rapporteur has carefully examined the impacts of IIAs, both BITs and FTAs, on the rights of indigenous peoples.[66] With special regard to the reform of the IIA-making process, the Special Rapporteur has raised a number of recommendations:

93. In accordance with the recommendations of the Special Rapporteur in her 2015 report to the General Assembly (A/70/301):

    a) Appropriate consultation procedures and mechanisms should be developed in cooperation with indigenous peoples in relation to the drafting, negotiation and approval of international investment agreements, and their right to consultation should be guaranteed prior to the ratification of the Trans-Pacific Partnership;
    b) Human rights impact assessments should be conducted of all trade and investment agreements, following the impact assessments carried out as part of the Guiding Principles on Business and Human Rights developed by the Special Rapporteur on the right to food.

94. States should negotiate international investment agreements in accordance with their international cooperation obligations under the International Covenant on Economic, Social and Cultural Rights and in keeping with the "clean hands" doctrine in relation to indigenous peoples' rights.
95. States should negotiate international investment agreements in accordance with their international cooperative on obligations under international human rights law, and in keeping with the "clean hands" doctrine, through the conduct of human rights impact assessments, appropriate due diligence and knowledge generation in relation to all potential impacts on indigenous peoples' rights, both at home and abroad.[67]

As can be seen from the above recommendations, while states should remain the negotiating parties of IIAs, such IIA-making power should be supplemented by two further requirements. First, states are required to undertake more procedural sustainable development obligations when negotiating IIAs and making relevant national policies. Second, adequate participation opportunities should also be made available for indigenous peoples to be involved in the IIA-making process.

Conclusion

The increase of the number of IIAs does not necessarily produce greater compatibility of IIAs with sustainable development. IIAs as a whole remain insufficiently capable of addressing sustainable development concerns associated with transnational investment activities for a number of reasons. First, IIAs as the major norm supplier for the global investment governance regime fail to supply sufficient sustainable development norms; second, some IIAs feature an ill-designed substantive-procedural balance; and third, the sustainable development provisions in IIAs lack sufficient normativity.

To respond to such a compatibility gap, serious reform of the IIA system needs to be carried out. Such reform should aim at three targets. First, enhancing the supply of sustainable development norms of IIAs, which could be achieved through the incorporation of more "balancing provisions" and "good governance provisions" into IIAs, referring to more external standards and norms and hardening of the soft-law rules of IIAs.

Second, harmonizing the sustainable development provisions in IIAs at the global level, which can be achieved either by inter-IIA harmonization towards greater normative convergence of these norms in IIAs or by intra-branch harmonization of sustainable development rules in IIAs with the conflicting norms in other branches of international law through proper treaty interpretation of the former rules.

Third, because traditionally states monopolize the treaty-making power, non-state actors are excluded from IIA-making. This is partly the reason that explains why the IIA system is insufficient and ineffective in addressing sustainable development concerns. To remedy such a democratic deficit, it is necessary to enhance the transparency and the engagement of non-state actors in the IIA-making process through appropriate ways. Understandably, non-state party participation in IIA-making is more a political issue than a legal one. The achievement of this goal requires profound institutional building and a policy-making paradigm shift by states at both national and international level.

It is important to note that, while this book proposes to reduce the incompatibility between IIAs and sustainable development, it does not suggest that IIAs should be made "omnipotent" so as to be able to address all types of concerns raised during the course of global investment governance. Besides, this book also readily recognizes that states remain the predominant players in global investment governances, thus they should enjoy a broad margin of appreciation and discretion in taking measures in IIA-making and ISA-reforming. In this sense, the international community should still aim at building greater consensus with regard to making IIAs more compatible with sustainable development in the future.

Notes

1   See B. Simma, "Foreign Investment Arbitration: A Place for Human Rights?" 60 (4) *International and Comparative Law Quarterly* 576 (2011), at 579.
2   K. Berner, "Reconciling Investment Protection and Sustainable Development", in S. Hindelang and M. Krajewski (eds.), *Shifting Paradigms in International Investment Law: More Balanced, Less Isolated, Increasingly Diversified* (Oxford: Oxford University Press, 2016), at 177–203.
3   In this regard, the CETA seems to be a plausible exception. Chapter 23 of the CETA is titled "Trade and Sustainable Development".
4   Article 12, 2012 U.S. Model BIT.
5   Article 13, 2012 U.S. Model BIT.
6   Article 18, 2012 U.S. Model BIT.
7   Article 24, 2012 U.S. Model BIT.
8   Article 23, China–Japan–Korea TIT.
9   Protocol C, China–Japan–Korea TIT.
10   Article 15, China–Japan–Korea TIT.
11   See e.g. T. Honkonen, *The Common but Differentiated Responsibility in Multilateral Environmental Agreements: Regulatory and Policy Aspects* (The Hague: Kluwer Law International, 2009), at 297–306.
12   See e.g. G. Gagne and J.-F. Morin, "The Evolving American Policy on Investment Protection: Evidence from Recent FTAs and the 2004 Model BIT", 9 *Journal of International Economic Law* 357 (2006), at 363; B. Kingsbury and S. W. Schill, "Public Law Concepts to Balance Investors' Rights with State Regulatory Actions in the Public Interest – The Concept of Proportionality", in S. W. Schill (ed.), *International Investment Law and Comparative Public Law* (Oxford: Oxford University Press, 2010), at 76.
13   See Chapter 3, 4, 5 and 6.
14   See e.g. R. S. Karmel and C. R. Kelly, "The Hardening of Soft Law in Securities Regulation", 34 (3) *Brooklyn Journal of International Law* 883 (2009); S. Bradshaw, "Internet Governance via Hard and Soft Laws: Choosing the Right Tools for the Job", available at www.cigionline.org/publications/internet-governance-hard-and-soft-laws-choosing-right-tools-job.
15   See e.g. J. B. Skjæseth, O. S. Stokke and J. Wettesta, "Soft Law, Hard Law, and Effective Implementation of International Environmental Norms", 6 (3) *Global Environmental Politics* 104 (2006).
16   R. S. Karmel and C. R. Kelly (2009), at 951.
17   Ibid., at 916–924.
18   The CETA contains separate chapter of sustainable development (Chapter 23), labour (Chapter 24) and the environment (Chapter 25); TPP also contains separate chapters dealing with labour (Chapter 19), the environment (Chapter 20) and development (Chapter 23) issues.
19   See EU, "EU–China 2020 Strategic Agenda for Cooperation", available at https://eeas.europa.eu/headquarters/headquarters-homepage/15398/eu-china-2020-strategic-agenda-cooperation_en, at 9–14.

20   See generally M. Koskenniemi (2006).

21   See e.g. J. P. Commission, "Precedent in Investment Treaty Arbitration: A Citation Analysis of a Developing Jurisprudence", 24 (2) *Journal of International Arbitration* 129 (2007), at 129–133; A. K. Bjorklund, "Investment Treaty Arbitral Decisions as Jurisprudence Constante", in C. Picker, I. Bunn and D. Arner (eds.), *International Economic Law: The State and Future of the Discipline* (Oxford: Hart Publishing, 2008), at 265–280.

22   See e.g. S. D. Franck (2005); C. N. Brower and S. W. Schill, "Is Arbitration a Threat or a Boon to the Legitimacy of International Investment Law?", 9 (2) *Chicago Journal of International Law* 471 (2009); D. Schneiderman, "Legitimacy and Reflexivity in International Investment Arbitration: A New Self-Restraint?", 2 (2) *Journal of International Dispute Settlement* 471 (2011); J. Kurtz, "Building Legitimacy Through Interpretation in Investor–State Arbitration: On Consistency, Coherence and the Identification of Applicable Law", in Z. Douglas, J. Pauwelyn and J. Viñuales (eds.), *The Foundations of International Investment Law: Bringing Theory into Practice* (Oxford: Oxford University Press, 2014), at 257–296.

23   See e.g. G. O. Zabalza, *The Principle of Systematic Integration: Towards a Coherent International Legal Order* (Zurich: Lit, 2012); D. Rosentreter, *Article 31(3) (c) of the Vienna Convention on the Law of Treaties and the Principle of Systemic Integration in International Investment Law and Arbitration* (Baden-Baden: Nomos, 2015); P. Merkouris, *Article 31(3) (c) VCLT and the Principle of Systemic Integration: Normative Shadows in Plato's Cave* (Leiden: Brill, 2015).

24   See e.g. C. McLachlan, "The Principle of Systemic Integration and Article 31(3) (c) of the Vienna Convention", 54 (2) *International and Comparative Law* 279 (2005), at 279–280.

25   J. d'Aspremont, "The Systemic Integration of International Law by Domestic Courts: Domestic Judges as Architects of the Consistency of the International Legal Order", in O. K. Fauchald and A. Nollkaemper (eds.), *The Practice of International and National Courts and the (De-)fragmentation of International Law* (London: Hart Publishing, 2012), at 148.

26   Ibid.

27   C. McLachlan (2005), at 282.

28   See C. McLachlan, "Investment Treaties and General International Law", 57 *International and Comparative Law Quarterly* 361 (2008).

29   See F. Ortino, "Investment Treaties, Sustainable Development and Reasonableness Review: A Case against Strict Proportionality Balancing", 30(1) *Leiden Journal of International Law* 71 (2017), at 77.

30   See ibid., at 78–81.

31   See e.g. A. Kulick (2012); Pia Acconci, Mara Valenti and Anna De Luca (eds.), *General Interests of Host States in International Investment Law* (Cambridge: Cambridge University Press, 2014).

32   See B. Choudhury, "Recapturing Public Power: Is Investment Arbitration's Engagement of the Public Interest Contributing to the Democratic Deficit?", 41 *Vanderbilt Journal of International Law* 775 (2008), at 782–783.

33   See Trinh Hai Yen, *The Interpretation of Investment Treaties* (Leiden: Brill, 2014), at 75–100.

34   See e.g. C. Schreuer, "Comments on Treaty Interpretation", in R. Hofmann and C. J. Tams (eds.), *International Investment Law and General International Law – From Clinical Isolation to Systemic Integration?* (Baden-Baden: Nomos, 2011), at 71–74.

35 D. Mason, "'Deliberative Democratising' of Australian Treaty Making: Putting into Context the Significance of Online Access to the Treaty Process", 24 (2) *Journal of Law, Information and Science* 1 (2016), at 4.

36 See e.g. Law Commission of New Zealand, *The Treaty Making Process: Reform and the Role of Parliament* (1997), available at www.lawcom.govt.nz/sites/default/files/projectAvailableFormats/R45-TreatyMaking.pdf, at 25.

37 S. Joseph, *Blame It on the WTO?: A Human Rights Critique* (Oxford: Oxford Scholarship Online, 2011), at 76–77.

38 Australian Parliament (Foreign Affairs, Defence and Trade Committee), *Blind Agreement: Reforming Australia's Treaty-Making Process* (26 June 2015), available at www.aph.gov.au/Parliamentary_Business/Committees/Senate/Foreign_Affairs_Defence_and_Trade/Treaty-making_process/Report, at 71.

39 See generally S. W. Schill, "Editorial: Five Times Transparency in International Investment Law", 15 (3–4) *Journal World Investment and Trade* 363 (2014), at 363–364.

40 L. Cotula, *Investment Treaties and Citizens' Power: Lessons from Experience* (7 September 2015), available at www.iied.org/investment-treaties-citizens-power-lessons-experience.

41 D. Mason (2016), at 1.

42 Australian Parliament (Foreign Affairs, Defence and Trade Committee) (2015), at 71–72.

43 Ibid., at 72.

44 Ibid., at 73.

45 The Australian Government (Department of Foreign Affairs and Trade), *Treaty Making Process*, available at http://dfat.gov.au/international-relations/treaties/treaty-making-process/pages/treaty-making-process.aspx.

46 See e.g. L. Cotula, "*Democracy and International Investment Law*", *Leiden Journal of International Law (2017)*, DOI: https://doi.org/10.1017/S0922156517000152,; C. Megan, "The Democratic Deficit in the European Union," *Claremont-UC Undergraduate Research Conference on the European Union* (2009), available at http://scholarship.claremont.edu/urceu/vol2009/iss1/5.

47 See e.g. the European Commission, "Online Public Consultation on Investment Protection and Investor-to-State Dispute Settlement (ISDS) in the Transatlantic Trade and Investment Partnership Agreement (TTIP)" (13 July 2014), available at http://trade.ec.europa.eu/consultations/index.cfm?consul_id=179.

48 S. W. Schill, "Transparency as a Global Norm in International Investment Law" (15 September 2014), *Kluwer Arbitration Blog*, available at http://kluwerarbitrationblog.com/2014/09/15/transparency-as-a-global-norm-in-international-investment-law/.

49 J. E. Alvarez, *International Organizations as Law-Makers* (New York: Oxford University Press, 2005), at 277.

50 See e.g. The Australian Government (Department of Foreign Affairs and Trade), *Treaty Making Process*, available at http://dfat.gov.au/international-relations/treaties/treaty-making-process/pages/treaty-making-process.aspx; U.S. State Senate, *Treaties*, available at www.senate.gov/artandhistory/history/common/briefing/Treaties.htm; Article 7, the Constitution of the People's Republic of China (1982).

51 J. E. Alvarez (2005), at 284.

52 R. Wolfrum and V. Röben (eds.), *Developments of International Law in Treaty Making* (Heidelberg: Springer, 2005), at 1.

53   See e.g. K. Raustiala, "NGOs in International Treaty Making", in Duncan B. Hollis (ed.), *The Oxford Guide to Treaties* (Oxford: Oxford University Press, 2012), at 150–173.

54   WHO, *Public Hearings on the WHO Framework Convention on Tobacco Control*, available at www.who.int/tobacco/framework/public_hearings/en/.

55   See W. J. Wilson, "Legal Foundations for NGO Participation in Climate Treaty Negotiations", 10 *Sustainable Development L. & Policy* 54 (2010), at 54.

56   Law Commission of New Zealand (1997), at 80.

57   For instance, since expert, technical views are often needed by officials at international negotiations, representatives from the States, Territories, industry groups and other NGOs often serve as advisers to Australian delegations. See Department of Foreign Affairs and Trade of the Australian Government, *Treaty Making Process*, available at http://dfat.gov.au/international-relations/treaties/treaty-making-process/pages/treaty-making-process.aspx.

58   K. Raustiala (2012), at 173.

59   Law Commission of New Zealand (1997), at 25–29.

60   OHCHR, *Report of the Special Rapporteur on the Rights of Indigenous People (Addendum, The Situation of Indigenous Peoples in Paraguay)* (13 August 2015) (Doc. Number: A/HRC/30/41/Add.1), available at http://unsr.vtaulicorpuz.org/site/images/docs/country/2015-paraguay-a-hrc-30-41-add-1-en.pdf, at 11.

61   A. Kaushal, "Revisiting History: How the Past Matters for the Present Backlash against the Foreign Investment Regime", 50 (2) *Harvard International Law Journal* 491 (2009), at 491.

62   Article 10(3), the TEU.

63   J. Mayoral, "Democratic Improvements in the European Union under the Lisbon Treaty: Institutional Changes Regarding Democratic Government in the EU" (February 2011), available at www.eui.eu/Projects/EUDO-Institutions/Documents/EUDOreport922011.pdf, at 4.

64   See generally A. Ott, "The European Parliament's Role in EU Treaty-Making", 23 *Maastricht Journal of European and Comparative Law* 1009 (2016).

65   OHCHR, *Report of the Special Rapporteur on the Rights of Indigenous Peoples* (11 August 2014) (Doc. Number: A/HRC/27/52), available at http://unsr.vtaulicorpuz.org/site/images/docs/2014-annual-hrc-a-hrc-27-52-en.pdf, at 15.

66   OHCHR, *Report of the Special Rapporteur on the Rights of Indigenous Peoples* (11 August 2016) (Doc. Number: A/HRC/33/42), available at http://unsr.vtaulicorpuz.org/site/images/docs/annual/2016-annual-hrc-a-hrc-33-42-AEV.pdf.

67   Ibid., at 20–21.

Final remarks

Will future IIAs be made more compatible with sustainable development?

With ongoing globalization, transnational investment activities have become a major driving force of global economic development. These activities not only bring about economic prosperity, but also often generate profound sustainable development concerns. Yet IIAs as the main norm supplier of the global investment governance regime seem insufficiently capable of addressing these concerns. Today, the international community shares a growing consensus that IIAs need to be made more compatible with sustainable development. As Judge Huber pointed out nearly a century ago, "international law, like law in general, has the object of assuring the coexistence of different interests which are worthy of legal protection".[1] The question that naturally follows is: will future IIAs be more compatible with sustainable development? This question has several inter-related aspects. First, from a conceptual perspective, how can one properly construe the investment–development relationship in IIAs? Second, from a normative perspective, what kind of IIAs can be deemed compatible with sustainable development? Third, from the governance perspective, how can IIAs be negotiated and enforced in a manner that is compatible with sustainable development?

The first sub-question relates to how the stakeholders, especially states, understand sustainable development within the specialized legal system of international investment law. Although an investment–development relationship has long been recognized in IIAs, development is understood predominantly as an equivalent to economic growth, while many other elements of sustainable development are not envisaged. Such a conceptual paradigm, to some extent, has led to the general view that investment protection and sustainable development are inherently conflictual and mutually exclusive in the context of IIAs. Consequently, as these two goals cannot be achieved simultaneously, making IIAs compatible with sustainable development would inevitably lead to a deficit in investment protection.

The second sub-question essentially relates to how IIA provisions should be designed and reformed to better reflect and implement the multiple aspects of sustainable development, especially its social aspect. IIA-making should achieve the goal of protecting foreign investments and investors without necessarily marginalizing the sustainable development needs of the host states and the international community at large. To achieve this goal, efforts should be made with regard to several aspects.

First, IIAs should feature a better balance between the protection of foreign investment and the preservation of state regulatory power (for taking sustainable development measures). This implies a fully fledged reform of the existing IIA system, and will inevitably touch upon a wide range of IIA clauses, covering substantive (expropriation and FET), exceptive, public interest, procedural and soft-law provisions IIAs.

Second, and at a deeper level, IIAs should embody the principles of good governance and the rule of law. There is no doubt that states have inherent sovereign power in regulating foreign investments; the question is how to exercise such power properly? The two principles, though insufficiently clear in their contents and boundaries, provide necessary standards for assessing state conduct. While FET clauses, commonly seen in modern IIAs, are a classical expression of the principles of good governance and rule of law, the procedural provisions of IIAs should also be reformed.

Third, IIAs should be made a better norm supplier of the global investment governance regime. IIAs can only be effective in addressing sustainable development concerns if they are able to supply effective and enforceable sustainable development provisions. In light of this, the normativity of the relevant IIA provisions, such as the public interest provisions, should be greatly enhanced.

The third sub-question explores how the IIA-making and IIA-enforcing processes could be improved, so that sustainable development concerns associated with transnational investment activities can be adequately considered and properly addressed by IIA-makers and IIA-enforcers.

First, with regard to IIA-making, the key issue is to democratize the IIA-making process. As global investment governance involves multiple types of stakeholders other than investors and states, public participation is central to the democratization efforts. The existing experiences of some states, especially the EU's treaty-making practice after the Lisbon Treaty, seem to suggest that there are several approaches. These include improvement of the transparency of the IIA-making process and the engagement of non-state actors in this process in an appropriate way. In particular, NGOs, civil society groups and various marginalized groups are also playing an increasingly important role in global investment governance, especially in the fields of environmental protection, human rights and CSR.[2] Their participation in the IIA-making process could be beneficial to states as well.

Second, with regard to IIA-enforcing, i.e. ISA, the key issue is to ensure that arbitrators are encouraged (or at least not impeded) to properly consider the sensitivities around sustainable development in investment disputes. While arbitrators are generally required to apply IIAs and other international law rules within the procedural boundaries set out by the applicable arbitration laws and rules, they do possess broad discretionary power. Through ISA, arbitrators not only weigh the conflicting goals of investment protection and sustainable development promotion, but also undertake a duty to ensure that the arbitral proceeding is conducted in a legitimate manner. Arbitrators may play a helpful role in addressing sustainable development concerns by improving the transparency of ISA and interpreting IIA provisions by using appropriate treaty-interpretation tools.

Finally, will future IIAs be more compatible with sustainable development? There is no easy answer. The answer to this question should be explored from three perspectives.

From a conceptual perspective, it depends on how the stakeholders of global investment governance, particularly states, conceptualize the investment–development relationship implied in IIAs. In this respect, this book submits that development should be perceived in all its dimensions, as sustainable development.

From a normative perspective, it depends on whether states will incorporate a larger number and higher quality of sustainable development provisions in IIAs. In this respect, it is submitted that a comprehensive IIA norm-making reform should be carried out. IIA provisions should be made with greater normativity (to be better enforced) and diversity (to capture the full dimension of sustainable development). These provisions should feature a better balance (in constructing state–investor relationships) and good governance (in constructing state–public relationships).

From a governance perspective, it depends on how the various major stakeholders of the international investment governance regime can play their respective roles in a more balanced and coordinated way. Despite the fact that states would remain playing a central role in this game, other stakeholders, investors, arbitrators and civil societies, should also be allowed and even encouraged to play a more constructive and active role in IIA-making and dispute settlement.

Notes

1   *The Island of Palmas Case* (PCA), Award of 4 April 1928, available at www.hague justiceportal.net/Docs/PCA/Island%20of%20Palmas%20PCA%20PDF.pdf, at 36.
2   See e.g. K. Miles, *The Origins of International Investment Law: Empire, Environment and the Safeguarding of Capital* (Cambridge: Cambridge University Press, 2013), at 100–119.

Bibliography

Primary sources

General treaties

Charter of the United Nations, signed 26 June 1945, entered into force 24 October 1945

Convention on the Settlement of Investment Disputes between States and Nationals of Other States, signed 18 March 1965, entered into force 14 October 1966.

Paris Agreement under the UN Framework Convention on Climate Change, signed 22 April 2016, entered into force 4 November 2016

Treaty on European Union, signed 7 February 1992, entered into force 1 November 1993

Treaty on the Functioning of the European Union, signed 25 March 1957, entered into force 1 January 1958

Treaty of Lisbon amending the Treaty on European Union and the Treaty establishing the European Community, signed 18 December 2007, entered into force 1 December 2009

UN Convention on Biological Diversity, signed 22 May 1992, entered into force 29 December 1993

UN Framework Convention on Climate Change, signed in May1992, entered into force March 1994

UN Convention on the Recognition and Enforcement of Foreign Arbitral Awards, signed 10 June 1958

UN Convention on Transparency in Treaty-Based Investor–State Arbitration, signed 10 December 2014, entered into force 18 October 2017

Vienna Convention on the Law of Treaties, adopted 22 May 1969, entered into force 27 January 1980

WTO/GATT documents

Agreement on the Application of Sanitary and Phytosanitary Measures, entered into force 1 January 1995

Agreement on Trade-Related Aspects of Intellectual Property Rights, entered into force 1 January 1995

General Agreement on Tariffs and Trade, signed April 1947, entered into force 1 January 1948

General Agreement on Trade in Services, signed December 1993, entered into force
   January 1995
Marrakesh Ministerial Decision on Trade and Environment, 15 April 1994,
   (GATT/MTN.TNC/MIN(94)/1/Rev.1)
WTO Secretariat, "GATT/WTO Dispute Settlement Practice Relating to GATT
   Article XX, Paragraphs (b), (d) and (g)" (WT/CTE/W/203)

Selected international investment agreements

ASEAN Comprehensive Investment Agreement, signed 26 February 2009, entered into
   force 29 March 2012
Australia–China Free Trade Agreement, signed 17 June 2015, entered into force 17
   December 2015
Bahrain–United States Bilateral Investment Treaty, signed 29 September 1999, entered
   into force 30 May 2001
Belgium–Luxembourg Economic Union–Colombia Bilateral Investment Treaty, signed 4
   February 2009
Belgium–Luxembourg Economic Union–Tajikistan Bilateral Investment Treaty, signed
   10 February 2009
Canada–Columbia Free Trade Agreement, signed 21 November 2008, entered into force
   15 August 2011
Canada–EU Comprehensive Economic and Trade Agreement, signed 30 October 2016
CARICOM–Cuba Bilateral Investment Treaty, signed 19 May 1998
Central America Free Trade Agreement, signed 28 May 2004, entered into force 1
   March 2006
China–ASEAN Free Trade Agreement, signed 4 November 2002, entered into force 1
   January 2010
China–Canada Bilateral Investment Treaty, signed 9 September 2012, entered into force
   1 October 2014
China–Korea–Japan Trilateral Investment Treaty, signed 13 May 2012, entered into
   force 17 May 2014
China–Madagascar Bilateral Investment Treaty, signed 21 November 2005, entered into
   force 1 July 2007
China–New Zealand Bilateral Investment Treaty, signed 22 November 1988, entered
   into force 25 March 1989
China–Singapore Bilateral Investment Treaty, signed 21 November 1985, entered into
   force 7 February 1986
China–Thailand Bilateral Investment Treaty, signed 12 March 1985, entered into force
   13 December 1985
Croatia–Oman Bilateral Investment Treaty, signed 4 May 2004
E.U.–Vietnam Free Trade Agreement (negotiation in process)
Investment Agreement for the Common Market for Eastern and Southern Africa,
   signed 3 May 2007
Germany–Pakistan Bilateral Investment Treaty, signed 25 November 1959, entered into
   force 28 April 1962
North American Free Trade Agreement, signed 12 August 1992, entered into force 1
   January 1994
Panama–United States of America Bilateral Investment Treaty, signed 27 October 1982,
   entered into force 30 May 1991

Peru–Singapore Free Trade Agreement, signed 28 May 2008, entered into force 1
   August 2009
Singapore–U.S. Free Trade Agreement, signed 6 May 2003, entered into force 1 January
   2004
Transatlantic Trade and Investment Partnership (negotiation in process)
Trans–Pacific Partnership, signed 4 February 2016
U.S.–Korea Free Trade Agreement, signed 30 June 2007, entered into force 15 March 2012

Model IIAs

Canadian Model BIT (2004), available at http://italaw.com/documents/Canadian
   2004-FIPA-model-en.pdf
IISD Model International Investment Agreement for the Promotion of Sustainable
   Development (2004), available at
   www.italaw.com/sites/default/files/archive/ita1027.pdf
Indian Model BIT (2016), available at:
   www.mygov.in/sites/default/files/master_image/Model%20Text%20for%20the%20
   Indian%20Bilateral%20Investment%20Treaty.pdf
SADC Model Bilateral Investment Treaty, available at: www.iisd.org/itn/wp-
   content/uploads/2012/10/sadc-model-bit-template-final.pdf
U.S. Model BIT (2012), available at
   www.italaw.com/sites/default/files/archive/ita1028.pdf

International organization documents

EC, Commission Proposes New Investment Court System for TTIP and Other EU Trade
   and Investment Negotiations, 16 September 2015, available at:
   http://europa.eu/rapid/press-release_IP-15-5651_en.htm
EC, "Communication from the Commission", 2006, available at:
   http://trade.ec.europa.eu/doclib/docs/2006/february/tradoc_127374.pdf
EC, Concept Paper: Investment in TTIP and Beyond – the Path for Reform, available
   at: http://trade.ec.europa.eu/doclib/docs/2015/may/tradoc_153408.PDF
EC, "Online Public Consultation on Investment Protection and Investor-to-State
   Dispute Settlement (ISDS) in the Transatlantic Trade and Investment Partnership
   Agreement (TTIP)", 13 July 2014, available at http://trade.ec.europa.eu/
   consultations/index.cfm?consul_id=179
EC, "Towards a Comprehensive European International Investment Policy",
   Communication, 7 July 2010, available at:
   http://trade.ec.europa.eu/doclib/docs/2010/july/tradoc_146307.pdf
EC, "Why the New EU Proposal for an Investment Court System in TTIP Is Beneficial
   to Both States and Investors", 12 November 2015, available at
   http://europa.eu/rapid/press-release_MEMO-15-6060_en.htm
EP, "European Parliament resolution of 9 October 2013 on the EU–China negotiations
   for a bilateral investment agreement", available at: http://eur-lex.europa.eu/legal-
   content/EN/TXT/PDF/?uri=CELEX:52013IP0411&from=EN
EU, "EU–China 2020 Strategic Agenda for Cooperation", available at:
   https://eeas.europa.eu/headquarters/headquarters-homepage/15398/eu-china-2020-
   strategic-agenda-cooperation_en

ICSID, "The ICSID Caseload – Statistics", available at:
    https://icsid.worldbank.org/apps/icsidweb/resources/pages/icsid-caseloadstatistics.aspx
ICSID Secretariat, "Possible Improvement of the Framework for ICSID Arbitration",
    ICSID Secretariat Discussion Paper, 22 October 2004
ICSID Secretariat, "Suggested Changes to the ICSID Rules and Regulations", *ICSID
    Secretariat Discussion Paper*, 12 May 2015
ILC, Articles on Diplomatic Protection with Commentaries, YBILC, 2006, Vol. 2, Part
    Two
ILC, Draft Articles on Responsibility of States for Internationally Wrongful Acts with
    Commentaries, YBILC, 2001, Vol. 2, Part Two
ILO, *Tripartite Declaration of Principles concerning Multinational Enterprises and Social
    Policy* (1977)
OECD, *Employment and Industrial Relations – 2008 Annual Report on the OECD
    Guidelines for Multinational Enterprise*, available at:
    www.oecd.org/corporate/mne/employmentandindustrialrelations-
    2008annualreportontheoecdguidelinesformultinationalenterprises.htm
OECD, *G20 Trade Ministers Meeting Statement*, 9–10 July 2016, Shanghai, available at:
    www.oecd.org/daf/inv/investment-policy/G20-Trade-Ministers-Statement-July-
    2016.pdf
OECD, *Guidelines for Multinational Enterprises* (2011 edn.), available at:
    www.oecd.org/daf/inv/mne/48004323.pdf
OECD, *Guidelines for Recipient Country Investment Policies Relating to National Security*,
    available at: www.oecd.org/investment/investment-policy/43384486.pdf
OECD, *International Investment Law: A Changing Landscape*, 2005, Paris: OECD Publishing
OECD, *International Investment Perspectives: Freedom of Investment in a Changing World*
    (Paris: OECD, 2007)
OECD, "The OECD Guidelines for Multinational Enterprises", *OECD Policy Brief* (June
    2001), available at: www.oecd.org/investment/mne/1903291.pdf
OECD, "Transparency and Third Party Participation in Investor–State Dispute
    Settlement Procedures", *OECD Working Papers on International Investment*, January
    2005, available at: http://dx.doi.org/10.1787/524613550768
OHCHR, *Report of the Special Rapporteur on the Rights of Indigenous Peoples*,
    (A/HRC/27/52), 11 August 2014, available at:
    http://unsr.vtaulicorpuz.org/site/images/docs/2014-annual-hrc-a-hrc-27-52-en.pdf
OHCHR, *Report of the Special Rapporteur on the Rights of Indigenous Peoples*,
    (A/HRC/33/42), 11 August 2016, available at: http://unsr.vtaulicorpuz.org/site/
    images/docs/annual/2016-annual-hrc-a-hrc-33-42-AEV.pdf
OHCHR, *Report of the Special Rapporteur on the Rights of Indigenous Peoples* (*Addendum,
    The Situation of Indigenous Peoples in Paraguay*), (A/HRC/30/41/Add.1), 13 August
    2015, available at: http://unsr.vtaulicorpuz.org/site/images/docs/country/2015-
    paraguay-a-hrc-30-41-add-1-en.pdf
UN, *Report of the Secretary-General on the Rule of Law and Transitional Justice in Conflict
    and Post-Conflict Societies* (2004)
UNCED, *Agenda 21* (1992)
UNCED, *Rio Declaration on Environment and Development* (1992)
UNCITRAL, Rules on Transparency in Treaty-Based Investor–State Arbitration
    (entered into force 1 April 2014)
UNCTAD, "Bilateral Investment Treaties 1995–2006: Trends in Investment
    Rulemaking (UNCTAD/ITE/IIT/2006/5), 2007

UNCTAD, "Denunciation of the ICSID Convention and BITs: Impact on Investor–State Claims", *IIA Issues Note*, No. 2, December 2010

UNCTAD, "Dispute Settlement: State–State", *UNCTAD Series on Issues of International Investment Agreements* (UNCTAD/ITE/IIT/2003/1), 2003

UNCTAD, "Expropriation", *UNCTAD Series of Issues of International Investment Agreements II* (UNCTAD/DIAE/IA/2011/7), 2012

UNCTAD, "Fair and Equitable Treatment", *UNCTAD Series on Issues in International Investment Agreements II* (UNCTAD/DIAE/IA/2011/5), 2012

UNCTAD, Investment Policy Framework for Sustainable Development (2012), available at: http://unctad.org/en/PublicationsLibrary/diaepcb2012d5_en.pdf

UNCTAD, Investment Policy Framework for Sustainable Development (2015), available at: http://unctad.org/en/PublicationsLibrary/diaepcb2015d5_en.pdf

UNCTAD, "Investor–State Disputes: Prevention and Alternatives to Arbitration", *UNCTAD Series on International Investment Policies for Development* (UNCTAD/DIAE/IA/2009/11), 2010

UNCTAD, "The Protection of National Security in IIAs" (UNCTAD/DIAE/IA/2008/5), 2009

UNCTAD, "The Role of International Investment Agreements in Attracting Foreign Direct Investment to Developing Countries", *UNCTAD Series on International Investment Policies for Development* (UNCTAD/DIAE/IA/2009/5), 2009

UNCTAD, "Towards a New Generation of International Investment Policies: UNCTAD's Fresh Approach to Multilateral Investment Policy-Making", *IIA Issue Note*, No. 5, July 2013

UNCTAD, "Transparency", *UNCTAD Series on Issues in International Investment Agreements* (UNCTAD/ITE/IIT/2003/4), 2004

UNCTAD, "Transparency in IIAs", *UNCTAD Series on Issues in International Investment Agreements II* (UNCTAD/DIAE/IA/2011/6), 2012

UNCTAD, *UNCTAD Facilitates G20 Consensus on Guiding Principles for Global Investment Policymaking*, 11 July 2016, available at: http://investmentpolicyhub.unctad.org/News/Hub/Home/508

UNEP, *Corporate Social Responsibility and Regional Trade and Investment Agreements* (2011),

UNESCAP, "What Is Good Governance?", available at: www.unescap.org/sites/default/files/good-governance.pdf

UNGA, 2005 World Summit Outcome (A/RES/60/1), 24 October 2005

UNGA, Declaration on the Establishment of a New International Economic Order (A/RES/S-6/3201), 1 May 1974

UNGA, "Permanent Sovereignty over Natural Resources", Resolution 1803, 14 December 1962

UNGC, *The Ten Principles of the United Nations Global Compact*, available at: www.unglobalcompact.org/what-is-gc/mission/principles

UNHRC, Guiding Principles on Business and Human Rights (2011) (HR/PUB/11/04), available at: www.ohchr.org/Documents/Publications/GuidingPrinciplesBusinessHR_EN.pdf

UNHRC, "What Are Human Rights", available at: www.ohchr.org/EN/Issues/Pages/WhatareHumanRights.aspx

WCED, *Our Common Future* (1987), available at: www.un-documents.net/wced-ocf.htm

WHO, Public Hearings on the WHO Framework Convention on Tobacco Control, available at: www.who.int/tobacco/framework/public_hearings/en/

WWSD, *Johannesburg Declaration on Sustainable Development* (2002), available at:
www.un-documents.net/jburgdec.htm

National entities' documents

Australian Government (Department of Foreign Affairs and Trade), *Treaty Making
Process*, available at: http://dfat.gov.au/international-relations/treaties/treaty-making-
process/pages/treaty-making-process.aspx
Australian Parliament (Foreign Affairs, Defence and Trade Committee), *Blind
Agreement: Reforming Australia's Treaty-Making Process*, 26 June 2015, available at:
www.aph.gov.au/Parliamentary_Business/Committees/Senate/Foreign_Affairs_
Defence_and_Trade/Treaty-making_process/Report
FTC, *Statement of the Free Trade Commission on Non-disputing Party Participation*,
available at www.state.gov/documents/organization/38791.pdf
Law Commission of New Zealand, *The Treaty Making Process: Reform and the Role of
Parliament* (1997), available at www.lawcom.govt.nz/sites/default/files/
projectAvailableFormats/R45-TreatyMaking.pdf
Ministry of Foreign Affairs, Trade and Development of Canada, *Final Environmental
Assessment of the Canada–China Foreign Investment Protection Agreement (FIPA)*,
available at: www.international.gc.ca/trade-agreements-accords-commerciaux/agr-
acc/china-chine/finalEA-china-chine-EEfinale.aspx?lang=en
MOFCOM, Regulations of Overseas Investment Management (19 August 2014),
available at: www.mofcom.gov.cn/article/b/c/201409/20140900723361.shtml (original
in Chinese).
MOFCOM, Spokesperson's Remarks on Outward Investment and Economic
Cooperation of the Ministry of Commerce Comments on China's Outward
Investment and Economic Cooperation in 2015, available at:
http://english.mofcom.gov.cn/article/newsrelease/policyreleasing/201602/2
0160201251488.shtml
U.S. Department of Justice (The Criminal Division) and U.S. Securities and Exchange
Commission (The Enforcement Division), "A Resource Guide to the FCPA U.S.
Foreign Corrupt Practices Act", 14 November 2012, available at:
www.justice.gov/sites/default/files/criminal-fraud/legacy/2015/01/16/guide.pdf
U.S. State Senate, *Treaties*, available at:
www.senate.gov/artandhistory/history/common/briefing/Treaties.htm

Secondary sources

Monographic books

Alvarez, J. E., *International Organizations as Law-Makers*, 2005, New York: Oxford
University Press
Bernasconi-Osterwalder, N., *Environment and Trade: A Guide to WTO Jurisprudence*,
2005, London: Earthscan
Birnie, P., Boyle, A. and Redgwell, C., *International Law and the Environment* (2nd edn.),
2002, Oxford: Oxford University Press
Birnie, P., Boyle, A. and Redgwell, C., *International Law and the Environment* (3rd edn.),
2009, Oxford: Oxford University Press

Bonanomi, E. B., *Sustainable Development in International Law Making and Trade*, 2015, Cheltenham: Edward Elgar Publishing

Bonnitcha, J., *Substantive Protection under Investment Treaties: A Legal and Economic Analysis*, 2014, Cambridge: Cambridge University Press

Brownlie, I., *Principles of Public International Law* (7th edn.), 2008, Oxford: Oxford University Press

Cassese, A., *Human Rights in a Changing World*, 1990, Cambridge: Polity Press

Dolzer, R. and Stevens, M., *Bilateral Investment Treaties*, 1995, The Hague: Martinus Nijhoff Publishers

Dolzer, R. and Schreuer, C., *Principles of International Investment Law* (1st edn.), 2008, Oxford: Oxford University Press

Dolzer, R. and Schreuer, C., *Principles of International Investment Law* (2nd edn.), 2012, Oxford: Oxford University Press

Fung, H., Law, S. and Yau, J., *Socially Responsible Investment in a Global Environment*, 2010, Cheltenham: Edward Elgar Publishing

Gallagher, N. and Shan, W., *Chinese Investment Treaties: Policies and Practice*, 2009, Oxford: Oxford University Press

Hobér, K., *Investment Arbitration in Eastern Europe: In Search of a Definition of Expropriation*, 2007, New York: Juris

Honkonen, T., *The Common but Differentiated Responsibility in Multilateral Environmental Agreements: Regulatory and Policy Aspects*, 2009, The Hague: Kluwer Law International

Huerta-Goldman, J. A., Romanetti, A. and Stirnimann, F. X. (eds.), *WTO Litigation, Investment Arbitration and Commercial Arbitration*, 2013, The Hague: Kluwer Law International

Joseph, S., *Blame It on the WTO?: A Human Rights Critique*, 2011, Oxford: Oxford Scholarship Online

Karavias, M., *Corporate Obligations under International Law*, 2013, Oxford: Oxford University Press

Kilovesi, K., *The WTO Dispute Settlement System: Challenges of the Environment, Legitimacy and Fragmentation*, 2011, Alphen aan den Rijn: Kluwer Law International

Kläger, R., *Fair and Equitable Treatment in International Investment Law*, 2011, Cambridge: Cambridge University Press

Komori, T. and Wellens, K. (eds.), *Public Interest Rules of International Law: Towards Effective Implementation*, 2009, Farnham: Ashgate Publishing

Kulick, A., *Global Public Interest in International Investment Law*, 2012, Cambridge: Cambridge University Press

Lowe, V., *International Law*, 2007, Oxford: Oxford University Press

Malanczuk, P., *Akehurst's Modern Introduction to International Law* (7th edn), 1997, London: Routledge

Martinez-Fraga, P. J. and Reetz, C. R., *Public Purpose in International Law: Rethinking Regulatory Sovereignty in the Global Era*, 2015, Cambridge: Cambridge University Press

Merkouris, P., *Article 31(3)(c) VCLT and the Principle of Systemic Integration: Normative Shadows in Plato's Cave*, 2015, The Netherlands: Brill

Miles, K., *The Origins of International Investment Law: Empire, Environment and the Safeguarding of Capital*, 2013, Cambridge: Cambridge University Press

Paparinskis, M., *International Minimum Standard and Fair and Equitable Treatment*, 2013, Oxford: Oxford University Press

Parra, A. R., *The History of ICSID*, 2012, Oxford: Oxford University Press

Raustiala, K., NGOs in International Treaty Making, in Hollis, Duncan B. (ed.), *The Oxford Guide to Treaties*, 2012, Oxford: Oxford University Press

Richardson, B. J., *Socially Responsible Investment Law: Regulating the Unseen Polluters*, 2008, New York: Oxford University Press

Rosenau, J. N. and Czempiel, E. O. (eds.), Governance without Government, 1992, Cambridge: Cambridge University Press

Rosentreter, D., *Article 31(3)(c) of the Vienna Convention on the Law of Treaties and the Principle of Systemic Integration in International Investment Law and Arbitration*, 2015, Baden-Baden: Nomos

Sacerdoti, G., Acconci, P., Valenti, M. and De Luca, A. (eds.), *General Interests of Host States in International Investment Law*, 2014, Cambridge: Cambridge University Press

Salacuse, J. W., *The Law of Investment Treaties* (2nd edn.), 2015, Oxford: Oxford University Press

Salacuse, J. W., *The Three Laws of International Investment: National, Contractual and International Frameworks for Foreign Capital*, 2013, Oxford: Oxford University Press

Schill, S. W., *The Multilateralization of International Investment Law*, 2009, Cambridge: Cambridge University Press

Schutter, O. De, Swinnen, J. and Wouters, J. (eds.), *Foreign Direct Investment and Human Development: The Law and Economics of International Investment Agreements*, 2013, Abingdon: Routledge

Shaw, M., *International Law* (5th edn.), 2003, Cambridge: Cambridge University Press

Sornarajah, M., *The International Law on Foreign Investment* (2nd edn), 2004, Cambridge: Cambridge University Press

Sornarajah, M. *The International Law on Foreign Investment* (3rd edn.), 2010, Cambridge: Cambridge University Press

Tladi, D., *Sustainable Development in International Law: An Analysis of Key Enviro-economic Instruments*, 2007, Cape Town: Pretoria University Law Press

Tudor, I., *The Fair and Equitable Treatment Standard in International Law of Foreign Investment*, 2008, Oxford: Oxford University Press

Vadi, V., *Public Health in International Investment Law and Arbitration*, 2013, Abingdon: Routledge

Van den Bossche, P., *The Law and Policy of the World Trade Organization: Text, Cases and Materials* (2nd edn.), 2008, Cambridge: Cambridge University Press

Van Harten, G., *Investment Treaty Arbitration and Public Law*, 2007, Oxford: Oxford University Press

Villiger, M. E., *Commentary on the 1969 Convention on the Law of Treaties*, 2009, Leiden: Martinus Nijhoff

Voigt, C., *Sustainable Development as a Principle of International Law: Resolving Conflicts between Climate Measures and WTO Law*, 2009, Leiden: Martinus Nijhoff Publishers

Wolfrum, R. and Röben, V. (eds.), *Developments of International Law in Treaty Making*, 2005, Heidelberg: Springer

WTO, *WTO Analytical Index* (3rd edn.), 2012, Cambridge: Cambridge University Press

Yen, T. H., *The Interpretation of Investment Treaties*, 2014, Leiden: Brill

Zabalza, G. O., *The Principle of Systematic Integration: Towards a Coherent International Legal Order*, 2012, Zurich: Lit

Zerk, J. A., *Multinationals and Corporate Social Responsibility: Limitations and Opportunities in International Law*, 2006, Cambridge: Cambridge University Press

Edited book chapters

Acconci, P., The Integration of Non-Investment Concerns as an Opportunity for the Modernization of International Investment Law: is a Multilateral Approach Desirable?, in Sacerdoti, G., Acconci, P., Valenti, M. and De Luca, A. (eds.), *General Interests of Host States in International Investment Law*, 2014, Cambridge: Cambridge University Press

Alschner, W. and Tuerk, E., "The Role of International Investment Agreements in Fostering Sustainable Development", in Baetens, F. (ed.), *International Investment Law within International Law: Integrationist Perspectives*, 2013, Cambridge: Cambridge University Press

Asada, M., Security Council Resolution 1540 and International Legislation, in Komori, T. and Wellens, K. (eds.), *Public Interest Rules in International Law: Towards Effective Implementation*, 2016, London and New York: Routledge

Asteriti, A. and Tams, C., Transparency and Representation of the Public Interest in Investment Treaty Arbitration, in Schill, S. W. (ed.), *International Investment Law and Comparative Public Law*, 2011, Oxford: Oxford University Press

Ayres, G. and Mitchell, A., General and Security Exceptions under the GATT and the GATS, in Carr, I., Bhuiyan, J. and Alam, S. (eds.), *International Trade Law and WTO*, 2013, Sydney: Federation Press

Berner, K., Reconciling Investment Protection and Sustainable Development, in Hindelang, S. and Krajewski, M. (eds.), *Shifting Paradigms in International Investment Law: More Balanced, Less Isolated, Increasingly Diversified*, 2016, Oxford: Oxford University Press

Binder, C., Necessity Exceptions, the Argentine Crisis and Legitimacy Concerns, in Treves, T., Seatzu, F. and Trevisanut, S. (eds.), *Foreign Investment, International Law and Common Concerns*, 2014, Abingdon: Routledge

Bjorklund, A. K., Assessing the Effectiveness of Soft Law Instruments in International Investment Law, in Bjorklund, A. K. and Reinisch, A. (eds.), *International Investment Law and Soft Law*, 2013, Cheltenham: Edward Elgar Publishing

Bjorklund, A. K., Investment Treaty Arbitral Decisions as Jurisprudence Constante, in Picker, C., Bunn, I. and Arner, D. (eds.), *International Economic Law: The State and Future of the Discipline*, 2008, Oxford: Hart Publishing

Born, G. B. and Shenkman, E. G., Confidentiality and Transparency in Commercial and Investor–State International Arbitration, in Rogers, C. A. and Alford, R. P. (eds.), *The Future of Investment Arbitration*, 2009, Oxford: Oxford University Press

Bungenberg, M. and Chi, M., Chinese Investment Law, in Bungenberg, M., Griebel, J., Hobe, S. and Reinisch, A. (eds.), *International Investment Law: A Handbook*, 2015, Baden-Baden: Nomos

Cottier, T., and Delimatsis, P., Article XIV bis GATS: Security Exceptions, in Wolfrum, R., Stoll, P. T. and Feinäugle, C. (eds.), *Max Planck Commentaries on World Trade Law – Trade in Services*, 2008, Leiden: Martinus Nijhoff Publishers

D'Aspremont, J., The Systemic Integration of International Law by Domestic Courts: Domestic Judges as Architects of the Consistency of the International Legal Order, in Fauchald, O. K. and Nollkaemper, A. (eds.), *The Practice of International and National Courts and the (De-)fragmentation of International Law*, 2012, London: Hart Publishing

Desta, M. G., Soft Law in International Law: An Overview, in Bjorklund A. and Reinisch, A. (eds.), *Soft Law and International Investment Law*, 2013, Cheltenham: Edward Elgar Publishing

Dimsey, M., Submission by a Third Person, in Euler, D., Gehring, M. and Scherer, M. (eds.), *Transparency in International Investment Arbitration: A Guide to the UNCITRAL Rules of Transparency in Treaty-Based Investor–State Arbitration*, 2015, Cambridge: Cambridge University Press

Gehring, M. W. and Kent, A., International Investment Agreements and Sustainable Development: Future Pathways, in Alam, S., Bhuiyan, J. H., Chowdhury, T. M. R. and Techera, E. J. (eds.), *International Investment Agreements and Sustainable Development: Future Pathways*, 2013, Abingdon: Routledge

Gehring, M. and Scherer, M., Public Interest in Investment Arbitration, in Euler, D., Gehring, M. and Scherer, M. (eds.), *Transparency in International Investment Arbitration: A Guide to the UNCITRAL Rules of Transparency in Treaty-Based Investor–State Arbitration*, 2015, Cambridge: Cambridge University Press

Hirsch, M., Investment Tribunals and Human Rights: Divergent Paths, in Dupuy, P. M., Francioni, F. and Petersmann, E. U. (eds.), *Human Rights in International Investment Law and Arbitration*, 2009, Oxford: Oxford University Press

Hirsch, M., Source of International Investment Law, in Bjorklund, A. K. and Reinisch, A. (eds.), *Soft Law and International Investment Law*, 2013, Cheltenham: Edward Elgar Publishing

Hobe, S., The Law Relating to Aliens, the International Minimum Standard and State Responsibility, in Bungenberg, M., Griebel, J., Hobe, S. and Reinisch, A. (eds.), *International Investment Law: A Handbook*, 2015, Baden-Baden: Nomos

Holzgrefe, J., The Humanitarian Intervention Debate, in Holzgrefe, J. and Keohane R. (eds.), *Humanitarian Intervention: Ethical, Legal and Political Dilemmas*, 2003, Cambridge: Cambridge: Cambridge University Press

Howse, R., Adjudicative Legitimacy and Treaty Interpretation in International Trade Law: The Early Years of WTO Jurisprudence, in Weiler, J. H. H. (ed.), *The EU, the WTO, and the NAFTA: Towards a Common Law of International Trade?*, 2010, Oxford: Oxford University Press

Khalfan, A., International Investment Law and Human Rights, in Segger, M. C. et al. (eds.), *Sustainable Development in World Investment Law*, 2011, Alphen aan den Rijn: Kluwer Law International

Kaufmann-Kohler, G., Interpretive Powers of the Free Trade Commission and the Rule of Law, in Bachand, F. (ed.), *Fifteen Years of NAFTA Chapter 11 Arbitration*, 2011, New York: Juris Publishing

Kilovesi, K., *The WTO Dispute Settlement System: Challenges of the Environment, Legitimacy and Fragmentation*, 2011, The Netherlands: Kluwer Law International

Kingsbury, B. and Schill, S. W., Public Law Concepts to Balance Investors' Rights with State Regulatory Actions in the Public Interest – The Concept of Proportionality, in Schill, S. W. (ed.), *International Investment Law and Comparative Public Law*, 2010, Oxford: Oxford University Press

Kurtz, J., Building Legitimacy through Interpretation in Investor–State Arbitration: On Consistency, Coherence and the Identification of Applicable Law, in Douglas, Z., Pauwelyn, J. and Viñuales, J. (eds.), *The Foundations of International Investment Law: Bringing Theory into Practice*, 2014, Oxford: Oxford University Press

Lafferty, W. M., From Environmental Protection to Sustainable Development: The Challenge of Decoupling through Sectoral Integration, in Lafferty, W. M. (ed.), *Governance for Sustainable Development: The Challenge of Adopting Form to Function*, 2004, Cheltenham: Edward Elgar Publishing

Legum, B., Options to Establish an Appellate Mechanism for Investment Disputes, in

Sauvant, K. (ed.), *Appeals Mechanism in International Investment Disputes*, 2008, Oxford: Oxford University Press

Liang, D. and Liu, J., Preventing Environmental Deterioration from International Trade and Investment: How China Can Learn from NFATA's Experience to Strengthen Domestic Environmental Governance and Ensure Sustainable Development, in Kong, H. and Wroth, W. (eds.), *NAFTA and Sustainable Development: History, Experience and Prospects for Reform*, 2015, Cambridge: Cambridge University Press

Lowe, V., Sustainable Development and Unsustainable Arguments, in Boyle, A. and Freestone, D. (eds.), *International Law and Sustainable Development*, 1999, Oxford: Oxford University Press

Maupin, J., Transparency in International Investment Law: The Good, the Bad and the Murky, in Bianchi, A. and Peters, A. (eds.), *Transparency in International Law*, 2013, Cambridge: Cambridge University Press

Mistelis, L., Confidentiality and Third-Party Participation: *UPS* v. *Canada* and *Methanex Corp.* v. *USA*, in Weiler, T. (ed.), *International Investment Law and Arbitration: Leading Cases from the ICSID, NAFTA, Bilateral Treaties and Customary International Law*, 2005, London: Cameron May

Muchlinski, P., Regulating Multinational Enterprises, in Bungenberg, M., Herrmann, C., Krajewski, M., and Terhecht J. P., (eds.), *EYBEL*, 2016, Switzerland: Springer International Publishing AG

Newcombe, A., Investor Misconduct, in de Mestral, A. and Lévesque, C. (eds.), *Improving International Investment Agreements*, 2013, London and New York: Routledge

Newcombe, A. and Paradell, L., *Law and Practice of Investment Treaties*, 2009, Alphen aan den Rijn: Kluwer Law International

Raimondo, F. O., *General Principles of Law in the Decisions of International Criminal Courts and Tribunals*, 2008, Leiden: Martinus Nijhoff Publishers

Reinisch, A., Legality of Expropriations, in Reinisch, A. (ed.), *Standards of Investment Protection*, 2008, Oxford: Oxford University Press

Reiner, C. and Schreuer, C., Human Rights and International Investment Arbitration, in Dupuy, P. M., Francioni, F. and Petersmann, E. U. (eds.), *Human Rights in International Investment Law and Arbitration*, 2009, Oxford: Oxford University Press

Reinisch, A., Expropriation, in Muchlinski, P., Ortino, F. and Schreuer, C. (eds.), *The Oxford Handbook of International Investment Law*, 2008, Oxford: Oxford University Press

Rose-Ackerman, S. and Tobin, J. L., Do BITs Benefit Developing Countries?, in Rogers, C. A. and Alford, R. P. (eds.), *The Future of Investment Arbitration*, 2009, New York: Oxford University Press

Schill, S. W., Tams, C. and Hofmann, R., International Investment Law and Development: Friends or Foes?, in Schill, S. W., Tams, C. and Hofmann, R. (eds.), *International Investment Law and Development: Bridging the Gap*, 2015, Cheltenham: Edward Elgar Publishing

Schreuer, C., Comments on Treaty Interpretation, in Hofmann, R. and Tams, C. (eds.), *International Investment Law and General International Law – From Clinical Isolation to Systemic Integration?*, 2011, Baden-Baden: Nomos

Schreuer, C., Denunciation of the ICSID Convention and Consent to Arbitration, in Waibel, M., Kaushal, A., Chung K. L. and Balchin, C. (eds.), *The Backlash against Investment Arbitration: Perceptions and Reality*, 2010, The Hague: Kluwer Law International

Segger, M., Gehring, M. W. and Newcombe, A. (eds.), *Sustainable Development in World Investment Law*, 2011, Alphen aan den Rijn: Kluwer Law International

Sjafjell, B., Quo vadis, Europe? The Significance of Sustainable Development as Objective, Principle and Rule of EU Law, in Bailliet, C. M. (ed.), *Non-State Actors, Soft Law and Protective Regimes: From the Margins*, 2012, Cambridge: Cambridge University Press

Taillant, J. D. and Bonnitcha,J., International Investment Law and Human Rights, in Segger, M. C. et al. (eds.), *Sustainable Development in World Investment Law*, 2011, Alphen aan den Rijn: Kluwer Law International

Tienhaara, K., Regulatory Chill and the Threat of Arbitration: A View from Political Science, in Brown, C. and Miles, K. (eds.), *Evolution in Investment Treaty Law and Arbitration*, 2011, Cambridge: Cambridge University Press

Treves, T., Seatzu, F. and Trevisanut, S. (eds.), *Foreign Investment, International Law and Common Concerns*, 2014, London and New York: Routledge

Vadi, V. S., Reconciling Public Health and Investor Rights: The Case of Tobacco, in Dupuy, P., Petersmann, E. and Francioni, F. (eds.), *Human Rights in International Investment Law and Arbitration*, 2009, Oxford: Oxford University Press

VanDuzer, J. A., "Sustainable Development Provisions in International Trade Treaties: What Lessons for International Investment Agreements?", in Hindelang, S. and Krajewski, M. (eds.), *Shifting Paradigms in International Investment Law: More Balanced, Less Isolated, Increasingly Diversified*, 2016, Oxford: Oxford University Press

Viñuales, J. E., Sovereignty in Foreign Investment Law, in Z. Douglas, Pauwelyn, J. and Viñuales, Jorge E. (eds.), *The Foundations of International Investment Law: Bringing Theory into Practice*, 2014, Oxford: Oxford University Press

Journal and yearbook articles

Abbott, K. W. and Snidal, D., Hard and Soft Law in International Governance, *International Organization*, Vol. 54, No. 3, 2000

Akande, D. and Williams, S., International Adjudication on National Security Issues: What Role for the WTO?, *Virginia Journal of International Law*, Vol. 43, 2003

Ala'i, P., Free Trade or Sustainable Development? An Analysis of the WTO Appellate Body's Shift to a More Balanced Approach to Trade Liberalization, *American University International Law Review*, Vol. 14, No. 4, 1999

Alford, R. P., The Convergence of International Trade and Investment Arbitration, *Santa Clara Journal of International Law*, Vol. 12, No. 1, 2014

Alford, R. P., The Self-Judging WTO Security Exception, *Utah Law Review*, Vol. 3, 2011

Allen, B. E. and Soave, Tommaso, Jurisdictional Overlap in WTO Dispute Settlement and Investment Arbitration, *Arbitration International*, Vol. 30, No. 1, 2014

Alston, P., "Core Labor Standards" and the Transformation of the International Labor Rights Regime, *European Journal of International Law*, Vol. 15, 2007

Alvarez, J. and Khamsi, K., The Argentine Crisis and Foreign Investors: A Glimpse into the Heart of the Investment Regime, *Yearbook of International Investment Law and Policy* 2008–2009

Anderson, L., Antiquated before They Can Ossify: States that Fail before They Form, *Journal of International Affairs*, Vol. 58, No. 1, 2004

Bagner, H., Confidentiality–A Fundamental Principle in International Commercial Arbitration?, *Journal of International Arbitration*, Vol. 18, No. 2, 2001

Bantekas, I., Corporate Social Responsibility in International Law, *Boston University International Law Journal*, Vol. 22, 2004

Barral, V., Sustainable Development in International Law: Nature and Operation of an Evolutive Legal Norm, *European Journal of International Law*, Vol. 23, No. 2, 2012

Bartholomeusz, L., The Amicus Curiae before International Courts and Tribunals, *Non-State Actors and International Law*, Vol. 5, 2005

Bastin, L., The Amicus Curiae in Investor–State Arbitration, *Cambridge Journal of International and Comparative Law*, Vol. 1, No. 3, 2012

Baughen, S., Expropriation and Environmental Regulation: The Lessons of NAFTA Chapter Eleven, *Journal of Environmental Law*, Vol. 18, 2006

Benvenisti, E., The Law of Global Governance, *Recueil des cours*, Vol. 368, 2013

Bhala, R., National Security and International Trade Law: What the GATT Says and What the United States Does, *University of Pennsylvania Journal of International Law*, Vol. 19, 1998

Bjorklund, A. K., Convergence or Complementarity?, *Santa Clara Journal of International Law*, Vol. 12, No. 1, 2014

Böckstigel, K., Commercial and Investment Arbitration: How Different Are They Today?, *Arbitration International*, Vol. 28, No. 4, 2012

Bridgeman, N. L. and Hunter, D. B., Narrowing the Accountability Gap: Toward a New Foreign Investor Accountability Mechanism, *Georgetown International Environmental Law Review*, Vol. 20, No. 2, 2008

Brower, C. N. and Schill, S., Is Arbitration a Threat or a Boon to the Legitimacy of International Investment Law?, *Chicago Journal of International Law*, Vol. 9, No. 2, 2009

Buckley, R. P. and Blyschak, P., Guarding the Open Door: Non-party Participation Before the International Centre for Settlement of Investment Disputes, *Banking and Finance Law Review*, Vol. 22, 2007

Bungenberg, M., Going Global? The EU Common Commercial Policy after Lisbon, *EYBIEL* 2010

Burke-White, W. W. and Von Staten, A., Investment Protection in Extraordinary Times: The Interpretation and Application of Non-Precluded Measures Provisions in Bilateral Investment Treaties, *Virginia Journal of International Law*, Vol. 48, No. 2, 2008

Buys, C. G., The Tension between Confidentiality and Transparency in International Arbitration, *American Review of International Arbitration*, Vol. 14, No. 1, 2003

Chaisse, J. and Polo, M., Globalization of Water Privatization – Ramifications of Investor–State Disputes in the 'Blue Gold' Economy', *Boston College International and Comparative Law Review*, Vol. 38, No. 1, 2015

Charnovitz, S., The WTO's Environmental Progress, *Journal of International Economic Law*, Vol. 10, No. 3, 2007

Chi, M., "Exhaustible Natural Resources" in WTO Law: GATT Article XX (g) Disputes and their Implications, *Journal of World Trade*, Vol. 8, No. 5, 2014

Chi, M., The "Greenization" of Chinese BITs: An Empirical Study of the Environmental Provisions in Chinese BITs and Its Implications for China's Future BIT-Making, *Journal of International Economic Law*, Vol. 18, No. 3, 2015

Chi, M., From Europeanization toward Americanization: The Shift of China's Dichotomic Investment Treaty-Making Strategy, *Canadian Foreign Policy Journal*, Vol. 23, No. 2, 2017

Choudhury, B., Democratic Implications Arising from the Intersection of Investment Arbitration and Human Rights, *Alberta Law Review*, Vol. 46, No. 4, 2009

Choudhury, B., Recapturing Public Power: Is Investment Arbitration's Engagement of the Public Interest Contributing to the Democratic Deficit?, *Vanderbilt Journal of Transnational Law*, Vol. 41, 2008

Chow, D. C. K., Why China Opposes Human Rights in the World Trade Organization, *University of Pennsylvania Journal of International Law*, Vol. 35, No. 1, 2013

Christie, G. C., What Constitutes a Taking of Property under International Law, *BYBIL*, Vol. 38, 1963

Chung, O., The Lopsided International Investment Law Regime and its Effects on the Future of Investor–State Arbitration", *Virginia Journal of International Law*, Vol. 47, 2007

Coe, J. J., Jr, Transparency in the Resolution of Investor–State Dispute – Adoption, Adaptation, and NAFTA Leadership, *Kansas Law Review*, Vol. 54, 2006

Commission, J. P., Precedent in Investment Treaty Arbitration: A Citation Analysis of a Developing Jurisprudence, *International of International Arbitration*, Vol. 24, No. 2, 2007

Compa, L., Labour Rights and Labour Standards in International Trade, *Law and Policy in International Business*, Vol. 25, 1993

Compa, L., The Multilateral Agreement on Investment and International Labour Rights: A Failed Connection, *Cornell International Law Journal*, Vol. 31, 2007

Connolly, K., Say What You Mean: Improved Drafting Resources as a Means for Increasing the Consistency of Interpretation of Bilateral Investment Treaties, *Vanderbilt Journal of Transnational Law*, Vol. 40, 2009

Cotula, L., Democracy and International Investment Law, *Leiden Journal of International Law*, Vol. 30, No. 2, 2017

Dabone, Z., International Law: Armed Groups in a State-Centric System, *International Review of Red Cross*, Vol. 93, 2011

De Ly, F., Friedman, M and di Brozolo, L. R., Confidentiality in International Commercial Arbitration, *Arbitration International*, Vol. 28, No. 3, 2012

Desierto, D. A., Necessity and Supplementary Means of Interpretation for Non-Precluded Measures in Bilateral Investment Treaties, *University of Pennsylvania Journal of International Economic Law*, Vol. 31, No. 3, 2014

Dhooge, L., The Revenge of the Trail Smelter: Environmental Regulation as Expropriation Pursuant to the North American Free Trade Agreement, *American Business Law Journal*, Vol. 38, 2001

Dolzer, R., The Impact of International Investment Treaties on Domestic Administrative Law, *New York University Journal of International Law and Politics*, Vol. 37, 2007

Douglas, Z., Nothing If Not Critical for Investment Treaty Arbitration: Occidental, Eureko and Methanex, *Arbitration International*, Vol. 22, No. 1, 2006

Ellison, K., Rio+20: How the Tension between Developing and Developed Countries Influenced Sustainable Development Efforts, *Pacific McGeorge Global Business and Development Law Journal*, Vol. 27, 2014

Emmerson, A., Conceptualizing Security Exceptions: Legal Doctrine or Political Excuse, *Journal of International Economic Law*, Vol. 11, 2010

Fitzmaurice, G., The Law and Procedural of the International Court of Justice 1951–1954, *BYBIL*, Vol. 33, 1957

Fontanelli, F., Necessity Killed the GATT – Art. XX GATT and the Misleading Rhetoric about 'Weighing and Balancing', *European Journal of Legal Studies*, Vol. 5, No. 2, 2012

Forcese, C., Does the Sky Fall?: NAFTA Chapter 11 Dispute Settlement and Democratic Accountability, *Michigan State University Journal of International Law*, Vol. 14, 2006

Fortier, Y., The Occasionally Unwarranted Assumption of Confidentiality, *Arbitration International*, Vol. 15, 1999

Fortier, L. Y. and Drymer, S. L., Indirect Expropriation in the Law of International Investment: I Know It When I See It, or Caveat Investor, *ICSID Review*, Vol. 19, No. 2, 2004

Foster, G. K., Investors, States, and Stakeholders: Power Asymmetries in International Investment and the Stabilizing Potential of Investment Treaties, *Lewis and Clark Law Review*, Vol. 17, No. 2, 2013

Franck, S. D., The Legitimacy Crisis in Investment Treaty Arbitration: Privatizing Public International Law through Inconsistent Decisions, *Fordham Law Review*, Vol. 73, No. 4, 2005

Gagne, G. and Morin, J-F., The Evolving American Policy on Investment Protection: Evidence from Recent FTAs and the 2004 Model BIT, *Journal of International Economic Law*, Vol. 9, 2006

Gaines, S., The WTO's Reading of the GATT Article XX Chapeau: A Disguised Restriction on Environmental Measures, *University of Pennsylvania International Economic Law Journal*, Vol. 22, No. 4, 2001

Gal-Or, N., The Concept of Appeal in International Dispute Settlement, *European Journal of International Law*, Vol. 19, No. 1, 2008

Galvez, C. C., Necessity, Investor Rights, and State Sovereignty for NAFTA Investment Arbitration, *Cornell International Law Journal*, Vol. 46, No. 1, 2013

Ghouri, A. A., The Evolution of Bilateral Investment Treaties, Investment Treaty Arbitration and International Investment Law, *International Arbitration Law Review*, Vol. 14, No. 6, 2011

Gómez, K. F., Rethinking the Role of Amicus Curiae in International Investment Arbitration: How to Draw the Line Favorably for the Public Interest, *Fordham International Law Journal*, Vol. 35, No. 2, 2012

Gruchalla-Wesierski, T., A Framework for Understanding 'Soft Law', *McGill Law Journal*, Vol. 30, 1984

Gu, B., Mineral Export Restraints and Sustainable Development – Are Rare Earths Testing the WTO's Loopholes?, *Journal of International Economic Law*, Vol. 14, No. 4, 2011

Gudgeon, K. S., United States Bilateral Investment Treaties: Comments on their Origin, Purposes, and General Treatment Standards, *International Tax and Business Lawyer*, Vol. 4, 1986

Guzman, A. T. and Meyer, T. L., International Common Law: The Soft Law of International Tribunals, *Chinese Journal of International Law*, Vol. 9, No. 2, 2008.

Haynes, J., The Evolving Nature of the Fair and Equitable Treatment (FET) Standard: Challenging its Increasing Pervasiveness in Light of Developing Countries' Concerns – The Case for Regulatory Rebalancing, *Journal of World Investment and Trade*, Vol. 14, 2013

Henkin, L., International Law: Politics, Values and Functions, *Recueil des cours*, Vol. 216, 1989

Hillgenberg, H., A Fresh Look at Soft Law, *European Journal of International Law*, Vol. 19, No. 3, 1999

ILA, New Dehli Declaration of Principles of International Law Relating to Sustainable Development, *International Environment Agreements*, Vol. 2, No. 2, 2002

Isakoff, P. D., Defining the Scope of Indirect Expropriation for International Investments, *Global Business Law Review*, Vol. 3, No. 2, 2013

Ishikawa, T., Third Party Participation in Investment Treaty Arbitration, *International and Comparative Law Quarterly*, Vol. 59, 2010

Ji, Y., Voluntary "Westernization" of the Expropriation Rules in Chinese BITS and its Implication: An Empirical Study, *Journal of World Investment and Trade*, Vol. 12, No. 1, 2011

Karmel, Roberta S. and Kelly, Claire R., The Hardening of Soft Law in Securities Regulation, *Brooklyn Journal of International Law*, Vol. 34, No. 3, 2009

Kaufmann-Kohler, G., Soft Law in International Arbitration: Codification and Normativity, *Journal of International Dispute Settlement*, Vol. 1, No. 1, 2010

Kaushal, A., Revisiting History: How the Past Matters for the Present Backlash against the Foreign Investment Regime, *Harvard International Law Journal*, Vol. 50, No. 2, 2009

Koskenniemi, M. and Leino, P., Fragmentation of International Law? Postmodern Anxieties, *Leiden Journal of International Law*, Vol. 15, 2002

Kurtz, J., Adjudging the Exceptional at International Investment Law: Security, Public Order, and Financial Crisis, *International and Comparative Law Quarterly*, Vol. 59, 2010

Kurtz, J., The Use and Abuse of WTO Law in Investor–State Arbitration: Competition and Its Discontents, *European Journal of International Law*, Vol. 20, No. 3, 2009

Lamy, P., Global Governance: From Theory to Practice, *Journal of International Economic Law*, Vol. 15, No. 3, 2012

Levine, E., Amicus Curiae in International Investment Arbitration: The Implications of an Increase in Third-Party Participation, *Berkeley Journal of International Law*, Vol. 29, 2011

Lowe, V., Regulation or Expropriation, *Transnational Dispute Management*, Vol. 1, No. 3, 2004

Mann, H., Reconceptualization International Investment Law: Its Role in Sustainable Development, *Lewis and Clark Law Review*, Vol. 17, 2013

Mantouvalou, V., Are Labour Rights Human Rights?, *European Labour Law Journal*, Vol. 3, 2012

Marlles, J. R., Public Purpose, Private Losses: Regulatory Expropriation and Environmental Regulation in International Investment Law, *Florida State Journal of Transnational Law and Policy*, Vol. 16, No. 2, 2007

Marks, S., State-Centrism, International Law, and the Anxieties of Influence, *Leiden Journal of International Law*, Vol. 19, 2006

Mason, D., "Deliberative Democratising" of Australian Treaty Making: Putting into Context the Significance of Online Access to the Treaty Process, *Journal of Law, Information and Science*, Vol. 24, No. 2, 2016

Meshel, T., Human Rights in Investor–State Arbitration: The Human Right to Water and Beyond, *Journal of International Dispute Settlement*, Vol. 6, 2015

McLachlan, C., Investment Treaties and General International Law, *International and Comparative Law Quarterly*, Vol. 57, 2008

McLachlan, C., The Principle of Systemic Integration and Article 31(3)(c) of the Vienna Convention, *International and Comparative Law Quarterly*, Vol. 54, No. 2, 2005

Moon, W. J., Essential Security Interests in International Investment Agreements, *Journal of International Economic Law*, Vol. 15, No. 2, 2012

Mostafa, B., The Sole Effects Doctrine, Police Powers and Indirect Expropriation under International Law, *Australian International Law Journal*, Vol. 15, 2008

Newcombe, A., Sustainable Development and Investment Treaty Law, *Journal of World Investment and Trade*, Vol. 8, No. 3, 2007

Newcombe, A. and Lemaire, A., Should Amici Curiae Participate in Investment Treaty Arbitrations?", *Vindobona Journal of International Law and Arbitration*, 2001

Ortino, F., Investment Treaties, Sustainable Development and Reasonableness Review: A Case against Strict Proportionality Balancing, *Leiden Journal of International Law*, Vol. 30, No. 1, 2017

Osofsky, H. M., Defining Sustainable Development after Earth Summit 2002, *Loyola of Los Angeles International and Comparative Law Review*, Vol. 26, 2003

Ott, A., The European Parliament's Role in EU Treaty-Making, *Maastricht Journal of European and Comparative Law*, Vol. 23, 2016

Pauwelyn, J., Recent Books on Trade and Environment: GATT Phantoms Still Haunt the WTO, *European Journal of International Law*, Vol. 15, No. 3, 2004

Peters, B. G. and Pierre, J., Governance without Government: Rethinking Public Administration, *Journal of Public Administration Research and Theory*, Vol. 8, No. 2, 1998

Peters, P., Recent Development in Expropriation Clause in Asian Investment Treaties, *Asian Yearbook of International Law*, Vol. 5, 1997

Potesta, M., Legitimate Expectations in Investment Treaty Law: Understanding the roots and the Limits of a Controversial Concept, *ICSID Review*, Vol. 28, No. 1, 2013

Poulsen, L. N. S., The Importance of BITs for Foreign Direct Investment and Political Risk Insurance: Revisiting the Evidence, *Yearbook on International Investment Law and Policy 2009/2010*, 2010

Pupolizio, I., The Right to an Unchanging World – Indirect Expropriation in International Investment Agreements and State Sovereignty, *Vienna Journal of International Constitutional Law*, Vol. 10, No. 2, 2016

Roberts, A., Clash of Paradigms: Actors and Analogies Shaping the Investment Treaty System, *American Journal of International Law*, Vol. 107, No. 1, 2013

Roberts, A., The Next Battleground: Standards of Review in Investment Treaty Arbitration, *International Council for Commercial Arbitration Congress Series*, Vol. 16, 2011

Roberts, A. and Sivakumaran, S., Lawmaking by Non-state Actors: Engaging Armed Groups in the Creation of International Humanitarian Law, *Yale Journal of International Law*, Vol. 37, 2012

Rose-Ackerman, S. and Billa, B., Treaties and National Security, *International Law and Policy*, Vol. 40, 2008

Sabater, A., Towards Transparency in Arbitration (A Cautious Approach), *Berkeley Journal of International Law*, Vol. 5, 2010

Sands, P., International Courts and the Application of the Concept of Sustainable Development, *Max Planck Yearbook of United Nations Law*, Vol. 3, 1999

Schill, S. W., Editorial: Five Times Transparency in International Investment Law, *Journal of World Investment and Trade*, Vol. 15, No. 3–4, 2014

Schill, S. W., Enhancing International Investment Law's Legitimacy: Conceptual and Methodological Foundations of a New Public Law Approach, *Virginia Journal of International Law*, Vol. 52, No. 1, 2011

Schill, S. W., Fair and Equitable Treatment under Investment Treaties as an Embodiment of the Rule of Law, *Transnational Dispute Management*, Vol. 3, No. 5, 2006

Schill, S. W., W(h)ither Fragmentation? On the Literature and Sociology of International Investment Law, *European Journal of International Law*, Vol. 22, 2011

Schill, S. W. and Briese, R., "If the State Considers": Self-Judging Clauses in International Dispute Settlement, *Max Planck Yearbook of Unite Nations Law*, Vol. 13, 2009

Schlemmer-Schulte, S., Fragmentation of International Law: The Case of International Finance & Investment Law versus Human Rights Law, *Pacific McGeorge Global Business and Development Law Journal*, Vol. 25, 2012

Schneiderman, D., Legitimacy and Reflexivity in International Investment Arbitration: A New Self-Restraint?, *Journal of International Dispute Settlement*, Vol. 2, No. 2, 2011

Schreuer, C., Fair and Equitable Treatment in Arbitral Practice, *Journal of World Investment and Trade*, Vol. 6, No. 3, 2005

Schreuer, C., From ICSID Annulment to Appeal: Half Way down the Slippery Slope, *The Law and Practice of International Courts and Tribunals*, Vol. 10, 2011

Schrijver, N., ILA New Delhi Declaration of Principles of International Law Relating to Sustainable Development, *Netherlands International Law Review*, Vol. 49, No. 2, 2002

Schrijver, N., The Evolution of Sustainable Development in International Law: Inception, Meaning and Status, *Recueil des cours*, Vol. 329, 2007

Shan, W., Towards a Common European Community Policy on Investment Issues, *Journal of World Investment*, Vol. 2, No. 3, 2001

Shan, W. and Wang, Lu., The China–EU BIT and the Emerging Global BIT 2.0, *ICSID Review*, Vol. 30, No. 1, 2015

Shan, W. and Zhang, S., The Treaty of Lisbon: Halfway towards a Common Investment Policy, *European Journal of International Law*, Vol. 21, No. 4, 2011

Shinn, D. H. The Environmental Impact of China's Investment in Africa, *Cornell International Law Journal*, Vol. 49, No. 1, 2016

Simma, B., Foreign Investment Arbitration: A Place for Human Rights?, *International and Comparative Law Quarterly*, Vol. 60, No. 4, 2011

Skjæseth, J. B., Stokke, O. S. and Wettesta, J., Soft Law, Hard Law, and Effective Implementation of International Environmental Norms, *Global Environmental Politics*, Vol. 6, No. 3, 2006

Stern, B., Civil Society's Voice in the Settlement of International Economic Disputes, *ICSID Review*, Vol. 22, No. 2, 2007

Swenson, D. L., Why Do Developing Countries Sign BITs?, *U.C. at Davis Journal of International Law and Policy*, Vol. 12, 2005

Tanaka, Y., Protection of Community Interests in International Law: The Case of Law of the Sea, *Max Planck Yearbook of United Nations Law*, Vol. 15, 2011

Teitelbaum, R., A Look at the Public Interest in Investment Arbitration: Is It Unique? What Should We Do about It?, *Berkeley Journal of International Law Publicist*, Vol. 5, No. 1, 2010

Thjoernelund, M. C. H., State of Necessity as an Exemption from State Responsibility of Investment, *Max Plank Yearbook of United Nations Law*, Vol. 13, 2009

Vandevelde, K. J., A Brief History of International Investment Agreement, *U.C. Davis Journal of International Law and Policy*, Vol. 12, No. 1, 2005

Vandevelde, K. J., Rebalancing through Exceptions, *Lewis and Clark Law Review*, Vol. 17, No. 2, 2013

VanDuzer, A., Enhancing the Procedural Legitimacy of Investor–State Arbitration through Transparency and Amicus Curiae Participation, *McGill Law Journal*, Vol. 52, 2007

Veeder, V. V., The Lena Goldfields Arbitration: The Historical Roots of Three Ideas, *International and Comparative Law Quarterly*, Vol. 47, 1998

Viñuales, J. E., Amicus Intervention in Investor–State Arbitration, *Dispute Resolution Journal*, Vol. 61, 2006

Wälde, T. W., Procedural Challenges in Investment Arbitration under the Shadow of the Dual Role of the State – Asymmetries and Tribunals' Duty to Ensure, Pro-actively, the Equality of Arms, *Arbitration International*, Vol. 26, 2010

Wang, H. and Rosenau, J. N., China and Global Governance, *Asian Perspective*, Vol. 33, No. 3, 2009

Wang, J., Ralls Corp. v. CFIUS: A New Look at Foreign Direct Investments to the US, *Columbian Journal of Transnational Law Bulletin*, 30, 2016

Wilson, W. J., Legal Foundations for NGO Participation in Climate Treaty Negotiations, *Sustainable Development Law and Policy*, Vol. 10, 2010

Wong, J. and Yackee, J., The 2006 Procedural and Transparency-Related Amendments to the ICSID Arbitration Rules, *Yearbook on International Investment Law and Policy 2009/2010*, 2010

Yasuaki, O., A Transcivilizational Perspective on International Law, *Recueil des cours*, Vol. 342, 2009

Internet resources

Åslund, A., The World Needs a Multilateral Investment Agreement, *Policy Brief of Peterson Institute for International Economics*, No. PB 13-01, available at: https://piie.com/sites/default/files/publications/pb/pb13-1.pdf

Bernasconi-Osterwalder, N. and Johnson, L. (eds.), *International Investment Law and Sustainable Development: Key Cases from 2000 to 2010*, available at: www.iisd.org/publications/international-investment-law-and-sustainable-development-key-cases-2000-2010

Born, G., Finizio, S. P., Ogden, D. W., Kent, R. D., Pierce J. V. H. and Bowker, D. W., *Investment Treaty Arbitration: ICSID Amends Investor–State Arbitration Rules*, available at: www.wilmerhale.com/pages/publicationsandnewsdetail.aspx?News PubId=90393

Bradshaw, S., *Internet Governance via Hard and Soft Laws: Choosing the Right Tools for the Job*, 20 March 2017, available at: www.cigionline.org/publications/internet-governance-hard-and-soft-laws-choosing-right-tools-job

Carim, X., Lessons from South Africa's BITs Review, *Columbia FDI Perspectives*, No. 109, 25 November 2013), available at: http://ccsi.columbia.edu/files/2013/10/No_109_-_Carim_-_FINAL.pdf

Chaisse, J. and Hamanaka, S., The Investment Version of the Asian Noodle Bowl: The Proliferation of International Investment Agreements, *ADB Working Paper Series on Regional Economic Integration*, No. 128, April 2014, available at: www.cuhk.edu.hk/law/proj/BITSel/download/Hamanaka_Shintaro.pdf

Commission on Global Governance, *Our Global Neighborhood*, available at: www.gdrc.org/u-gov/global-neighbourhood

Cotula L., *Investment Treaties and Citizens' Power: Lessons from Experience* (7 September 2015), available at www.iied.org/investment-treaties-citizens-power-lessonsexperience

Dugard, J., *Articles on Diplomatic Protection*, United Nations Audiovisual Library of International Law, available at: http://legal.un.org/avl/pdf/ha/adp/adp_e.pdf

Ferrarini, B., *A Multilateral Framework for Investment?*, available at:
www.cid.harvard.edu/cidtrade/Papers/ferrarini_wti_investment.pdf

Gallagher, K. P. and Shrestha, E., Investment Treaty Arbitration and Developing
Countries: A Re-Appraisal, *Global Development and Environment Institute Working
Paper No. 11-01*, 2011, available at: https://ase.tufts.edu/gdae/Pubs/wp/11-
01TreatyArbitrationReappraisal.pdf

Gomezperalta, C. M., *How States Can Cope with the Growing Threat of Arbitration*, May
2010, available at: www.robertwraypllc.com/how-states-can-cope-with-the-growing-
threat-of-arbitration

Gordon, K., Pohl, J. and Bouchard, M., Investment Treaty Law, Sustainable
Development and Responsible Business Conduct: A Fact Finding Survey, *OECD
Working Papers on International Investment*, January 2014, available at:
www.oecd.org/investment/investment-policy/WP-2014_01.pdf

Greenwood, C., *Sources of International Law: An Introduction*, available at:
http://legal.un.org/avl/pdf/ls/greenwood_outline.pdf

Johnson, L. and Bernasconi-Osterwalde, N., *New UNCITRAL Arbitration Rules on
Transparency: Application, Content and Next Steps*, available at:
http://ccsi.columbia.edu/files/2014/04/UNCITRAL_Rules_on_Transparency_
commentary_FINAL.pdf

Kiguel, M., *Argentina's 2001 Economic and Financial Crisis: Lessons for Europe*, available
at: www.brookings.edu/wp-content/uploads/2016/06/11_argentina_kiguel.pdf

Lestor, S., *Improving Investment Treaties through General Exceptions Provisions:
The Australian Example*, available at: www.cato.org/publications/commentary/
improving-investment-treaties-through-general-exceptions-provisions

Mann, H. and Von Moltke, K., *Protecting Investor Rights and the Public Good: Assessing
NAFTA's Chapter 11*, available at: www.iisd.org/sites/default/files/publications/
investment_ilsd_background_en.pdf

Mann, H., Cosbey, A., Peterson, L. and Von Moltke, K., *Comments on ICSID Discussion
Paper, "Possible Improvements of the Framework for ICSID Arbitration"*, available at:
www.iisd.org/pdf/2004/investment_icsid_response.pdf

Mayoral, J., Democratic Improvements in the European Union under the Lisbon
Treaty: Institutional Changes Regarding Democratic Government in the EU,
February 2011, available at: www.eui.eu/Projects/EUDO-Institutions/Documents/
EUDOreport922011.pdf

McGraw, S. L. and Rufe, S. E., *The Foreign Corrupt Practices Act: An Overview of the
Law and Coverage-Related Issues* (21 March 2014), available at:
http://apps.americanbar.org/litigation/committees/insurance/articles/janfeb2014-
foreign-corrupt-practices-act.html#_edn6

Megan, C., The Democratic Deficit in the European Union, *Claremont-UC
Undergraduate Research Conference on the European Union*, 2009, available at:
http://scholarship.claremont.edu/urceu/vol2009/iss1/5

Neumayer, E., Nunnenkamp, P. and Roy, M., Are Stricter Investment Rules Contagious?
Host Country Competition for Foreign Direct Investment through International
Agreements, *WTO Working Paper ERSD-2014-04*, 10 March 2014, available at:
www.wto.org/english/res_e/reser_e/ersd201404_e.pdf

Newcombe, A., *General Exceptions in International Investment Agreements*, available at:
www.biicl.org/files/3866_andrew_newcombe.pdf

Peterson, L., *Human Rights and Bilateral Investment Treaties: Mapping the Role of Human
Rights Law in Investor–State Arbitration* (2009), available at:

http://publications.gc.ca/collections/collection_2012/dd-rd/E84-36-2009-eng.pdf

Philip Morris International Inc., *Submission by Philip Morris International Inc. in Response to the National Center for Standards and Certification Information Foreign Trade Notification No. G/TBTIN/CAN/22*, available at: www.essentialaction.org/tobacco/pmresponsetonoi.pdf

Public Citizen, *Only One of 44 Attempts to Use the GATT Article XX/GATS Article XIV "General Exception" Has Ever Succeeded: Replicating the WTO Exception Construct Will Not Provide for an Effective TPP General Exception*, available at: www.citizen.org/documents/general-exception.pdf

Porterfield, M. C. and Byrnes, C. R., *Philip Morris v. Uruguay: Will investor-State Arbitration Send Restrictions on Tobacco Marketing Up In Smoke?*, available at: www.iisd.org/itn/2011/07/12/philip-morris-v-uruguay-will-investor-state-arbitration-send-restrictions-on-tobacco-marketing-up-in-smoke

Reed, L., *Scorecard of Investment Treaty Cases against Argentina since 2001*, available at: http://kluwerarbitrationblog.com/2009/03/02/scorecard-of-investment-treaty-cases-against-argentina-since-2001

Reich, S., *What Is Globalization: Four Possible Answers*, Kellogg Institute Working Paper, December 1998), available at: www3.nd.edu/~kellogg/publications/workingpapers/WPS/261.pdf

Schill, S. W., *Transparency as a Global Norm in International Investment Law* (15 September 2014), Kluwer Arbitration Blog, available at: http://kluwerarbitrationblog.com/2014/09/15/transparency-as-a-global-norm-in-international-investment-law/

Sewlikar, A., *Introduction of Labor Standards in Investment Arbitration*, available at: http://kluwerarbitrationblog.com/blog/2014/03/18/introduction-of-labour-standards-in-investment-arbitration

Shirlow, E., *A Step toward Greater Transparency: The UN Transparency Convention*, available at: http://kluwerarbitrationblog.com/2015/03/30/a-step-toward-greater-transparency-the-un-transparency-convention

Stichele, M. V. and Van Bennekom, S., Investment Agreements and Corporate Social Responsibility (CSR): Contradictions, Incentives and Policy Option, *SOMO Discussion Paper*, 1 November 2015, available at: www.somo.nl/wp-content/uploads/2005/12/Investment-agreements-and-Corporate-Social-Responsibility.pdf

Swiss Alliance of Development Organizations, *FTA between Switzerland and China: Human Rights on the Scrap Heap* (19 July 2013), available at: www.alliancesud.ch/en/policy/trade/fta-between-switzerland-and-china-human-rights-on-the-scrap-heap

VanDuzer, J. A., Simons, P. and Mayeda, G., *Integrating Sustainable Development into International Investment Agreements: A Guide for Developing Countries* (Prepared for the Commonwealth Secretariat), 2012, available at: www.iisd.org/pdf/2012/6th_annual_forum_commonwealth_guide.pdf

Weiss, T. G., Seyle, D. C. and Coolidge, K., The Rise of Non-State Actors in Global Governance: Opportunities and Limitations, *One Earth Foundation Future Discussion Paper*, available at: http://acuns.org/wp-content/uploads/2013/11/gg-weiss.pdf

Wilkie, D., *UNCITRAL Unveils New Transparency Rules – Blazing a Trail towards Transparency in Investor–State Arbitration?*, available at: http://kluwerarbitrationblog.com/2013/07/25/uncitral-unveils-new-transparency-rules-blazing-a-trail-towards-transparency-in-investor-state-arbitration

Other documents

Harvard Draft Convention on the International Responsibility of States for Injuries to Aliens (1961)

Kazemi, L., *Monopoly Broken? Investment Governance beyond the Sovereign State* (Thesis for Doctor of Philosophy) (UMI Number: 3420848, 2010), at 1

Koskenniemi, M., *Fragmentation of International Law: Difficulties Arising from the Diversification and Expansion of International Law,* (Report of the Study Group of the International Law Commission), A/CN.4/L.682 (13 April 2006)

Tietje, C. and Baetens, F., *The Impact of Investor–State-Dispute Settlement (ISDS) in the Transatlantic Trade and Investment Partnership* (Study prepared for the Minister for Foreign Trade and Development Cooperation, Ministry of Foreign Affairs, The Netherlands), Reference: MINBUZA-2014.78850

Index

For Product Safety Concerns and Information please contact our EU
representative GPSR@taylorandfrancis.com
Taylor & Francis Verlag GmbH, Kaufingerstraße 24, 80331 München, Germany

www.ingramcontent.com/pod-product-compliance
Ingram Content Group UK Ltd.
Pitfield, Milton Keynes, MK11 3LW, UK
UKHW021849240425
457818UK00020B/786